# SANTA TERESA DE AVILA

by

## HELMUT A. HATZFELD

This book stresses the literary qualities of Santa Teresa rather than her great mystical and reformatory importance, her mastery of the language rather than the high caliber of her spirituality. It revaluates the Saint as a prose writer and poet. The author offers an abridged reading with a commentary of her main works—*Vida, Castillo interior, Camino de Perfección,* and *Poesías*—with stress on the images, their cohesion and disruption, Teresa's structural purpose and stylistic rambling. The visions and the letters are analyzed from the viewpoint of their stylization.

By scrutinizing certain of Santa Teresa's expressions in their context, Dr. Hatzfeld brings her human qualities to the fore. She is situated within her epoch and her place is fixed in the history of Spanish and religious literature.

## ABOUT THE AUTHOR

Helmut A. Hatzfeld holds the degree of Ph.D. from the University of Munich, and honorary degrees from Grenoble, Catholic University, George Washington, Notre Dame, and Marquette. He is a corresponding member of the Hispanic Society of America and of the Bavarian Academy of Arts and Sciences. Long interested in Spanish, French and comparative literature, he has devoted much time to investigations of Cervantes, mysticism, and the Baroque. The fruits of these investigations are three books: *El Quijote como Obra de Arte del Lenguaje, Estudios literarios sobre Mistica española*, and *Estudios sobre el Barroco*.

Professor Hatzfeld has taught in the Universities of Frankfort, Koenigsberg, Heidelberg, Louvain and, for 28 years, at the Catholic University of America in Washington, D.C. He was visiting professor at the Universities of Munich and Goettingen and has lectured at different American and French institutions of higher learning. He has read papers at many national and international conventions. Three of his publications have won awards in the United States, Spain and France respectively.

A Survey of the World's Literature

Sylvia E. Bowman, Indiana University

GENERAL EDITOR

## TWAYNE'S WORLD AUTHORS SERIES (TWAS)

*The purpose of TWAS is to survey the major writers —novelists, dramatists, historians, poets, philosophers, and critics—of the nations of the world. Among the national literatures covered are those of Australia, Canada, China, Eastern Europe, France, Germany, Greece, India, Italy, Japan, Latin America, New Zealand, Poland, Russia, Scandinavia, Spain, and the African nations, as well as Hebrew, Yiddish, and Latin Classical literatures. This survey is complemented by Twayne's United States Authors Series and English Authors Series.*

*The intent of each volume in these series is to present a critical-analytical study of the works of the writer; to include biographical and historical material that may be necessary for understanding, appreciation, and critical appraisal of the writer; and to present all material in clear, concise English—but not to vitiate the scholarly content of the work by doing so.*

# Santa Teresa de Avila

By HELMUT A. HATZFELD

*Catholic University of America*

Twayne Publishers, Inc.    ::    New York

# *Preface*

THE mystical writings of Santa Teresa of Avila belong to literature because of their originality, spontaneity, their imagery and pedagogical skill in the expression of concepts usually considered ineffable. The literary critic should restrict himself to his capacity to pass judgment on these qualities of the famous Saint as a writer. The literary historian knows that he has to elucidate these writings in the sense of the Saint's intentions as she reports on her spiritual experiences. In the interpretation of these experiences themselves Santa Teresa speaks as a Roman Catholic Spanish woman of the sixteenth century. Her burning faith and her opposition to the Reformation of Northern Europe were shared by many Spaniards of her time. Her mysticism was shared by a few. The form in which she expresses the mystical development is her own spiritual and literary contribution. It is this ineffable development, for which she has found the adequate images and terms, with which we will be confronted in the main part of this book. It would be quite beyond the range of his knowledge for the philologist *qua* interpreter of texts to make a decision as to the parapsychological or metaphysical character of her stages of prayer and visions. This is a matter of belief which may be strengthened in the one or the other direction only after a careful reading of her works. One point, however, is more than clear from historical evidence, namely that the so-called erotic language (very slight in Santa Teresa) has rhetorical and not sexual implications.[1]

On the other hand, some knowledge of traditional Catholic mysticism is the *sine qua non* for the understanding of Teresa's classical writings. For this mysticism, however, the works of Santa Teresa are themselves source, substance and commentary. Therefore an additional theoretical introduction would be superfluous here, and out of place. There are two excellent French studies which approach the mystical phenomenon in Santa Teresa from a supernatural and from a natural viewpoint. The one by Louis Bertrand treats of the visions of the Saint as "open windows upon a new world," [2] the other by Henri Delacroix as psychic hallucinations.[3] Whatever the merits of these books may be, the first evaluates, the second devaluates Santa Teresa. The literary achievements of the Saint are of course to be evaluated, too, in accordance with their significance for mankind and not as curiosities for the psychiatrist. Teresa the writer is not only Teresa the visionary; she is also Teresa the reformer of the Carmelite Order, the founder of many convents, the legislator, the letter writer, and the poet. She is even the clear-minded business woman and the patient who analyzes her sufferings nosographically as she analyzes her mystical experiences psychologically. In her own understanding of the interrelationship between suffering and creativity she is an early forerunner of Dostoevski.[4] By her supreme handling of the Spanish language she has become a classic, like the author of the *Celestina* before her and the great Cervantes after her.

All quotations, as indicated in the Bibliography, are taken from the Spanish Aguilar edition, Madrid, 1940, of Teresa's *Complete Works*. All translations are my own, the English Standard translation by Edgar Allison Peers, however, having been often consulted. Since in the bridal mysticism of Santa Teresa the soul appears as the spouse of the Divine Groom, it seemed fit to treat the soul in this context as feminine. References to the mystical soul are therefore given as "she," not as "it."

I wish to express my gratitude to Professor Catherine Dunn of the Department of English of the Catholic University of America for her kindness in reading the manuscript of this book and for her careful criticism of it as well as her suggestions for its improvement.

HELMUT A. HATZFELD

*Washington, D.C.*

# Contents

# Contents

Preface

Chronology

# Chronology

1515    March 28: Teresa de Cepeda y Ahumada born in Avila.

1528    Death of Teresa's mother, Doña Beatriz de Ahumada.

1531    Teresa's visits with her cousins as boarder and pupil of the Augustinian Sisters in Avila (Convent of Our Lady of Grace).

1535    Reads Francisco de Osuna's *Tercer Abecedario Espiritual* (*Third Spiritual Primer*), decisive for her development.

1536    Enters as a Carmelite nun the Incarnation Convent of Avila.

1537    Professes at the Incarnation.

1538    Falls ill. Stays with her married sister in Castellanos and with her uncle Pedro in Hortigosa.

1540    Returns to Incarnation.

1543    Death of Teresa's father, Don Alonso Sánchez de Cepeda.

1557    Teresa's first vision.

1558    First raptures.

1559    The so-called Transverberation or Piercing of her heart by the spear of a Cherub.

1562    August 24: Teresa's first foundation of the Carmelite reform, San José in Avila, where she herself stays from 1563 to 1567.

1562    *El Libro de su Vida* (*The Book of Her Life*), first draft.

1563    *Constituciones* (*The Constitutions*), Rules for the Discalced Carmelites.

1563    *Relaciones espirituales* (*Spiritual Reports*), finished in 1579.

1565    Composition of the *Camino de perfección*.

1567    Final form of *El Libro de su Vida*.

1567–    Foundations of six reformed convents (Medina, Malagón,
1570    Valladolid, Toledo, Pastrana, Salamanca).

1571–    Prioress of the Incarnation in Avila.
1574

1571–  Ten new foundations (Alba de Tormes, Segovia, Beas, Se-
1582    villa, Caravaca, Villanueva, Palencia, Soria, Granada, Bur-
        gos).

1572    Spiritual marriage.

1573–  *Libro de las Fundaciones* (*The Book of the Foundations*).
1582

1574    *Conceptos del Amor de Dios* (*Concepts of the Love of
        God;* that is, Thoughts on the Song of Songs).

1575    First meeting with Father Gracián, her confessor, co-
        founder, provincial and main correspondent.

1577    *El Castillo Interior* (*The Interior Castle*), written in To-
        ledo, Segovia and Avila during the greatest opposition to
        Teresa's reform.

1579    The *Spiritual Reports* finished.

1580    Death of Teresa's brother Lorenzo de Cepeda y Ahumada.

1582    *Modo de visitar los Conventos* (*Manner of Visiting Con-
        vents*), written in Toledo. October 4: Death in Alba de
        Tormes.

# CHAPTER 1

## Introduction: Life and Times of Santa Teresa

### I  The First Years

IN the following biographical sketch an attempt will be made
to explain the life of Santa Teresa by the important events in
the political and religious life which surround her, and which mo-
tivate her decisions. Since the appreciation of the Saint as writer is
reserved for the literary part of our presentation, the emphasis in
this first chapter will be on the reformer of the Carmelite Order,
the foundress of convents, the mystic and the saint.

Teresa de Cepeda y Ahumada was born in Avila on March 28,
1515, only twenty-three years after Isabella of Castile and Ferdi-
nand of Aragon, the so-called "Catholic Majesties," had broken
the last Moorish resistance against the *Reconquista* and at the
same time, thanks to the glorious discovery of Christopher Co-
lumbus, had begun the conquest of Latin America. Since the
Catholic Majesties had resided for years in Teresa's very Avila,
this fortress-city still was filled with noble families to which her
father's kin, the Cepedas, belonged, as well as the family of her
mother, the Ahumadas. In these families there lived the spirit of
adventure, daring enterprise, honor and willpower, but also the
spirit of religion, missionary zeal evoked by the American enterprise, even intolerance as evident in the kingdom's policy of the
expulsion of the Jews, and fanaticism, as evidenced by the Inquisition and the *autos de fe*. This was the spirit inherited by the
Saint, who seriously believed she would undo by her prayers and
sacrifices the division of the Church through the Lutheran reformation, which had begun only two years after her birth. Atonement for the Protestant Reformation and missionary zeal for the
Indians in America are the major incentives of Teresa's religious
activities.

Teresa's father, Alonso Sánchez de Cepeda (1485–1543), married in 1507 his second wife, Beatriz de Ahumada y Tapia

11

(1495–1528). In her short life, full of suffering, Doña Beatriz bore him twelve children, of whom Teresa was the third. Retelling her children the novels of chivalry which she used to read together with the heroic legends of the saints, Doña Beatriz implanted in them religious enthusiasm coupled with the taste for dangerous adventure. She actually could not help exciting the emotions of Teresa and her brother Rodrigo (born 1511), so that one day Teresa and Rodrigo set out to die the death of martyrs in the land of the Moors in order, as they assumed, to achieve Heaven in the quickest and easiest way. Brought back by their father, they changed the object of their youthful religious enthusiasm by playing hermits and constructing hermit cells and oratories with stones from their garden. But little Teresa also tried to give alms from her small possessions and to play nuns with other girls. And when her mother died in 1528, the thirteen-year-old Teresita threw herself at the feet of a statue of the Blessed Virgin and begged her to be her mother from that time onwards.

Teresa's "virtuous and Godfearing" highly principled father certainly was a good educator for her. He did not bother her with Latin, however, although the daughters of other genteel families used to learn it, even when they did not enter religion. So did Beatriz Galindo, María Mendoza and the still more famous products of Hispanic-Erasmian humanism like Doña Lucía de Medrana, who taught at Salamanca, and Francisca de Nebrija, who taught at times for her father, the famous grammarian Antonio de Nebrija, in the chair of rhetoric at the new University of Alcalá de Henares, founded by the Cardinal Jiménez de Cisneros. Teresa at the age of sixteen was sent to a finishing school and spent two years as a boarder at the Augustinian Convent outside the walls of Avila (1531–1533). The convent was called Our Lady of Grace. At that time she did not feel any urge to become a nun; on the contrary, she knew that she was a beautiful girl, liked fine clothes and perfumes, took good care of her person, particularly her hands and hair. She liked the company of her male cousins, who used to visit her at home and in the convent school. Acknowledging the perfect personalities of most of the nuns and particularly that of her tutor, Doña María de Briceño y Contreras, who loved her and inspired her with religious ideas, Teresa nevertheless was at that time decidedly hostile to religious life, "*enemiguísima de ser monja,*" *Vida* (*Life*), Ch. 2, p. 6. The reader is reminded that it is the 1940 edition of Teresa's *Complete Works* to which we refer.

Teresa's attitude, naturally, raised the question of her possible marriage. But this prospect seemed to her virginal nature still more unacceptable, *"también temía el casarme," Life*, Ch. 3, p. 7. Thus conversations with María de Briceño and a nun from the Incarnation Convent of Avila's Calced Carmelites, Doña Juana Suárez (whom Teresa visited sometimes, clad in an orange-colored dress trimmed with black velvet ribbons), tipped the scales in the direction of the convent. But it was a hard struggle for Teresa, a terrible crisis which ended with the conviction that life in a convent could not be worse than Purgatory, anyway, and would lead her directly to Heaven. In this crisis Teresa fell ill. She suffered from fever, swoonings and pains about her heart. She spent about two years at home and used her convalescence to read the letters of St. Jerome in a new translation. Under the influence of this reading she informed her father of her decision to become a Carmelite nun.

Meanwhile the spiritual climate of Spain had changed. Charles V, King of Spain since 1516 and German Emperor of the Holy Roman Empire since 1519, wanted to expand his colonial possessions and to strengthen the orthodoxy of Spain. The humanism of Erasmus had become taboo. It was maliciously identified with Lutheran tendencies, and in all the processes against the Alumbrados, a group of religious people similar to the gnostics, who believed in private illuminations, the name of Erasmus appears. Reading Erasmus, says the founder of the Jesuit Order, Ignatius of Loyola, according to his biographer Ribadeneyra, means destroying one's spirituality. And Ignatius, who was allowed to found his Order under Pope Paul III (1537), emphasizes against Luther and the Augustinian tradition the importance of the will in the balance of grace and human cooperation with it.

## II   *First Years in the Convent*

In this atmosphere of spiritual energy and contempt toward humanism, Teresa entered the Carmel of Avila, the already-mentioned convent of the Incarnation, with its relaxed rule, in November, 1536. She assumed the name of Sor Teresa de Jesús and put her strong will to saving her soul, but she had not as yet discovered the radical love of God as the only valid incentive to a dedicated life in the cloister. Her difficulties in mental prayer were somewhat offset by her serious ascetic spirit. This latter made her see what was wrong in the convents: friendships between nuns, frequent visits from outside at the grill, etc. She made her perpetual vows one year later, on November 3, 1537.

But in the autumn of 1538 Teresa's illness returned. She ascribed it to the kind of life and food so different from what she was accustomed to (*Life*, Ch. 4, p. 10), but also to the wrong guidance she received from poorly trained confessors, "*confesores medio letrados*," *ibid.*, Ch. 5, p. 13. As a matter of fact, she had to leave the convent to get medical care and treatment, and was absent for almost two years. In an attempt to get a rest, she went first to her paternal uncle Pedro Sánchez de Cepeda in Hortigosa. This uncle was a very pious man and ended his life as a widower in the cloister of the Hieronymites. He understood his niece's spiritual difficulties and gave her as reading matter the so-called *Third Spiritual Primer* of the Franciscan, Francisco de Osuna (*ibid.*, Ch. 4, p. 10). Osuna, under the double influence of the Northern mystics like Ruysbroek and the Catalan Ramon Lull, who had undergone on his part the influence of the Arabic-Mohammedan Sufism, demonstrated exactly wherein lay the decisive point between active and passive prayer or between asceticism and mysticism. He explained the techniques of active recollection, i.e. the highest concentration in prayer combined with the most radical detachment from everything that is not God. He taught that when the powers of the soul, understanding, will, and memory unite or rather fuse in a kind of intuition, excluding discursive and analytical procedures of meditation, God himself interferes and keeps the soul recollected. Thus the changing of active recollection into passive contemplation (imperfections and weaknesses becoming more perceptible) means the beginning of mystical prayer in a darkness which God may illuminate with all kinds of spiritual insights in order to unite the soul with Himself directly without any means (*media*) or methods (*modi*).

The reading of the *Third Spiritual Primer* laid in Teresa the very foundations for her later development as a mystic. But her illness directed her first of all to a radical abandonment to the will of God, so far as this illness was concerned. First, she seemed to recover when spending the winter of 1538 in the house of her married half-sister (a relationship due to the first marriage of her

father) in the village of Castellanos de la Cañeda. But in 1539
things became worse, and her father insisted on a medical treatment in Becedas, where a woman healer (*curandera*) perhaps
worsened the young girl's serious illness. In August of 1539 Teresa
had such a serious attack of catalepsy that she received extreme
unction, was unconscious for four days and remained helpless in
bed for eight months.

As a semi-invalid she returned to her convent around Easter of
1540. She began to make progress in prayer, thanks to her knowledge of the Osuna *Spiritual Primer* and because of some clear-
sighted Dominican and Jesuit confessors. The Dominican, her father's confessor, was Padre Vicente Barrón, from the monastery of
St. Thomas in Avila. But Teresa's terrible suffering did not subside, and the partly paralyzed young nun was not capable of
much activity until 1542, tortured as she was by severe pains and
incessant vomiting. (*ibid.*, Ch. 7, p. 23) She read the history of
Job in the *Moralia* of St. Gregory (*ibid.*, Ch. 5, p. 14), and tried to
imitate the virtue of perfect patience. However one may explain
her eidetic temptations or excitements in a superstitious sixteenth-
century Spain where second sight (*vislumbramiento*) was neither
extraordinary nor as yet conjured away by Cervantes' *Don Quijote,* she swears to have seen during three years with her bodily
eyes a gigantic toad (*ibid.*, Ch. 7, p. 22) which of course she identified with the devil. As a heavenly helper she chose a particular
patron, according to the custom of the convent. Her choice fell on
St. Joseph, and she thus came to propagate his devotion, until
then very little developed in Spain. On December 24, one day
before Christmas, in 1543, the father of Teresa died a holy death
or, as the Spaniards say with an Arabic paradox, he died like an
angel. (*ibid.*, Ch. 7, p. 24)

For a period of twelve years Teresa struggled in her convent for
the right way to find a more intense love of God, a sense of His
presence; in brief, she is waiting for the grace of God in order to
see her initial contemplation develop into something higher. She
thinks at that time that contemplation would be the usual way of
the Christian. But in the convent and in herself she believes she
discovers so much vanity that a real retreat to the very depth
(*hondón*) of the soul seems impossible. The question arises: what
to do?

Meanwhile the Council of Trent convenes in 1545. It stresses

internal and external reform of all organizations within the
Church. Rejecting the Protestant iconoclasts, it recommends as
the way to promote piety and devotion the traditional use of holy
pictures. This appeals to Teresa's eidetic propensities. There is a
famous sonnet of these times called "To the Crucified Christ"; it
paraphrases freely thus: "Lord, I am not moved to love you (*No
me mueve, mi Dios, para quererte*) by the fear of Hell or the
reward of Heaven; it is only my burning love for you that moves
me, for if Hell and Heaven did not exist, I would still love you."
And this love arose in many of the faithful when praying before a
crucifix. The sonnet looks like a refined use of the principles of the
Spiritual Exercises of Ignatius of Loyola, exercises which around
1555 had become a common practice in Spain under the guidance
of members of the Order. The world had become more devout, as
is proved by the retreat of Charles V to the Monastery of San
Yuste.

### III   *The Santa's Middle Years*

The young Jesuit priest Diego de Cetina (1531–1567) who later
taught at the University of Salamanca, became Teresa's first important confessor, probably in 1554. He was followed in 1555 by
the rector of the Jesuit College in Avila, Father Juan de Prádanos
(1528–1597). The latter became a lifelong friend of the Saint. The
Jesuit direction soon bore its fruit with her, too. One day in 1555
she entered the oratory and saw by chance an *Ecce Homo* picture
(not Christ at the column, as was often reported) which had been
recently stored there. Looking at the suffering face and wounds of
Christ, she became totally disturbed at seeing this price paid for
our sins. (*Life,* Ch. 9, p. 31) Immediately she underwent what the
Jesuits used to call a second conversion. From then onward her
love of God was radical and it happened to her often that she felt
Christ close to her like a loving friend. For the first time she starts
wondering whether she would ever be able to produce this presence by an act of will, and she fears that she may not be able to
do this by discursive meditation nor by any act of memory. She
thus discovers that she has entered a higher stage of contemplation than that of mere passive recollection, and she realizes that
what occurred to her is no vision in the eidetic sense but a presence. She adds ingenuously: "I think they call this mystical theology." (*ibid.,* Ch. 10, p. 33)

## IV  *Mystical Experiences*

As Teresa's mystical graces grew, devout persons like the saintly layman Francisco de Salcedo or the theologian Maestro Gaspar Daza considered her a victim of illusions. Despite the encouragement of her Jesuit confessors and even of St. Francis Borgia who met her in 1557, she became frightened and anticipated the fate of Sister Magdalen of the Cross, who had been persecuted by the Inquisition as an illusionist (*alumbrada*). But new spiritual books, such as Bernardino de Laredo's *La Ascensión del Monte Sion por la Vida Contemplativa* (*The Ascension of Mount Sion through the Contemplative Life*), consoled her. In 1558 she made the vow of trying for the highest perfection, had her first ecstatic rapture and, as her first gesture towards putting her ideas into practice, began her discussions about the reform of the Carmelite Order.

In 1559 the radical local Index of the Spanish Inquisitor General, Fernando de Valdés, deprived Teresa of her preferred books dealing with mysticism, but she found at the same time a Jesuit Father from the College of St. Giles (*San Gil*) who understood her spiritual problems very well. This was Padre Baltasar Alvarez (1533–1580), whom Teresa praised for his severity. (*ibid.*, Ch. 26, p. 104) At the same time Teresa was visited by one who was to have much influence on her. This was the Franciscan mystic and reformer of his own Order, San Pedro de Alcántara (1499–1562), who seemed to her almost like the roots of a tree in the ascetic shape of his body. (*ibid.*, Ch. 27, p. 110) It was with him and her saintly lady friend María Díaz del Vivar that Teresa developed her reformist ideas.

Among the many visions and divine utterances which the Saint sensed at that time, the most important is the so-called transverberation or transfixion, because this mystical phenomenon produced an unquenchable burning love of God in her and it is at that moment that she feels what she later confided to a poem: "I am dying from not being able to die." The Saint describes the experience (which Bernini later translated inadequately into his sculpture in the Roman church Santa Maria della Vittoria): A Cherub pierced her heart with an iron-headed spear with a flaming gold tip and then departed, leaving her with a boundless desire for God. (*ibid.*, Ch. 29, p. 121) This happened in 1559. In the next two years, according to her own reporting, Teresa experienced

many diabolic temptations during which, however, she preserved
her marvelous lucidity. During these two years, with the financial
help of her young niece María de Ocampo and the rich widow
Doña Guiomar de Ulloa, she worked out the plans for her first
foundation, St. Joseph's of Avila. The Provincial of the Carmelites
agreed to the project on the condition that the new Discalced
branch would not contain more than thirteen nuns. Thus, despite
all the resistance of the city and of the Convent of the Incarnation, called the Convent of the Observance, Teresa's well-to-do
sister Juana de Ahumada bought and furnished her a house; the
bishop of Avila, Don Alvaro de Mendoza, took the new foundation under his protection, and Pius IV authorized not only the
foundation but also the new constitution, drawn up by Santa Teresa, in a brief dated February 7, 1562. To avoid trouble Teresa
now, at the order of the Provincial, stayed outside the Convent of
the Incarnation and lived with the widow Doña Luisa de la
Cerda, daughter of the Duke of Medinaceli, in Toledo. There she
wrote the book of her life, her *Vida*. In the spring of 1563 she was
authorized to enter, with three companions, her new house of St.
Joseph's in Avila, the first Discalced Carmelite convent.

## V   Teresa the Foundress

Santa Teresa considered the five years she stayed at St. Joseph's
the most tranquil ones of her life. (*Fundaciones* [*Foundations*], I,
467) It is there that she received as Prioress the apostolic visitor
and General of the Carmelites, Father Rossi, called Rubeo in
Spain. He came to enforce the decrees of the Council of Trent in
all the Spanish Carmelite houses and was delighted to see at least
one convent of the Carmel restored to the original austerity. Impressed by the saintly personality of Teresa, he gave her permission to found in Castile other convents, priories, and even monas-
teries for men. In her inner life, Teresa went on to become more
perfect and more free. She loses entirely her fear of death and
acquires a great contempt for the world. (*Life*, Ch. 28, p. 173)
She has the vision o fthe Holy Spirit (*ibid.*, Ch. 28, p. 175) and
many raptures. (*ibid.*, Ch. 28, p. 176) She is delighted at the striking of the clock, which is the sign of her drawing closer to death
and thus to permanent union with the Lord. (*ibid.*, Ch. 40, p. 192)
The year 1565 sees the finishing touches to Teresa's autobiography, whose original shorter version dated from 1562.

In 1567 Santa Teresa, having thirteen nuns waiting for her reform, also two from the Incarnation and two from St. Joseph's, founds in Medina del Campo her second reformed convent. Having arrived at 2 o'clock in the morning of August 15, the nuns had their first mass in the portal of an old house. This was the new convent. (*Foundations,* Ch. 3, p. 514) There Teresa met for the first time her future collaborator in the Reform, a mystic and a poet, San Juan de la Cruz (1542–1591); he enthusiastically joined her intentions, insisting on founding a priory and accompanying her to Valladolid. It is in the shadow of Santa Teresa that San Juan de la Cruz became the great mystical theologian who finally surpassed her in mystical experience, poetical vision and scientific interpretation of mystical phenomena. He will remain her most beloved spiritual son. St. Teresa mentions in her book of the foundations (Ch. 4, p. 476) that she established six more convents within the next four years, those at Valladolid (1568), Malagón (1569), Toledo (1569), Pastrana (1569), Salamanca (1570), and Alba de Tormes (1571). Her mention of the foundations as her main concern may demonstrate how, for the devout, contemplation may well be combined with the active life, if the burning love of God is the guide-line for any activity in His service.

The year 1568 saw Teresa's foundation of the first priory for friars at Duruelo with Fray Antonio de Jesús (Heredia), 1510–1601, as Prior, and San Juan de la Cruz as sub-Prior and Novice-Master. Santa Teresa at the time developed more and more as a "Psychagogue," leader of souls, as far as her nuns in the new foundations are concerned. With the help of her confessors and with an admirable clarity she distinguished real piety from hysterical complexes, of which she gives a dramatic example in her dealings with two nuns of Medina del Campo, the saintly M. Alberta Bautista and the unfortunate Sor Inés de la Concepción. (*Foundations,* Ch. 6, p. 436) She instructed the superiors to watch the dispositions of the sisters as to their disciplined or undisciplined desire to receive Communion and to distinguish their willed enjoyment (*ternura*) from divine consolation (*gusto*).

Teresa got the difficult task of reforming her old Convent of the Incarnation; this at first was inhabited by recalcitrant nuns who opposed her as their austere superior because she had been appointed Prioress without their having been consulted. After three years the convent, however, was reformed, the spiritual and financial questions were solved, and now the nuns loved Teresa; harmony and peace were restored to the house. Before her term as Prioress ended (1573), Teresa made still another foundation, in Segovia (1572). Meanwhile in Salamanca Teresa had had some bad experiences with hysterical nuns. In such cases the humane Mother Foundress who used to sing and dance with the novices is extremely severe; they have to be treated harshly. If one month of seclusion is not sufficient, they may be confined for four months. (*Foundations*, Ch. 7, p. 490) If they cry and suffer, well, they have their purgatory here instead of having it there. (*ibid.*, Ch. 7, p. 491) But in Valladolid, conversely, she knew a holy sister who loved to suffer for Christ and died a holy death after a long sickness, Madre Beatrix de la Encarnación. (*ibid.*, Ch. 12, p. 503) In Toledo she had a vision of Christ at the deathbed of Sor Petronila de San Andrés, (*ibid.*, Ch.16, p. 517) opening His arms to receive her. Thus Teresa witnessed everything in her houses; sickness, revolt, obedience, sanctity.

For the foundation of the Carmel in Segovia (1574), St. Teresa was financially helped by Doña Ana de Jiménez who, as a widow, entered the Carmel together with her daughter and became, as Madre Ana de Jesús, one of the outstanding helpers of the Saint. The following year (1575), rich in events, brings two new foundations, Beas and Sevilla; the Saint meets for the first time her greatly beloved Padre Gracián (1545–1614); her two brothers Lorenzo and Pedro return as well-to-do gentlemen from America and bring their sister some practical help, and last but not least, Teresa writes to King Philip II, asking that he intercede with the Pope to create a separate province of the Discalced Carmelites and to have Father Gracián as the Provincial. The Nuncio Ormaneto agrees to forward both petitions, the Archbishop of Seville helping, as he protected the Discalced movement in Andalusia. It was, indeed, not easy for Gracián and Teresa to overcome the difficulties raised by the Calced Carmelites, who with all their power opposed the reform of the Order at its critical stage.

## VI  *The Latter Years*

Teresa in her mystical evolution meanwhile has become quite another person from the one she was at the beginning of her foundations. Since she had been graced with the highest mystical union "without means and modes," the so-called spiritual marriage (1572), she now is entirely adjusted to the fact of her detachment from the world. She does not sigh any longer that she is dying because she can not physically die; she is at peace, in biblical terms; she enjoys that peace which the world cannot give or, in the most literal sense, she does not live herself but Christ is living in her. With a particular ease she continues describing the foundations of Seville and Caravaca, adding the picturesque Sevillian incidents of the procession, the fireworks and their endangering of the convent by fire, the flames of which fortunately, were quickly extinguished. (*Foundations,* Ch. 26, pp. 554–55) On the other hand she feels urged also to report on her higher mystical stages not included in her *Life.* Thus in June of 1577 she starts writing her great classic, the mystical *Castillo Interior* (*Interior Castle*), also called *Las Moradas* (*The Mansions*). In November this masterwork was completed.

Teresa lived at that time in a simple but comfortable cell in her convent in Toledo. She was in good health and of excellent spirits despite the peak of the struggle between Discalced and Calced Carmelites, the latter protected and helped by the new Nuncio, Filippo Sega, who disliked Teresa, calling her a restless gadabout (*femina andariega*). To Teresa's personal satisfaction, the Calced opposition prevented her reelection as Prioress of the Incarnation of Avila, but to her grief the Calced imprisoned at the same time San Juan de la Cruz. Out of all this trouble finally came the independent Discalced province granted by a brief from Rome. (*Foundations,* Ch. 29, p. 583) This brief was the crowning of Teresa's reformist enterprise (1580). Meanwhile, visiting her different convents, she had written, mostly in Avila, another work, *Camino de Perfección* (*The Way of Perfection*), a guide to sanctity, which she submitted to Don Teutonio de Braganza, Archbishop of Evora (1579).

With the full liberty given to the Discalced reform, Santa Teresa was free to continue her foundations. Early in 1580, she established the Convent of Villanueva de la Jara. She tried to do the same in Madrid, but failed to get the permission of the Archbishop. Despite the beginning of her serious illness, the aging Foundress on one of the last days in December, 1580, laid the cornerstone of the Convent of Palencia. Suffering, however, and almost forced to give up her activities, the Saint considers her situation a great misery. (*Foundations,* Ch. 29, p. 577) Fortunately, the canon Reinoso of Palencia volunteered to take over the financial problems. (*ibid.*, Ch. 29, p. 579). With a last effort the ailing Foundress, who had again been elected Prioress of St. Joseph's in Avila (1581), went to Soria (1581), Granada (1582), and Burgos (1582) to set up new establishments. And when Teresa thought that she was unable to go to this last-named northern city because of her weakness and the cold January weather, she believed that she heard Our Lord telling her: "Don't worry about the cold, because I am the real Warmth." (*ibid.*, Ch. 31, p. 591) And so she went to Burgos. This foundation the sixty-seven-year-old Saint had established under the most difficult conditions. Occupied with visiting her nuns everywhere up to the last moment, she died far away from her priory, in Alba de Tormes, on October 4, 1582. It was for a very curious reason that her death occurred in this place: It was the devout whim of the daughter of the Duchess of Alba, one of Teresa's old friends and sponsors, that the saintly Prioress should be present at the birth of her child. Even for this event the exhausted nun was late, and paid for her last human and charitable effort with her own fatal collapse.

What the *conquistadores* had done for the political and military greatness of Spain during the lifetime of Santa Teresa, the Saint had done for the spiritual grandeur of her country. Shortly after her death the "invincible" *Armada* was vanquished by the British fleet (1588), the glory of Spain was going into decline, the mystical life deteriorated into quietistic and visionary movements. But Santa Teresa's example and reform spread out to other countries, particularly to France, and her spirit lived on in the art of her former Toledan fellow-citizen, El Greco.

# CHAPTER 2

# *The Literary Method of Santa Teresa*

## I  *Her Imagery*

SANTA Teresa, as was already mentioned in the Preface, belongs to Spanish literature, but not because she wrote ascetical, mystical treatises. She belongs to it for one reason: she knew how to write. She wrote in a light, almost conversational, often elliptic and oral style with great individual syntactical liberties, with a plethora of diminutives revealing her human tenderness for her nuns,[1] with spontaneous exclamations of genuine piety and a striking, affective word order. But most of all she belongs to literature because she knew how to clothe her unique mystical experiences in an overwhelming and impressive imagery. This imagery is of a pedagogical rather than of a poetical kind and is arranged in such a way that an overall image chosen at the start undergoes a considerable extension, and produces a galaxy of accompanying images taken from quite different domains to make the experimentally gained insights clearer and clearer.

The matters to be clarified are the most lofty imaginable, namely, statements about man's contact with God. These images (some strictly traditional, some modified, some highly individual), do not aim at being literarily original—which they are anyway—but at illustrating a method. They try to show how to prepare the soul for receiving grace and how the experimental love relations with God assume specific forms of visions, utterances, and direct embraces. If, in the modern "God-is-dead" times, certain theologians reject the existence of God because they are unable to experience Him by ordinary natural means, Santa Teresa makes bold to demonstrate that the God experience is quite possible here below, but only as a reward for a life of the highest moral purity and the most ardent loving prayer. All the mystics of the Orient and the Occident have maintained this, but in a metaphysical rather than in a psychological way, and in an abstract rather than in a concrete manner. All have described the arduous way of ascetic ascent, crowned by the mystical graces, and all have done it with such an overwhelming conviction that William James, the great psychologist of religion, once remarked that the experiences of the mystics are a better proof of the existence of God than all those elaborated by the theologians.

## II  *The Meaning of God for the Saint*

For Santa Teresa, of course, God, to start with, is the unquestioned, most living reality, offering to let His creatures know Him through loving intuition. What the Saint then wants to describe through her imagery is the development of this love exchange due to the progress in prayer of a purified soul. The two literary masterpieces which explicate the description of this progress are:

1. *El libro de su vida,* in which is explained in Chapters 11–22 the simile of the four ways of Watering the Garden of the Soul, and
2. *El castilla interior,* a full-length book.

In order to attempt an understanding of Teresa's literary perfectioning, we shall concentrate first on these two works, and then shall deal with others in a more summary way.

Although there exists information about the detached similes of Santa Teresa, about their didactic character and their development into allegories,[2] as well as about their necessity for the identification of the mystical stages (inception, transition and termination),[3] we know less about their role as stepping-stones between definitions and periphrases in the mystical works themselves. Therefore we shall first review the structure of Teresa's main works under this particular aspect; this seems also the easiest way of an introduction to Teresa's doctrine and spiritual progress in the light of her literary art.

## III  *Ways of Watering the Garden* (Life, *Chaps. 11–22*)

Within the *Book of her Life,* Santa Teresa has inserted twelve chapters on her experiences of prayer. She tries to make clear that those who really want to progress in the spiritual life must go through four phases of ascetic and mystic purification, each of which is fraught with difficulties of its own distinctive kind.[4] The first stage of active meditation is disturbed as far as concentration in prayer is concerned by the critical intellect, the imagination, the memory, and a will not strong enough to eliminate these disturbances. If, however, the will gradually achieves the reduction of these disturbances, God takes over and grants first the necessary quiet of the mind; then He elevates the soul by spiritual illuminations and leads her to intermittent ecstasies, and finally to more enduring forms of union with the Divinity. Now, to make clear how this is possible, Santa Teresa introduces her famous comparison of the four ways of watering the garden which, in her modesty, she says she probably has read somewhere but does not remember when and where.

It seems to me that one may water a garden in four ways, either by getting the water from the well, which means a great effort for us, or by means of a chain, pump and buckets, which is done with a wheel (I myself have drawn water that way several times): this means less work than the other way, and one also gets more water; or directly from a river or brook; this kind of irrigation is still much better, because the earth is better filled with water, need not be watered so often and makes much less work for the gardener; or by means of much rain so that our Lord waters the garden without any effort of course and this is incomparably much better than anything mentioned before. (*Life*, Ch. 11, p. 38)

After this extremely condensed synthesis of her allegory to be developed, Teresa makes new excuses that she is attempting the whole difficult explanation, not by her own wish, but under the order of her confessor; this is probably Father García de Toledo. Witty as she is, even when discussing the most sacred problems, and sincere as always, she adds that as far as her own experience goes, the rain comes only in the form of drops but she hopes for much more in the future. Actually her later work, *El Castillo Interior*, will show her as still more advanced in mysticism than the *Life*. She adds a second hilarious *bon mot*: The Lord may laugh, and her exposition may appear sheer nonsense (*desatino*) to Him.

Then she explains as though talking to her sisters what drawing water from a well does mean: to try not to be absentminded when praying; seriously to repent one's sins, even if pride says there are none; meditating on the passion of Christ again and again, even if it seems tiresome. Since after all this one may not feel closer to God than before, the temptation to give up seems normal. But here the Santa injects a new idea into the garden simile, namely that the owner of the garden is the Lord himself and that the gardener who really loves Him does not raise the question of what he is getting from the gardening for himself. And the allegory begins to be filled with new images. Is not dryness a *cross?* And is not refusing dryness a refusal to help Christ the Lord to *carry His cross?*, to *empty the chalice of suffering* with Him? And she comes back to her main allegorical line: "If the Lord wishes that the plants and flowers grow . . ." (Ch. 11, p. 40) He finally will achieve this. To overcome weaknesses means *building on firm ground.* Forgetting about her central simile at this point, Teresa stresses the desperate soul as a *prisoner of the body*—almost a recurrent Neoplatonic theme with her—and the *body as a bad host* to her. Thus she says, do make this *host* some concession: recreation. The time will come when the *host* has to make concessions to the *guest.* And if spiritual dryness is accepted as an aid to the Lord by carrying His *cross,* in due time he will help to *carry ours.* And she closes the chapter with the most radical facing of the facts within her allegory, to which she adds the new, clearcut dryness, now in the literal and imagistic sense of the waterless garden: "If the *well* does not flow we are simply not able to get *water* from it." (Ch. 11, p. 41)

Until the well flows again, Teresa recommends following the advice of Fray Alonso de Madrid in his ascetical work *Arte de servir a Dios* (*The Art of Serving God*), namely to put always before one's eyes the humanity of Christ and thus fall in love with Him anew. Santa Teresa with this often-repeated recipe is in full conformity with the Ignatian Spirit to provoke spiritual progress by mental pictures that compel responses of love. The already mentioned famous sonnet "To Christ the Crucified," the unknown author of which, however, certainly cannot be identified with Teresa, as some erroneously believed, at least reveals exactly what Teresa is driving at. It reflects a gradual development from a negative dryness in love to a fiery meditation on love before the Crucifix, which finally enraptures the soul into loving contemplation:[5]

> *No me mueve, mi Dios, para quererte,*
> *el cielo que me tienes prometido,*
> *ni me mueve el infierno tan temido*
> *para dejar por eso de ofenderte.*

*Tú me mueves, Señor: muéveme el verte*
*clavado en una cruz y escarnecido,*
*muéveme el ver tu cuerpo tan herido,*
*muévenme tus afrentas y tu muerte.*

*Muéveme al fin tu amor, y en tal manera*
*que aunque no hubiera cielo, yo te amara*
*y aunque no hubiera infierno, te temiera.*

*No me tienes que dar porque te quiera;*
*porque aunque lo que espero no esperara,*
*lo mesmo que te quiero te quisiera.*

(I am not moved, my God, to love Thee so,
By that fair Heaven which Thou has promised me;
Nor am I moved to fear offending Thee
By terror of that dreaded Hell below;

*Thou* movest me, my Lord; my heart does glow
To see Thee nailed upon that shameful tree;
To see thy body wounded piteously,
To see Thee die, with agonizing throe;

Thy love, in sooth, doth move me in such wise,
That, if there were no Heaven, my love would burn
And if there were no Hell, my will would bow;

I love Thee not for hopes beyond the skies,
For did my every hope to nothing turn,
I'd love Thee still, as I do love Thee now.)
                                    (Translation by Gibson, 1887)

"This method of drawing ourselves close to Christ," says Santa Teresa, "is helpful in all stages and is a most secure means to make progress in the first stage of prayer and soon to reach the second." (Ch. 12, p. 42) But by no means can the soul make this step simply by her will. Trying this she would have the experience of a man who wants to start to *jump* while others *hold* him *back*. He would use his forces without any effect. The soul makes plans to rise, to fly, but like a little bird with no wings gets *tired* and remains below. Thus she has to be guided with discretion, neither to be for ever a *toad*, nor to be satisfied with hunting newts or lizards. The soul has to understand that there is not always *Sunday*;

*restless working* is the normal condition of man. (Ch. 13, p. 46)
*Eating* always the *same kind of food* can be helpful for adequately
*sustaining life;* (Ch. 13, p. 47) such food is meditating on Christ
fastened to the column in sorrow, pain and loneliness. Teresa in
her visual evocations of the life and suffering of Christ is a faithful
pupil of St. Ignatius. The soul, despite apparently gigantic progress, has to be a little child through humility and eat together with
*any food,* as delicate as it may be, the healthy *bread* of self-
knowledge (but even this with measure), and give it up when the
Lord on his part puts *better food* before her. For the right dis-
cernment, *light* is necessary and an *enlightened* confessor, i.e. one
who can give *light* to others, since he has it himself. (Ch. 13, p.
48) During the present *tempests* of the Church, God *holds* us by
His *hand* precisely through such confessors. "I have gone purposely away," says Santa Teresa, "from what I started to explain,
but those who set out to find so *high* a *way,* first ought to be put
on the *right way.*" (Ch. 13, p. 49)

Teresa actually has gone far away from her watering can; this
distancing is symbolic of the difficulty of oral prayer and meditation. The eidetic nun has defrosted a group of frozen metaphors
and has identified the watering task with a painful effort, with
carrying a cross, emptying a bitter chalice, tolerating, as guest, an
unfriendly host, learning that not every day is Sunday, eating a
monotonous food important for one's health, relying on light from
the confessor, particularly in these times—Reformation in the
North—when the ship of the Church is tempest-tossed and God's
hand is needed as support for one to be put on the right way. One
single time she turned to her original simile when, speaking of
dryness, she explained it by the well which temporarily has ceased
to flow. Thus we get a first insight into what has been called the
nosegay of metaphors. But now, speaking of the "second water,"
she returns to her original allegory:


So far it has been said with how much effort the garden is irrigated
by one who has to get the water from the well with the strength of
his own arms. Let us explain now the second method which the
owner of the garden has arranged in such a way that the gardener
with some artificial means, like the wheel and the buckets, gets more
water with less effort and may relax without working continuously.

(Ch. 14, p. 49)

Teresa anticipates that she will apply this simile to the first form of passive or supernatural prayer, the prayer of quiet. She lacks here a theological distinction of "supernatural in fact" and "supernatural in kind" (*supernaturaliter in re* and *supernaturaliter in modo*). She uses the term, of course, in the second sense and again clarifies by new metaphors the inceptive half—passivity of interior recollection due to a stronger direct aid.

The Santa even narrows down the original simile, saying that some kind of effort is necessary also for turning the wheel and emptying the buckets. But the garden has got sufficient water. Then the diverting metaphors start again. The powers of the soul do not *sleep;* only the loving will feels like a *prisoner* of God who has tied it fast in order that it may love only Him. Unfortunately Imagination and Memory behave like *doves* which stupidly are not satisfied with the food they get in their dovecote, without doing anything on their part. They flutter around looking for other food; they return again not having found what they wanted. (Ch. 14, p. 50) Here occurs a slight return, almost with a witticism, to the *water* symbol. Actually, the understanding, as it works slowly, gets much more *water* than once when drawing it from the well, and the *tears* beginning to flow are granted, not procured *water,* i.e. the passive gift of loving tears takes place, a *water* which *makes* the virtues *grow.* The *concavity* of the soul is *filled* with a delight and satisfaction not earthly. At this point the Saint definitely and consciously returns to the core of her major allegory and expands on it conspicuously:

Now let us go back to our *orchard* or better *flower garden* and let us see how the trees begin to become pregnant in order to bloom and then produce fruit, and the flowers, particularly the carnations, start to exhale perfumes. This comparison pleases me so much because very often, at my beginnings, it was for me a great delight to look at my soul as a garden and at the Lord who walked in it. (Ch. 14, p. 52)

Teresa had implored Him then that He might *increase* the *perfume* of the *little flowers* of her virtues and *cut* those He wished, since she knew better ones would begin to bloom. But, when the flowers were cut, everything appeared dry and the gardener had to see that what he himself had done, to sustain the garden by watering seemed lost labor. There is a time of *pruning* and *weed-*

*ing out* the tiniest grass until the *waters* of grace produce *new flowers*. Teresa then implores the Lord for her own present stage not to cut the *flowers* again, since then her miserable garden would be turned anew into a *dungheap* (*muladar*).

Also the beginners have a good moment when, under the spell of the recollected will, understanding and memory are helping so that the *little spark* of divine love does *not get extinguished*, (Ch. 15, p. 53) this little *spark* that has been *kindled* by the Lord himself. No one should, however, try by himself to bring this *spark* to a *burning fire;* this process would mean putting *water* on it to *kill* it. But if one does not kill this very *little spark*, it will develop into *a great fire* and *throw out flames*. (Ch. 15, p. 54)

The effort of one's arms—she uses another picture again—would only put *logs of wood* upon the *spark* and thus *stifle* it. The will in quietude must *keep away* from the *grinder* of "understanding" like a wise *bee*, because if *none of the bees* was to enter the *beehive*, and, outside of it, one would hinder the other bees from doing so, no *honey* could be *accumulated*. (Ch. 15, p. 55) What we ourselves may *add* to the *fire* by spiritual activity are at best *small straws* but *no wood*. The loving will, behaving correctly, dare not *lift up the eyes*, like the *publican*, and this is a better act of gratitude than the whole *effort* of the *understanding* using all its *rhetoric*. The Saint repeats here her image of forgetting self by being eager only to *help* Christ to *carry his cross*, and, she adds, to imitate the good *knights* who want to *serve* their king *without any reward* (*sin sueldo*). Forgetting self and seeking humility are the roots of the soul's growth, and it is normal that a *child*, after having *grown*, should keep the body of a *man* and not shrink again to a *smaller body*. (Ch. 15, p. 56) Therefore again: Go the *way of the cross* which is made easier now. The *flowers* are *budding* and on the point of *blooming*. With this closing image Teresa thinks again of her now more adequately irrigated garden.

Keeping to the image of the garden in principle, Santa Teresa has made clear, as far as the second stage of prayer is concerned, that in the inceptive stage of passive, loving contemplation God Himself has drawn the human will to Him. The disturbances coming from the imagination, the attempt to understand what happens to the soul as well as to the memory can be kept at bay if the soul actually abandons herself to the felt love of God. Teresa started out by saying that the loving will becomes a *fettered pris-*

*oner,* while the other powers of the soul behave like *fluttering doves.* The water procured easily by wheel and buckets makes the trees begin to *bloom,* the tears of love to *flow,* the *virtues to grow,* the carnations to exhale perfume. The Lord, however, does some painful pruning, cutting and weeding in the garden. He has kindled the *spark* of love destined to become a great *fire* if not stifled by *logs* of wood (which the soul tries to put on by herself), but helped rather by the little *straws* of meditation of which she is capable. The *bee* of soul is not to be busy outside the *hive* but to prepare the *honey* inside, i.e. in the solitude of recollection. Concentrated on love, the soul is a good *knight,* serving the king, not thinking of a reward. The principle of the spiritual *growth* is comparable to that of the corporal growth from *child* to *man.* It is guaranteed by humility only, and by attention to the quiet in the garden with the *budding blossoms* on the point of coming out.

### IV   *The Third Way of Watering the Garden*

The introduction to the third way of irrigation is at the outset again a masterly reprise and condensation of Teresa's spiritual problem.

Let us now speak about the third water by which this garden is irrigated. It is a running water from a river or a fountain so that the irrigation demands less work, although still some in order to canalize this water. Here the Lord wants to help the gardener and does everything alone. This means the sleep of the powers of the soul, which are neither entirely non-functioning nor capable of understanding how they operate.                                    (Ch. 16, p. 57)

Then the Saint shifts her original water image, saying, as if her original image were a water perilous to cross because of the danger of drowning: "The *water* rises to the throat of this *graced soul* so that she *cannot move forward* and would not know how, nor is she able to *turn backward.*" (Ch. 16, p. 58) And an avalanche of clarifying similes follows: The soul here is comparable to a *dying* person in his agony, *in whose hands* one has already put, according to Catholic ritual, the *candle* of the dying. The soul, however, loves this *dying to all the things* in the world. One is in this stage out of one's mind and almost *inebriated* because, returning to the overall image of the garden, the Saint exclaims: Now, now the *flowers* really break open and exhale their *perfume.* The soul feels jubilant like the *martyrs* amidst their *torments*. The heaviest *cross* appears light. One understands now the lack of effect which the preachers have on the people: The *flame of love* stifled by criticism (*seso*) does not give warmth.

But since in this third stage of prayer *God* is the gardener, the soul gets a *rest*. (Ch. 17, p. 60) She leaves herself in the *arms* of the *Lord* to be *carried* wherever He wants, to Heaven or even to Hell where she would not feel pain, being in the company of her supreme *Good*. The soul is astounded to see that the *Lord* is such a good *gardener* that He leaves her no work at all, but wishes that she may rejoice in the *smelling of the flowers*. And Teresa says in autobiographical retrospect: *More water* than the gardener was able to accumulate in twenty years has been provided *by the celestial gardener* in only a moment and *in a direct way*. It is He who makes the *fruit grow* and *mature* so that the gardener now can provide his living from the garden. But he does not as yet get permission to distribute the fruits, until he himself is *strong enough* from the *nourishment of these fruits*. (Ch. 17, p. 61) He is not fit as yet for apostolic work through transmission of the fruits of contemplation. Having confused somewhat the concepts of garden and gardener, Teresa enters a new series of comparisons.

## V  *Further Comparisons and Similes*

The Santa explains that the will being bound and the other powers being free, it is as though while *we are talking to a person, another person starts talking to us*. Or it is as though a person, satisfied *after a meal*, does not feel a need of further eating and yet the stomach would not reject all the food offered; the person would still have appetite enough to eat *some good food*. (Ch. 17, p. 62) This means that there is always room for more divine love but not for other things. Or more correctly, the soul seems as it were to disintegrate trying to cling to the loving will whilst memory and imagination still try to tear her away. But these are already powerless like small *night moths* that can only flutter about and yet become bothersome without causing real hurt. With the patience of Jacob who had to endure Leah before enjoying Rachel, the soul has to wait until the moth *burns itself* up in the flame of the *candle* of divine love.

The series of Teresa's exemplifications of the third way of irrigating the garden is impressive. The abundance of water is now

an overflowing river and would reach up to the neck of a person
trying to cross it. No movement is possible for this person, as for
one on his deathbed. But this passivity in the spiritual life is the
proof that some flowers of the garden have opened already and
we are inhaling their perfume. The soul is as though inebriated
and feels like playing the harp and singing, as the martyrs did
while glorying in their torment. The Lord has taken over the work
of the gardener.

## VI  *The Fourth Way of Watering*

The fourth degree of watering, that of the rain, the Saint explains, means the union of all the powers of the soul. (Ch. 18, p.
64) There is no thinking, remembering or feeling, but only delec-
tation. The soul enjoys without understanding what she is enjoying. Of course, she is experiencing the presence of God in rapture
or ecstasy. The Saint tries now to describe the ecstatic situation,
the actual ecstasy in passive prayer and her post-ecstatic and inter-
ecstatic periods. At the moment when Teresa describes her life,
she has not as yet experienced the so-called habitual mystical
union, and consequently is not in a position to report on this. It
will receive consideration in her *Castillo Interior*. What she tries
to clarify now is the actual mystical union. To explain ecstasy,
Teresa introduces the simile of the burning flame of love, a concept on which her pupil San Juan de la Cruz wrote a whole book.
Teresa only says as a commentary:

The soul sometimes goes out of herself like a fire which is burning
and has become a flame, and sometimes this fire grows impetuously.
The flame rises far above the fire, but not for this reason is it different
from the fire; it is the very flame which is also within the fire. (*loc. cit.*)

Then Teresa addresses God directly in five similes referring to
herself as the unworthy receptacle of God. She is a *breakable vase*
afraid to contain a *precious liquid* and always fearing to *spill* it.
She is a repository unworthy of such a valuable treasure. She is an
unworthy, cowardly *governor of a castle* who at the first attack
may *deliver the keys* to the enemy. She has not the right appreciation for the *jewels* given to her and may *lose* them. She may not
only hide the *talents* given to her but may *bury* them.
Teresa says all this as things become more and more difficult to

explain by similes. The water has been replaced by fire and flame. Starting from this change in her unified picture, Teresa tries to clarify further how it is possible that in the stage of the unification of the powers of the soul, there still occurs the momentary close union with God as felt in the form of a fleeting rapture (*arroba-miento*); that is, as a complete absorption in God. To clarify this, she compares the soul with an *iron* put *into a fire*. After a certain time the iron *glows* and seems to *lose its substance* entirely. (Ch. 18, p. 65) The iron's having become fire is the habitual state; the fire's developing a flame is the actual condition of the soul at this point. Making this departure from the overall picture of the watering process, Teresa comments that *there is not always rain* but that it *stops* at times. Otherwise, the gardener would be put to rest for good, and there *never* would be *winter* again; instead, there would always be *spring* with flowers and *summer* with fruits. No, the gardener is *surprised* by the *rain* when he least expects it, God chooses the moment to put the tired little *bird* into its *nest* that it may rest for a while. Returning from the rapture slowly, all the powers *having drunk* from the divine wine, they are still intoxicated for a time, but not totally inebriated. The wings of the restless moth, called memory, have been *burnt* and will not flutter now. The *water*, the gift of sweet *tears*, now seems actually *rain* from the clouds, and paradoxically *kindles* still more the *fire* of love instead of extinguishing it. Image and reality come here so close to each other that the Saint fears she is speaking nonsense in her effort at self-expression (*parece esto algarabía*).

In this lofty state of grace the soul sees her conditions as miserable in comparison with the purity of God: the soul is a *room* lighted by the *sun*, where all the *cobwebs* are discernible; (Ch. 19, p. 68) she is not the room, she is in the room, alone with God. All the *doors* to the outside world are *closed*. The understanding has not to go *ahunting* anymore; it finds its *food cooked* and prepared. The soul sees herself changed from *unclean refuse* to clear *water* for God's own *table*. Her *fruits* are recognized as God's and are ready to be distributed now; also the *perfume* of the flowers has become so strong that *others* smell and desire them. The *garden is never dry*, since God sends the necessary rain. If the garden's irrigation were the gardener's business now, it would be lost. God has the *medicine* and the *ointment* for our wounds. It would be absurd to *flee* from the light and go *stumbling* by one's self, absurd that a man being *anchored* and fastened should look for a column to lean on or a *cane* for support. (Ch. 19, p. 70) God has protected the little *bird* which has tried to fly from its nest although it cannot as yet *fly alone*. Even when the soul falls, she will be *helped back* as belonging to the people of *the house,* having eaten from this *bread.* The Lord never gets tired of giving from His *inexhaustible mercies* and we ought not to get tired of receiving them. (Ch. 19, p. 72)

Only after this excursus on the right cooperation does Teresa come back to the explanation of the temporary ecstasis within the habitual state of the union of the soul's powers. And she makes bold to do it with the central water-simile itself after the iron-fire simile has seemed to her insufficient to clarify the satisfaction which the soul gets from the rapture:

Let us consider now that this last water we have mentioned is so abundant that, if the soil does not refuse to absorb it, we may believe that the great cloud of the divine Majesty stays here with us on this earth. But if we are grateful for this great good, helping with our good works according to our power, then the Lord takes up our soul in the way the cloud takes up the vapors of the earth and lifts it up entirely, and the Lord like the cloud mounts to the sky and takes with Him the soul and begins to show her things of the kingdom prepared for her. I do not know whether the comparison is fitting but as far as the truth is concerned this is exactly what happens.          (Ch. 20, p. 72)

Teresa, as so often, has become entangled in her similes: the soul is the *soil* absorbing the rain of the cloud and is also the moisture of the air absorbed by the cloud at the same time. She adds therefore that instead of using the cloud simile she could say that a *mighty eagle* catches us with his wings. Trying to resist the impetus of such a rapture means struggling with a strong *giant* who—as she adds from her experience—leaves one *dead tired* if one can resist at all.

What this resistance and particularly what exterior levitation means defeats any attempt at comparison: "One simply feels as though he were being torn to pieces." (Ch. 20, p. 73) Having come back to herself, the soul feels a loneliness as though she were on the *roof* of the housetop of herself, comparable to the bird of Psalm 101, 8. At other times in the periods of dryness in the fourth stage she feels *crucified between Heaven and Earth,*

neither as though she were lifted up to God nor as though she
were attracted by the world. She feels like a person with a *rope
around his neck* gasping for breath. The Santa senses also that
through this new kind of suffering the soul is *refined like gold* in a
crucible, so that the *enamel* of the supernatural gifts of God may
be more easily set in. (Ch. 20, p. 76) The rapture as *transformation* into or as *engulfment* in God is of short duration; then the
powers of the soul, except the will, start to vibrate again like the
*pointer* of the *sun dial*. However, these restless faculties are
weaker than before; they are like a *person who, not quite asleep
and dreaming, is still not fully awake.* (Ch. 20, p. 77) But the
result of all this in terms of growth of virtue means that the once
tiny bird has *grown wings*, the down has disappeared, the bird
can fly. *The captain* of the *fortress* was able to mount and *hoist
the standard* on the top of the *highest tower*. Thinking of her
forgotten overall simile, the Saint remarks tongue-in-cheek: "Be-
hold the *gardener* has become the *captain* of a fortress!" He is free
from everything and would not even like to possess as his own a
pear tree of the *orchard*, for the *keys* of his will belong to the
Lord.

## VII  *Further Similes*

The Saint envisions now the other expression for rapture,
namely the flight of the spirit (*vuelo del espíritu*) and by implication the prayer for the *wings of a dove* according to Psalm 55, 6. It
is the *flight above* all creation and first of all of one's self, but "It is
a sweet flight, a delightful, noiseless flight." (Ch. 20, p. 78) The
Santa understands also that her life before this flight was a *prison*.
The soul has become very clean, so that no *cobwebs* would be
seen in the beams of the *sun* nor even a little *speck* of dust; it is as
though the sun were fully and directly shining on the *water in a
vessel*. The soul is not as yet the daughter of an eagle to face the
sun. She is tempted to *close her eyes* again, having at one time
seen those specks in her *troubled waters*. The little dove can neither look into the *brightness* of the *sun* nor at the residue of *mud*
in her *soul*. She is *dazzled* or *blinded*. She becomes a nothingness
in humility. She experiences the Lord as the gardener and *distrib-
utor* of the *fruits* when and to whom He pleases. Drinking only
one drop of this fourth *water* from Heaven, Teresa continues, one

will have a distaste for everything terrestrial and will have a foretaste of being entirely *engulfed* in this *water*. (Ch. 21, p. 80)

This is Teresa's famous experience that "everything is nothing"
(*es todo nada*), except following God's will.(Ch. 21, p. 81) The
soul is now on a *high watchtower* from which *one sees* the *true*
things, which are opposed to the "farce" of life, the earthly sleeping and eating. One sees clearly one's prison and cries for liberty.
The soul wants *to go out of the body*, with a particular impetus, as
though it were *being sold* in a *foreign country* where the inhabi-
tants do not understand her desire. Here the *flowers* of the garden
exhale more perfume for others also. The *fruits* are brought to the
*barn.* Everything earthly appears to the soul like *child's play*
(*juego de niños*) and she cannot help *laughing* at the preoccupa-
tion with honor on the part of religious persons. *Wealth* is not
only contained in the *short sips* of ecstatic delight, but also in
standing thus fortified below the cross with St. John. (Ch. 22, p.
85) The entrance door to the *bliss* of the divine secrets remains,
however, as in every situation, the *humanity of Christ.* If, in this
lofty state of less than actual rapture, the meditation, whenever it
is possible, on the humanity of Christ were neglected, this would
mean trying to *walk on air* and to be *Mary* before having labored
like *Martha.* (Ch. 22, p. 86). Here the Saint touches, without
knowing it, on the essence of Christian versus Oriental mysticism:
never to abandon oneself to a self-made pseudo-spirituality or
psychological suicide, but to reorganize always anew one's God-
given creative energy.[6]

On the dogmatic level Teresa stresses that the way *to the Father* leads always through the Son.[7] Therefore the Saint continues
with her metaphors, saying that we are not spiritual *angels* and
*need anchorage,* i.e. someone to lean on. For mounting higher we
need *His hand.* The *cement* of prayer is *humility.* The soul which
*bows down* will be *raised.* Yes, says Teresa, we have to tread
along like *little donkeys* to turn the *waterwheel* we mentioned, the
donkeys which, although they keep *their eyes closed* and do not
understand what they are doing, will draw more water than the
gardener with all his effort. (Ch. 22, p. 87) Teresa, not watching
her similes, thus falls back to her second water in the earlier passage we have examined. One must go on with courage, since *His
Majesty* wants us to *rise to the secret service* in his *chamber,* else

we have to serve at lowly tasks and will not be seated at a coveted position at *His table*. Teresa's metaphoric consolations and admonitions become here quite numerous. If somebody has a poor voice, she continues, he may make the greatest *efforts to sing* a song but the voice does not become better. If *God desires* to give one a good voice, he need not shout before this happens. It is a great favor to kneel with *Magdalen* at the feet of Christ and not to be sent away. In order that we may be given strength, God may carry us to the *desert*.

Teresa repeats: Rapture cannot be organized. It is as though a *giant* takes a *straw* with irresistible strength. We are *toads* and do not take off from our mud for any flight on our own. Teresa feels her sisters might be frightened by the fact that the habitual state between raptures of the advanced soul seems to represent a much greater dryness than the state beween the illuminations of the earlier stages. How then explain it? She submits to her confessor a solution of this apparent anomaly in the form of a new simile: There is excellent *food* from which at the beginning many persons taste a portion and keep the good taste for a short time, but in the advanced stage the few persons concerned *take much* of this excellent food for sustaining their life and the taste persists; they would prefer death to *touching any other food* which would destroy this taste. (Ch. 22, p. 88) Thus the Saint, not knowing as yet the wave rhythm of progress in spirituality, clarifies her own experienced tortures of Tantalus on the spiritual level, the tortures of an *insatiable love*. In order not to become in the situation *as dry as a stick*, she has already indicated that the return to the meditation on the humanity of Christ will be a healing medicine.

## VIII   *Some Conclusions*

In conclusion, let us say that Teresa, explaining the "fourth water," has clarified the difficulties of her figure of speech quite well. She started with the imagery for actual rapture. It is like a flame rising within a fire, it is a burning iron becoming flame itself, it is putting the little bird for a short time into its nest, it is the cloud taking the soul like vapors up to the sky, it is an eagle which lifts her up on his wings, it is the noiseless flight of a dove, it is an engulfing in the divine water, it is the lifting up of a straw by a giant.

The other images do not involve the actual rapture; they concern the habitual behavior of the soul after and between such raptures. Teresa feels all the more like a fragile vase, a governor after hoisting the flag on the highest tower and now threatened by cowardice, like an unworthy receptacle of treasures of jewels, of "Talents," like a person half drunk from wine, like a room still full of cobwebs, or clear water murky with specks visible under the sun. She feels also like a garden with mature fruits and fragrant flowers that represent the growth in virtue. On the psychological level the soul feels like a person lonely on the top of the house roof, or as hanging between heaven and earth, or as a criminal with a rope around his neck. All of this represents a thirsting for limitless divine love. In this temptation of despair waiting for help, the soul should be the little donkey patiently circling his waterwheel with eyes closed.

Our explanation of Santa Teresa's four stages through her garden-images and the complementary derivations from them shows that she neither wants, nor is able to keep strictly to her clarifying, overall allegory. Not writing as a poet, she is not interested in esthetic but in spiritual pursuits. But the particular reason is that she works on three levels: (1) clarification for herself of what is passive recollection in its growth, sleep of the powers of the soul, union of the powers and the actual event as well as the state of rapture; (2) clarification for her confessor, who has ordered her to write for his own understanding of her experiences; (3) clarification finally for her nuns, who have to be instructed, helped and warned in recognizing similar stages in the possible progress of their own spiritual life. If we still think of the constant interruption of her report and her mystagogical specifications by metaphor, by prayer and self-criticism, we cannot but admire a random causerie on such a level. Teresa apparently often forgets what she had written. Nevertheless her repetitions and parallels offer an almost circular presentation of doctrinal terms and they lay bare the logical skeleton around which the *charla* (*"chat"*) *developed in an almost inexhaustible imagery.*

Finally, the method of subordinating all kinds of metaphors to larger symbols and of subordinating to those symbols new expository comparisons, corresponds to Teresa's habit of thinking. It is the same way in which she builds up her sentences syntactically, a main clause producing primary and secondary subordinate clauses with the same consequence of an open ending, at times in the form of an anacoluthic sentence structure. Let us call this method of thinking and its expression "concatenation."

If Santa Teresa's watering allegory were a poem, she certainly would have been obliged to develop her central symbol in such a way as never to deviate from it and rather to proliferate and amplify it by details springing from the major metaphor. But Teresa chooses to explicate a treatise on prayer in didactic prose. She makes a concatenation, with changing stresses on ascetical effort, on progress in humility and love, and on mystical graces by which the effort becomes easier and the progress in perfection more comprehensible, the love more burning.

In other words, the open image-concatenation has its counterpoint and *raison d'être* in Teresa's motif combination; here too we have to look for her open and anacoluthic kind of concatenation. There is no doubt that Teresa shows on all levels of structure this same stylistic attitude. Let us clearly recognize this principle of her writing, that she actually does not expatiate on her watering symbol, but uses it together with other metaphors to comment on her ideas, ideas primarily expressed motivistically:

When we begin to be the slaves of love, in order to follow Him who loved us so much, along with determination to love, abandoning everything else the better to surrender to this love . . . , to possess this perfect love, this true love of God, . . . His Divine Majesty does not want one to enjoy such a precious possession without paying a great price. (Ch. 11, p. 36) May it please the Lord to give it to us drop by drop, although it may cost us all the effort in the world. (Ch. 11, p. 37) Speaking of the beginnings of those who are determined to pursue such a good, it is in these beginnings that the greatest effort lies, because the beginners are those who work with the greatest effort, the Lord giving the award; for in the other stages of prayer the greater part is enjoyment, although all degrees, the first, the middle and the last, have their crosses, . . . blessed sufferings. (Ch. 11, p. 37)

Without this ideological concatenation certain additions to the watering simile would not make sense, but in its light they appear illuminating.

## IX   *God the Gardener*

With the second degree of prayer all of a sudden God becomes the gardener. Teresa laughs at such shifts of hers; she knows what she is doing. The sufferings become more passive and interior and so God is already at this stage the gardener, who cuts the branches of the trees in the orchard (into which the garden has changed) and takes out the weeds which a human gardener would not have seen. This catachresis shows that God by passive help instills true *humility* into the quiet soul, (Ch. 15, p. 57) which is now primarily a pruned orchard, whilst the watering with the buckets, filled by a wheel, has been pushed into the background. So little is the pedagogical skill of the Saint interested in the poetic success of her primary image.

From the river of the third stage comes so much water that it goes up to the "neck" of the soul (Ch. 16, p. 57) which is no longer a garden but a mystical lover, who cannot live without the love of God in which he is already almost drowned since he loves in *profound humility.* (Ch. 17, p. 61) Again the relationship between ascetic effort, humility, and *love* is much more important to the Saint than what happens in detail in the garden and its budding flowers.

The rain-image would not explain at all the ecstatic love of the last stage nor the sufferings and the ascetic life prevailing even on the highest level. These important problems were not provided for in the famous introductory water simile, perfect as far as it goes in its condensation. Consequently, at the end of this masterly treatise on prayer, definitions have to take over and explain anew the constantly present but not self-evident triad: ascetic effort, humility, and love, with the final accent on love.

Whoever has understood Teresa's principles of anacoluthic concatenation will consider the recurrent watering simile with its often shifted meaning as the main aid for interpreting the motivistic interrelation of ascetic effort, humility, and love. He will read the text with sympathetic appreciation. Anyone who would start reading the text only as a commentary on the watering simile itself would be disturbed on every page by a suspected inability of Teresa to develop a symbol. He would misinterpret her literary method. He would misread also her masterwork *El Castillo Interior,* called also *Las Moradas.*

# CHAPTER 3

# *The Masterwork:* The Interior Castle

## I *The Seven Mansions*

*EL CASTILLO INTERIOR* (1571) was written at the wish of Padre Gracián. It is the most systematic work of Santa Teresa within her informal "improvisations," and contains her whole spiritual development from her practice of oral prayer to her so-called mystical marriage.[1] The soul is conceived of as a kind of crystal or diamond with seven mansions. In the cold outer courtyard, close to the fences and ditches, there are creeping poisonous creatures, snakes, vipers, and toads. In the outer mansions, close to the yard, there are lodgings for the servants and lower functionaries of the castle. As one proceeds toward the interior, the mansions, furnished for persons of greater distinction, are more comfortable. In the innermost mansion of all the Lord Himself is lodged. Each of the seven mansions or apartments contains many rooms. The three mansions most toward the outside represent imperfections in the spiritual life, in oral and meditative prayer; the four interior mansions represent the life of contemplation: quiet, the sleep of the powers, mystical betrothal, mystical marriage. This last stage, the mystical marriage, shows that Teresa has made progress in her spiritual life during the fifteen years since the redaction of her *Life.* Comparable to the confusion or coincidence of garden and gardener in the earlier parable, here the soul is both the castle and its governor. Of this the shrewd Saint, however, is fully aware.

Within the structure of the work there is also a decisive thread: the presence of God, at first only lovingly in Teresa's imagination, but later experienced as a real presence in the soul. Here the explanation of hallucination[2] seems weak and is heavily challenged by an interpretation that takes Teresa's metaphysical fact literally, that the soul responds mysteriously to the signaling, the "whistling" of the Lord within. (*Interior Castle,* IV) [3] It is the similes of the seventh mansion that are difficult, but even so the theologically untrained Saint can compete in clarity even with the learned formulations of her theologically tutored disciple, St. John of the Cross.[4]

*The Interior Castle* consists of twenty-seven chapters; five are dedicated to the ascetic life and active meditation as discussed in the first three mansions, eleven to the passive trials of the spiritual betrothal which St. John of the Cross would call the passive dark nights (the sixth mansion). Thus there remain three chapters for the fourth, four for the fifth and four for the seventh mansion. Again it appears that guided by Teresa's own allegory, plus accompanying similes and metaphors, the reader will not need a special theological commentary for the understanding of her doctrine, which is so overwhelming that Fray Francisco Boyl said: "We knew very little about God before there was a Santa Teresa." [5] An interpretative aid may be found in a recent symposium on the different aspects of her doctrine.[6] As to the text, Padre Gracián has slightly corrected Santa Teresa's autograph which Fray Luis de León edited as the text of the Saint.[7]

Just as in the watering allegory, Santa Teresa starts here with a programmatic simile:

When I was beseeching Our Lord this very day to speak . . . , it was offered to me, what I shall say now, to begin with a certain foundation: One ought to consider our soul like a castle made entirely out of a diamond or very clear crystal in which are many apartments as in Heaven there are many mansions. Actually, if we consider the situation closely, Sisters, the soul of the just man is nothing else than a paradise in which God, as He says, takes His delight. What then, do you think an apartment has to be, in which a king, so mighty, so wise, so pure, so full of goodness has His delight? (Part I, Ch. 1, p. 324)

Teresa's idea is not independent of literary sources, however; she had read Ramon Lull, Ludolphe of Saxony, Francisco de Osuna.[8] Teresa has references from the beginning to the most interior apartment of the diamond castle where the Lord is waiting for the soul-spouse. She shrewdly is aware from the beginning of her catachrestic image, according to which the soul has to enter into herself, (I, 1, p. 325) becoming bridal chamber and spouse at the same time. But the Spanish language in which *ensimismarse* means "to enter into oneself" gives her a splendid justification for

the ambiguous image. Her pedagogical interest in the nuns, however, lets her ask why the soul chooses to preserve the beauty
of the pure diamond rather than to enter into herself? Her answer's relation to the spiritual and ascetic aspect of the question
silences all aesthetic objections to the simile: because we have
interest only in the rough frame and setting of the diamond, or
rather in the outer wall of the castle, for the frame and the outer
wall both mean our body. (I, 1, p. 324) Some prefer to stay in the
courtyard of the castle with the guards; they do not enter at all,
not even being aware of the mansions which the castle contains.
(I, 1, p. 325) They do not seem disturbed even by the reptiles
crawling about. And now the Saint compares these souls in the
courtyard with palsy-stricken persons who cannot use their limbs,
i.e. in this case have lost the habit of prayer, and therefore have
become beasts rather then men, and feel at home in the courtyard
with the animals. They will be turned into pillars of salt like Lot's
wife, if, given the chance to enter the castle, they try to look backwards instead of looking into themselves.[9]

By way of this excursus on spiritual atrophy, Teresa leads to the
entrance door of the castle. This is, of course, prayer. Worldly
persons, thinking only occasionally of God, may steal into a room
of the first mansion, but there is risk that some of those filthy
animals are slipping in with them. If this is the case, the room will
remain in complete darkness; the divine sun present in the center
of the mansions can not reach this outermost apartment of sin
with its rays, since it is as though this first crystal apartment were
covered by a black cloth against the sun. The unpurified senses,
then, roaming about in the dark rooms, can do so because they
are entirely abandoned by the careless governors, stewards, and
butlers of the castle which are the atrophied powers of the soul.
(I, 2, p. 327)

## II   The Rooms of the Castle

Teresa has spoken of mansions and rooms in the castle. The
rooms diversify the mansions of the castle and are located above,
or below, in the middle, or on the sides of them and are of variant
importance, the most significant being the room of self-knowledge. The mansions, built in a concentric form around the center
mansion of the Lord, are compared to the layers of the palm tree
around the tree's heart. (II, 2, p. 328) The Santa adds still another

elucidation. Whenever a soul is admitted to a more interior mansion, she is free to return to the exterior mansions, too, and particularly to that important room of self-knowledge where, like a bee, she sips the nectar of flowers of humility before returning to her beehive closer to the center to make the honey of virtue. This bee simile is one of the favorite comparisons of the Saint. We have encountered it in the *Life.* (Ch. 15) It occurs also in *El Camino de Perfección* (*The Way of Perfection*) and in the *Fundaciones* (*Foundations*).[10] If anyone is capable of entering a room of the first mansion from the outside, his task is to clean it from the sinful poisons, i.e. sinful animals. (I, 2, p. 380) There are innumerable rooms in the first and outermost mansions, but each one is infested by sin and evil spirits—snakes, vipers—which hinder the passage to the interior of the castle. The light from the center floods the first rooms; they appear darkened, however, to those who enter from outside, because those persons have the dust of their earthly interests in their eyes and are not able to open them to the light. The Saint is a genius in variations: The black veil over the diamond has become dust in the eyes. All the more these persons are in danger of being bitten by the poisonous reptiles. Such danger will beset the soul as far as the third mansion, since—and the Saint says she repeats her old comparison from *The Way of Perfection* (Ch. 28)—the Devil works as noiselessly as a file. (I, 2, p. 331)

### III   *The Second Mansion*

In the second mansion the soul is more alert than in the first, but in her increased awareness she questions the superiority of the religious life as compared with the secular life of her relatives and friends, and she hears the battle of demons with the clash of arms and noise of artillery directed against her. (II, 1, p. 333) But she remembers the Host of her castle and wants to remain there, not to eat the food of pigs like the prodigal son, lest in her critical pride she experience the same misfortune as that which happens to a person bitten by a viper; the body gets poisoned and swells. It is difficult to heal such a person (II, 1, p. 334) because of his pride. Before reaching the mansions where it rains manna, one has to embrace the Cross. And if the poisonous beetles of bad thoughts bite us, we have to take the experience as a trial and guard ourselves against evil. We have to consider our situation like that of a pharmacist who takes poison in order to try the power of the antidote he wishes to sell. With this attitude of careful watchfulness the soul will become sure that "His Majesty will bring her from the one mansion to the others." (II, 1, p. 335) The only condition is not to fall back or to forget that the entrance door of the castle was prayer.

## IV   *The Third Mansion*

The third mansion rewards perseverance in the spiritual life with a greater security against temptations. Those who are there are not living any longer with enemies at their doors and cannot sleep and eat without weapons and without the fear that at one weak spot enemies may invade the fortress. (III, 1, p. 336) The nuns here are vassals of God, with the hope of being admitted later to the King's chamber. (III, 1, p. 338) This comparison is frequent; the vassals are sometimes called knights or subjects; the comparison occurs as something quite commonplace even in Teresa's correspondence. But a nun, disquieted about her lack of fervor in prayer, and yet after being rather free from sin and other temptations in this third mansion, is like a rich man without children who has lost a part of his possessions but still has more than enough for himself and his house. If this man were to behave as though not a piece of bread were left to him, how could he respond to the wish of the Lord that he abandon everything for His sake? Only humility remains as salve for our wounds until the Surgeon comes to heal us. (III, 2, p. 340) The travel from one country to another, i.e. from the first three to the second group of four mansions, is a travel through wind, snows and floods on endless roads. The best procedure is not to linger in one's fatigue but to speed up to meet the Lord at the end of the road. Obedience and imitation of perfect persons let us act here like little birds which eagerly observe their parents, gradually learning how to fly. (III, 2, p. 342) This simile too is frequent in the writings of the Saint, since the featherless ascetic will become the winged mystic. In this particular passage the bird should neither try to fly too high, e.g., already attempting to preserve others from sin, nor to return to the first mansion. At the borderline of the two groups of mansions the Carmelite rule has a particular significance: "To try to live always in silence and hope."

## V  *The Fourth Mansion*

The fourth mansion is closer to the King and brings delicate delight. If sometimes the poisonous creatures creep in by chance, they are harmless to do evil. The soul here experiences sweetness in prayer, i.e. natural delights such as those when a person acquires some valuable property, or meets a dear friend, or brings a business transaction to the desired conclusion, or when a woman finds her husband alive at home when he was said to have died; the soul also takes joy in divine consolations. We know the difference between imagined (*ternuras*) and real (*gustos*) consolations from the *Life*. (Ch. 12) The Saint explains here that her nuns have to do with love and understanding, not with thought and imagination, and she is not sure of the meaning of these distinctions, although she understands that the loving and understanding soul may be close to the Lord while the thought is wandering about in the outskirts of the castle. But alas, her head aches; it roars as though it were full of mighty rivers, and then as though the waters were rushing downwards, again it is as though many little birds were trilling, not in her ears but in the upper part of her head, (IV, 1, p. 345) and she learns something from her terrible headaches: "Let the mill clapper go on and let us grind our flour, neither the will nor the understanding must stop working." (IV, 1, p. 436) These distinctions permit us to recognize of what the soul is morally responsible and of what not.

One of those who know Santa Teresa best, Padre Crisógono de Jesús Sacramentado, wonders why Teresa starts this difficult chapter with psychological and moral rather than with theological and metaphysical distinctions. Actually, Santa Teresa herself senses the illogical procedure. (IV, 3, p. 352) P. Crisógono explains that in the fourth mansion the walls of a treasure chest become transparent.[11] This means: what has been believed as certainly present is now vaguely seen or rather sensed. But an analogous image in harmony with the castle allegory is lacking.

The Saint herself is aware that she has delayed in explaining the distinction between self-induced delight and divine consolation. Finally she links the first to meditation, the second to passive contemplation. Surprisingly, however, she does not do this in the framework of her mansions simile but reverts to a variation of her water simile from the *Life*. Both the meditation and the passive contemplation have their origin in the same divine source, but the water of meditation comes from a long distance to a basin through many aqueducts and noisy artifices; the water of contemplation fills a basin close to the fountain quite noiselessly and makes it constantly overflow. This quiet flowing consequently has its origin in the seventh mansion of the castle; it reaches out to the other three mansions of the interior castle (IV, 2, p. 347) and produces in the fourth that sweetness and quiet which are felt not in the heart but in the interior of the soul.[12] We are like silly shepherd boys and cannot understand such a marvel. Teresa, however, has now created something like a more inward locality of the soul, logical within the structure of the diamond castle, something like Dante's Purgatory in contradistinction to his antipurgatory. But for the moment the castle seems forgotten and to the eidetic Saint this interior becomes a kind of bottom of a concavity (*hondón*) where down below a brazier is standing, and on this sweet perfumes are burnt. Farther above one cannot see the flame or feel the warmth, but one smells the fragrance, causing delight. This is the way of expressing the human kind of permitted participation in the purest gold of divine wisdom despite one's own inferior metal. We cannot get at the stream of overflowing water by our own devices; it surprises us unawares. San Juan de la Cruz would identify this first bestowal of grace, causing a painful desire for more, with the first dark night of the spirit.[13]

Teresa knows that the traditional mystics, without using new comparisons, explain this mystic posture by saying: "The soul enters into itself" or "The soul mounts above itself." But this kind of language, Teresa says, she does not understand. This is all the more striking as, in the first mansion, Teresa herself made this paradoxical point that the soul enters into herself, although she jestingly states that she enters being already inside. She made the point to explain the symbolic framework of her *Castle*. Now neither the castle allegory nor the theological terminology helps her to say how the senses and faculties become united to make passive contemplation possible. Thus she must have recourse to other comparisons. The senses and the powers of the soul still dallying around like stray sheep suddenly hear the sweet and delicate whistle of the gentlest Shepherd. One does not hear this whistling with the corporeal ear but in the depth of the soul. (IV, 3, p. 350) Then, thanks to this mysterious call the powers unite and contract and retreat into themselves like the hedgehog and the tortoise. If this contraction (*encogimiento*) does not take place, we must simply like beggars beseech a great and rich emperor to grant it, and cast down our eyes. But if it occurs, a marvelous interior widening takes place as though the waters of a spring which cannot flow away would be collected in a larger basin around the very fountain. This enlargement means freedom; the soul loses the fear of possible damnation, and she feels the love of God increasing. The soul then has to keep to this life-giving love, else she will feel like the mystical infant she still is, that a tiny creature giving up its mother's breast cannot help facing death. (IV, 3, p. 352)

### VI  *The Fifth Mansion*

The Saint must have been aware that her castle simile was not well used in the fourth mansion and she begins her fifth mansion with the hint that for the entirely mystical and supernatural stages which remain to be discussed no comparison is valid. (V, 1, p. 354) She rather says with biblical allusions that, since the full mystical life means enjoying Heaven on earth, we have to plead for the strength to dig until we find the hidden treasure in ourselves. The soul has died to the world entirely to come closer to God. It is a delightful death, a breaking loose from all activities. The soul becomes like a person who, after a swooning, does not move either foot or hand, so that one believes she is dead. Teresa, aware that all this is no further clarification of the complete absorption of the soul's powers, her famous "sleep of the powers" from the *Life,* is only beating around the bush. She knows that she speaks "a lot of nonsense" in the hope at least at one point of making clearer the secrets of God. (V, 1, p. 355) Weakly continuing the castle simile, she states only negatively that there are no lizards in the fifth mansion, no wandering thoughts. The fifth mansion is already too close to the center of the castle, which is the wine cellar of Solomon's Song (Vulgate I, 3 and II, 4) from which the Lord does not come through the door of the faculties but mysteriously, as he appeared to his disciples after the resurrection, bringing them peace, saying *Pax vobis,* and as he left His sepulchre without moving the stone. (V, 1, p. 357) Then the castle allegory is abandoned for quite a while.

The beginning of the second chapter of the fifth mansion contains instead the famous simile of the silkworm's becoming a

beautiful butterfly; this illustrates in retrospect the soul's hard ascetic work until God grants her a capacity, with all the powers
united, of having wings to fly and to join with Him:

You may have heard . . . how a seed which is like small peppercorns
(I have never seen it but only heard about it, and so, if anything
turns out twisted, it is not my fault) with the beginning heat when
the mulberry trees start to have leaves, begins to get life; and before
it was able to get this sustenance it was dead. Now these living little
creatures feed on the mulberry leaves until after they have become
larger, one puts them on some twigs and there with their tiny mouths
start to spin the silk by themselves, and fabricate very tight cocoons
in which they enclose themselves. And it happens that the big and
ugly worm dies and that out of the very same cocoon rises a sweet,
white and graceful butterfly. (V, 2, p. 358)

Teresa has made her point with the most convincing simile:
The active recollection ends when the cocoon-mansion is built and
this mansion turns out to be that of the Lord Himself. Thus Teresa will understand the biblical statements that our life is Christ
and she adds, as one who is not accustomed to reading the Bible
or to recognizing a quotation like *Colossians* III, 3 ("Your life is
hid with Christ in God"): "I think I read or heard (this) somewhere." And enthusiastically she beseeches her sisters to think of
the difference between an ugly worm and a white butterfly,
which, coming out of the cocoon, has wings to fly upwards and is
not forced to crawl. But since the butterfly cannot simply fly to
Heaven, it is restless and so too is the advanced soul who is now
suffering vicariously for sinners, so much so that she feels as
though minced and ground into bits. But this suffering is as passive as the pleasing raptures. Since the soul in the wine cellar was
filled with the spiced wine of charity, she left there sealed with
the seal of the Lord. The seals are imprinted in wax and actually
"the soul here does not do more than the wax when another puts
the seal on it, since it does not imprint itself; it is only amenable,
namely soft and even for this disposition; it does not soften itself
but only is quiet and consenting." (V, 2, p. 360)
   After the interlude of the seal and the wax, Santa Teresa ab-
sentmindedly remarks: "Now let us turn to our little dove!" Apparently she wanted to say "to our butterfly," since she is speaking
about the good seeds for other creatures left by the one which

rose from the silkworm. But the silkworm's difficult death is the precondition for the butterfly's union with God. This will not occur when the soul remains wrapped up in prayer, fearing any disturbance from outside, but when she fasts in order to give her food to a starving woman. (V, 3, p. 364)

Speaking now about the soul as the little dove when one really expects "butterfly," [14] Teresa asks what the dove shall do, not finding a place to rest and in addition feeling constrained to fly higher. To become more explicit she changes the dove into a loving turtledove and by this bridge of thought she changes the tenor of comparison and speaks for the first time of the mystical betrothal between God and the soul as something traditionally known. She adds, however, writing as a dedicated virgin to virgins, that the comparison between the union with God and the sacrament of marriage seems a rather rough one, even though fitting. The comparison is inaccurate because on the one hand the bodily and psychological predispositions of those who have made up their minds to get married, and on the other the spiritual dispositions of the souls destined to be united to God in a clean and delicate, really inexpressible way, are quite different indeed. And yet the comparison is fitting, because in both cases there are three circumstances which seem to correspond: a first meeting of the spouses, their official betrothal, and their marriage. Now the union with the will of God, or the prayer of union, corresponds to the short moment of the first interview of the future bride with the spouse, who fills her so much with love that she is ready to do everything in order to become worthy of him and eager that the betrothal be carried through. (V, 4, p. 365)

To the modern American reader living within a culture of dating and "going steady" before an engagement, Teresa's concept of "love at first sight" in a society that practices arranged marriages may appear strange. The self-evident implication is, however, that this particular divine spouse has such fascinating qualities that his partner cannot help but be overwhelmed. This correctly understood, the insertion of a first meeting of the spouses before the betrothal to interpret the slow progress within the mystical life, is one of the most ingenious strokes of Teresa's spiritual didacticism or mystagogy.[15] The symbolism of bride and groom stems from St. Bernard's interpretation of Solomon's Song in *Sermons on the Canticle.*[16] (LXI, 2)

## VII   *The Sixth Mansion*

The sixth mansion begins with the fact that the adoring soul has been wounded by love. The not as yet fully requited love becomes unbearable.[17] This is an event on an advanced level. Now, old friends poke fun at her, saying she fakes being a saint. But because of the soul's perseverance all the blame as well as the still more unbearable praise finally appear as sweet music. (VI, 1, p. 369) The bride-to-be is enduring a last trial of love and patiently bears with her illnesses and her terrible pains, to which an actual martyrdom would be preferable, the more so as inexperienced confessors increase her torments. She feels that situation as fully comparable to the pains of Hell, since in this spiritual tempest there is no consolation. She is unable to concentrate her thoughts, even to grasp the meaning of a Spanish book. But all of a sudden the Lord by an utterance or some show of love takes all the clouds away and the sun is shining again. The soul feels like a soldier after the victory in a dangerous battle. The soldier sees clearly that the Lord has achieved the victory and not he, since all the weapons were in the hand of the adversary and were turned against him.

But, says Teresa, we have forgotten our little dove which, thanks to our sufferings, has become capable of taking a higher flight. Now in this sixth mansion the high flights of rapture actually begin. The Lord at times awakens the soul-dove, which is not even thinking of God at this moment. Then the soul experiences something like a swift comet passing, or like a noiseless thunderbolt. The soul feels a most delicious wound without realizing how she was wounded. She feels, however, that she was wounded by her absent Spouse because she hears His penetrating whistle coming from the seventh mansion where He is. As to the pain she feels, it goes to the very heart, and when the one who wounded the heart pulls out the arrow it seems that he pulls out the heart together with it. Here Teresa does not mention a Cherub as she did in her *Life*. Instead, she continues by saying that her best comparison would be this: that from the divine firebrand a spark was falling on the soul, not sufficient to consume her completely, but just sufficient to cause her the pain of burning love. There is often an experience like hearing a voice, or sometimes it is as though a perfume were suffusing all the senses. The Saint cautions: This again is a comparison. But as to the mystical fact, it is an irresistible reality, even though some confessors may say it is pure nonsense, since the spark in the soul is alive while the senses are in a state of slumber, so that the soul hears the utterance of the Voice clearly, loudly, and distinctly, whilst voices created by the imagination and wishfully composed bit by bit, rather seem to be heard by the ear as in a half dream. The soul cannot turn away from listening by any means since she is aware that the Lord who governs the castle is speaking.

"Is there no rest for our poor little butterfly?" asks the Saint, changing from the dove back to the butterfly. No, since new trials have to strengthen the bride-to-be, so that she may have the courage to unite herself with so great a Lord as her spouse. Now the betrothal occurs; the Lord enraptures the soul and takes her completely out of her senses; meeting the Spouse in full consciousness probably would mean death. Continuing her precious image of the spark, Teresa says that God lets it grow to the point that the soul becomes aflame like the phoenix; the soul assumes a new life and in its new purity is united to God in a fashion only He and she understand. The soul coming back to herself is within herself aware of her bliss; this, however, is not like a person after a swooning. (VI, 4, p. 389) She is so much awake and so close to the spouse that she feels the door between the sixth and the seventh apartments to be ajar. Otherwise the intellectual visions could not start here, and they are so lofty that they give truer insights into things divine than the imaginary vision of Jacob's ladder. (*Genesis* XXVIII, 12)

Teresa cannot cast into words, however, this type of vision, any more than Moses was able to relate what he envisioned in the burning bush. A lowly worm cannot understand the greatness of God. Here the butterfly-superior speaks humbly to her silkworm-sisters, not as yet changed into a chrysalis. Nevertheless Teresa dares one of her most charming comparisons of what she has experienced in her unitive passing raptures. She once visited her friend, the Duchess of Alba, and saw in her drawing room many precious objects and bric-a-brac; when she had left, she still had the impression of having seen pretty things, but had forgotten them as single objects. The same thing happens to the soul: united with God in the empyrean Heaven of our innermost being, she has seen marvelous things, but having returned from her ecstasy

can no longer recall particular details. (*Life*, 4, p. 381) Ecstasy
(*arrobamiento*) within the castle means that God closes all the
outer doors and also those between the mansions; He keeps open
only the one to the seventh apartment where He is, the apartment
where He often enraptures the soul-bride.

To try to resist such exalted rapture would be as useless, says
the Saint, as a straw resisting its being lifted up by the magnetic
power of amber. At this point, Teresa remembers the quiet basin
of water mentioned in the fourth mansion and uses it for a parallel
comparison. God unleashes now the sources from which the water
flowed to the nearby basin and thus creates a tremendous wave
by which the ship of the soul is tossed high up. No pilot can do
anything against such a wave. Then the Saint asks whether the
soul tossed up in rapture leaves the body. She concludes that it
does not and compares the phenomenon to the sun which remains
in its place, although it is sending out its rays. The quickness by
which the flight of the spirit occurs is comparable to a bullet leaving the gun although no sound is made. Visions granted in rapture
are like tokens from the Promised Land. (*Numbers* XIII, 18–24)
These raptures and visions are the gifts of the spouse for the
bride, and they remain deeply impressed in her memory.

Since the little butterfly (*mariposica*) in her situation of an en-
gaged spouse-to-be has a burning desire to be united to the spouse
forever, the raptures in the sixth mansion become more frequent,
indeed quite regular. Nevertheless, the poor butterfly (*maripo-
silla*) still is fettered with many chains which do not always let
her fly as she may wish. (VI, 6, p. 387) Passive tears of sorrow are
distilled from her fiery heart as by an alembic. But God is doing
the distillation, and coming back to the great allegory of the four
ways of irrigation from the *Life*, Teresa affirms that the passive
tears are the superabundant rain from Heaven which still flows
when one's dry earth has been thoroughly soaked to produce fruit.
If we should try to produce this rain, we should toil in vain and
not even fill a small pond with water. (VI, 6, p. 389) It is interesting that Teresa does not stress as much the details of the espousals
of the soul as she does her feelings. Now, powers and senses taking part consciously in the union with the Lord consolidate the
stage of the betrothal. The soul feels like the father of the prodigal
son, wants to arrange feasts and to summon the whole world to
the praise of the Lord. She is like a man who has drunk so much

that he is not master of his senses. All these are, however, the Saint adds, inadequate comparisons for such precious experiences, but she is incapable of finding better ones.

There is a rich stream in the soul which carries gifts from time to time but also bears always the slime of sin. This is a cross for the memory. (VI, 7, p. 390) To alleviate the burden of this cross, one has to meditate on the humanity of Christ again and again. He is the way and the light, i.e. the guide through these sublime apartments. And the rational meditation blows heat into the dying fire which used to enkindle the soul to burning love. (VI, 7, p. 392) This flame has always to be rekindled by ourselves and not by a miracle. Then, to the soul-bride-to-be in the sixth apartment the raptures will turn out as flashes revealing in an inkling an imaginary vision of Christ. It is true, of course, that Christ is ever present to the soul in such a lofty state. But the difference is like that of the presence of a precious stone with healing qualities within a reliquary, and the surprising opening of the reliquary by the one who has the key to make this stone truly visible for a moment. This brilliance experienced for a moment will remain a precious and unforgettable memory for life. It is like a particularly beloved person whom one has really seen once and whom one will never forget.

In this prenuptial stage the soul also realizes that God Himself is the palace in which she is living and consequently that He would be deeply hurt by the slightest sin, just as we might be hurt by a word spoken in our absence. Teresa, with this comparison, thanks to her incorrigible causerie, falls back to her central image in reverse: Now the soul lives in God as her palace, as at the outset God lived in the soul's palace. But the Saint, despite this new figure, has not forgotten what she had said earlier. Therefore she starts the last (eleventh) chapter of the sixth mansion by returning to her dove or butterfly:

Will all the favors which the spouse has granted the soul not suffice that the little dove or the little butterfly (don't think that I have forgotten her!) may finally be satisfied and find a quiet place to die? (VI, 9, p. 404)

The answer is, of course, no: before the mystical death in the consummation of the spiritual marriage, the soul has first to undergo still greater sufferings of a purifying and passive nature. The desire for the ultimate and permanent union, as a state lacking emotional equilibrium, is often like the receiving of a blow or like a new wound from a burning arrow. The person going through this stage is crying aloud and suffers like the souls in purgatory. The soul feels like a person hanging, who can neither reach the ground nor ascend to Heaven, or like a person burning with thirst and not able to reach the water. In this lack of emotional stasis, the slightest occasion (e.g. hearing a spiritual hymn) produces an irresistible rapture. Trying to resist would be the same as though a person thrown into a fire were to tell the flames not to give out their heat.

## VIII   *The Seventh Mansion*

In the seventh mansion the Saint speaks of the Spiritual Marriage, which, she hopes, Our Lord will grant also to her daughters. This marriage will be consummated in the apartment which belongs to His Majesty alone and therefore this apartment is another Heaven. With a mystagogical parenthesis Teresa remarks that the light of the sun of justice shining there will reach all the souls in the palace, if they are not in the darkness of the outer rooms by their own fault; such souls would be like a man who has his hands tied behind his back by a strong chain and is fettered to a post, and who is dying from hunger although surrounded by delicious food which he cannot reach. We would be cruel not to try to help this person. But then, Teresa continues, she will not speak of the souls of darkness now but of the souls of light who, admitted to this bridal chamber, experience like a cloud of greatest clarity the presence (*compañía*) of God's Unity in Trinity there, i.e. in the very depth of the soul ("the spirit of the soul"). Here God is the companion of the soul and is habitually with her. She is sure of His presence in the way one is sure of the presence of friends in a room although all of a sudden the shutters should be closed. Then one feels the presence of the friends although one does not see them. To see more clearly the soul has to wait until God opens the windows of the understanding again. ( VII, 1, p. 410)

In the spiritual marriage one thing is fundamental and distinct from the spiritual betrothal. In the spiritual, as in the human marriage, the partners are so united that they cannot be separated again. ( VII, 2, p. 411) In other words: the spirit of the soul has

become one (*una cosa*) with God. Here enters opportunely the
ingeniously "magnificent" [18] comparison between mystical betrothal and mystical marriage:

In the betrothal it is as though two wax candles were brought together
so closely that the whole light is only one or that the wicks and the
light and the wax all together are one; and yet afterward one may
well separate again the one candle from the other and there are two
candles again or the wick may be separated from the wax. But here
(in the spiritual marriage) it is as though rain from the skies were to
fall into a river or a fountain where everything is water, so that it is
impossible to divide or separate the water of the river and the water
which came from the skies. Or it is as though a small brook would
enter the sea; there is no means to separate the two. Or as though a
room had two windows through which much light would enter; although it enters divided, within the room it becomes one light. (VII,
2, p. 412)

And Teresa identifies her new comparison with her old one: the
butterfly dies with the greatest delight, since its life is now Christ.
But still the tiny soul-fountain (*esta fontecita pequeña*), absorbed
by the mighty divine stream, feels from time to time the irresistible
aspirations as actual motions of the water—apparently the actual
embraces in this lofty state of spiritual marriage of the pure spirit
of the soul in celestial union with the uncreated Spirit. (VII, 2, p.
413) Then it is as though a person suddenly were thrown into
cold water and as though milk streaming from the Divine Breasts
would flow to sustain the whole castle. Then the mover of water,
the giver of light, the shooter of arrows in the center of the soul-
castle becomes evident as the Lord. But also the fruits of the soul
whose spirit is now united to the celestial water are considerable,
and comparable to those of a tree planted by the streams of water,
which is fresher and extremely fertile due to the nature of the
ground.

What still remains to be understood is that the soul is now in
complete peace, although the spiritual combat on earth necessarily continues. It is like a kingdom at war where only the king
remains quiet in his palace; or it is like a body plagued by pains
while the head is sound, and the fact that the body suffers is no
reason for the head to suffer, too.

After all, the little butterfly-soul has died with the greatest joy

on finding Christ living in her. Consequently, as a fire does not
direct its flames downwards but upwards, now the internal movements come from the center of the soul and awaken its powers
(VII, 3, p. 415) by sweet and penetrating touches. These are like
a personal message or a letter written with so much affection that
the writer wants the receiver to understand that the answer can
only be love. In this temple of God where the soul now is, there is
the same perfect quiet which was observed during the building of
the temple of Solomon. God and the soul have mutual joy in the
greatest silence.[19] The understanding gets only now and then a
chance to look at what happens through a small aperture, as it
were. This means that the faculties in the stage of the mystical
marriage are not eliminated but only dazed. When the poor little
butterfly was still lonesome and frightened, a devotional song or
picture was sufficient to make her fly upward in ecstasy; now she
is with her divine spouse; in such a close companionship nothing
can distract her, and the external raptures and levitations of a
former time would appear to the soul as weaknesses. And jubi-
lantly the Saint adds: Here the soul comes to herself, thanks to the
kiss for which the bride besought the divine groom. Here the
wounded hind gets water in abundance, here the dove sent out by
Noah finds the olive branch, as a sign that the storm is over and
that she has found firm ground amidst the waters and the tempests of this world. (VII, 3, p. 417) And yet since these souls,
even though graced with the mystical marriage, do not as yet
enjoy the durable peace of eternal bliss, they will do well to be on
guard lest their ship overladen with gifts sink into the abyss of the
sea. But under normal conditions the storms pass like waves,
quickly, and the good weather returns, since the presence of the
Lord causes all else to be forgotten.

In the closing chapter the Saint hints again at her central negative motif of temptation, i.e. things in the outer castle may con-
spire to avenge themselves; they may indeed rage for a short time,
but it will be in vain. And the brides have to see to it that their
spiritual marriage is fruitful, that good works are born. This is
Teresa's focal point: The mystical graces enable the soul to do
apostolic work. That is the reason why the graces are given. Her
life has proved it. There will not be a lack of occasions to perform
valid actions even in the corner of the cloister. Mystical brides
have to be slaves of God, since they are branded with His sign of

the Cross as a token that they have given up their freedom for
Him. The best foundation of the castle is humility. Without it the
castle will not rise very high; consequently a firm foundation has
to be laid lest the structure crumble. The soul has drunk from the
wine in the cellar of the spouse, wine which has the power to give
strength to the body, as the food which goes to the stomach gives
strength also to the head and to the whole body. (VII, 4, p. 720)
We must be Mary and Martha together, not only sitting at the
Lord's feet but giving Him something to eat, that is, bringing Him
souls to be saved. Within the cloister this may be done by showing
toward the other sisters a charity which, like a fire, will enkindle
their aspirations toward higher virtues. This is the foundation of
even the highest towers of the castle.

The Saint closes with one of her sacred jokes. Considering the
enclosures of the nuns and their infrequent opportunity for enter-
tainment, she has built them this castle which they may enter and
in which they may roam about even without asking permission
from their superiors. They never ought to try to force the entrance, however, beyond the third area of apartments. But waiting there with humble patience, they may find themselves by
grace of the Lord of the castle soon in the fifth and even in the
seventh mansion. And in each of the mansions there are many
rooms upstairs, downstairs, around the whole ring of the mansions, with gardens and fountains inviting them to lose themselves
in praising the Lord.

In contradistinction to the treatment in a previous chapter of
the four ways of watering the soul-garden, in discussing the *Interior Castle,* I wanted to present the "stream of consciousness" of
the Saint in mixing central and peripheral imagery, without my
own extended critical interruption. We should now understand all
the better her manner of presentation.

## IX  *A Brief Critique of* The Interior Castle

Since the Saint's forte is improvisation, it is clear that her rambling occupies more space than her systematization. Since she
wants at the same time to report on her spiritual progress to her
confessor, and to guide her nuns in the spiritual life, as also to
clarify the greatest mysteries for herself, she finds it needful to
move from one set of images to another, to mix them, to return to
the one or to the other of her symbols at will and none-the-less

maintain the central allegory of the castle. This allegory, however, is eliminated for a period by the allegory of the silkworm's becoming a butterfly. The butterfly is confused with the dove. The dove finally becomes spouse and bride. The interior castle constructed at the beginning of the great allegory is rebuilt at the end. There is no doubt that all these somewhat uncontrolled mental pictures and stylistic catachreses may add zest and charm to the presentation. The *Interior Castle* actually is a test case of what Fray Jerónimo de San José in his *History of the Discalced Carmel* wrote in 1637 of the jumping-about style of Santa Teresa: "She starts a problem, and when another important one comes to her mind, she interrupts the first and follows the second, and she returns to the first and blends the two with such skill that, being sometimes quite different things, they form a texture and marvelous harmony." [20] With closer scrutiny, however, one is aware that this blending of extreme images does not always go so smoothly.

The plan of *The Interior Castle* is well detailed in the very first chapter of the first mansion, but runs at once into the difficulty that the soul is the diamond-castle as well as the person moving through it. There is, for the modern reader, at least, an unnecessarily long description of the poisonous creatures in the outer castle, the entrance door of prayer and the three ascetic mansions. But with the fourth mansion, the recurrence of the water-simile actually drowns the castle-simile. In the fifth mansion the castle is forgotten and the silkworm-butterfly simile takes over. The butterfly as the winged soul is again and again confused with the dove, and the spouse of the future betrothal and marriage is introduced. The main link with the Castle is always this, that in the seventh mansion the Lord and Groom is waiting. In the sixth mansion comes the open door to the seventh, an image serving rather than dominating the now stronger symbol of betrothal and marriage. The seventh mansion thus turns out to be the bridal chamber, even underscored by an involuntary sacred humor of the peeping intellect at the chink; but again the image is obscured by the new splendid comparisons of the united flames of two candles versus the indistinguishable waters of the river and the sea.

The catachretic aspect of the castle image is offset by a host of minor metaphors. The souls outside in the courtyard are palsy-stricken by sin. When they enter the first apartment they do not see the sun shining from the interior but see the diamond as though covered by a black cloth because the dust of imperfection is in their eyes. They are exposed to the poisonous beetles of bad thoughts and have to try the antidote of prayer on them like clever pharmacists. They are little birds who slowly have to learn how to fly. When the first passive consolation comes, the soul feels like a woman who surprisingly finds her husband living after he was thought to have died; she does not care that the clanging of the senses goes on and on while she smells the fragrance and feels the warmth of an internal divine flame. The stray sheep hears the whistle of the gentle shepherd. The wax has been disposed to receive the seal. Like a victorious soldier the soul gives the glory of conquest over the senses to the Lord, the more so as she feels His touches and presence as a passing comet or a noiseless thunderbolt, a strange voice, a perfume, a spark enkindling the fire which Moses experienced in the burning bush. The superabundant tears of bliss now water the soul-tree and make it bear fruit, Noah's dove brings back the olive branch of peace within the tempest of the world.

It is as though, at the beginning of the baroque age, Santa Teresa were attempting something like a mirror technique, something like a theater within a theater, a picture within a picture. A great symbol develops a new imagery and this imagery proliferates into almost numberless new metaphors. The frame almost cannot contain this plethora of imagination. The complexity is, however, exactly what fascinates the reader; he forgets his temptation to bring order into the fullness and is carried on by an imagistic creativity which at the same time both clarifies the most mysterious of all the human experiences and shows the way to sanctity.

# CHAPTER 4

## *The Style of Moderation:*
## The Way of Perfection

### I  *The First Two Chapters*

SANTA Teresa at an early date (1562) wrote a kind of testament for her nuns of St. Joseph in Avila in one single book of forty-two chapters. It is called *El Camino de Perfección* (*The Way of Perfection*), and through it she wants to teach her sisters the best kind of prayer according to her experience; consequently the whole treatise is a kind of grandiose paraphrase of the Paternoster. She wants to educate her nuns to see the social needs of the Church as well as her central problem: the salvation of souls. In this book there is no mention of a single vision, no demonstration of complicated truth by lengthily developed comparisons. But there is a large view of the spiritual life vibrating with deep concern for mankind. Teresa tries to put the prayer and the rule of her cloistered nuns on the level of the fighters for the Church, of the preachers and the theologians. Nuns are not in the convent to pray for personal favors or, God forbid, for money for the convent; they are there to save France from Protestantism. The progress made there by "those Lutherans" (*estos luteranos*), as she still calls the Calvinists in 1563, breaks her heart, since she is afraid so many souls may be lost every day. At the high points of her concern, her language turns oratorical, almost Ciceronian, although she never knew Latin, and her rhythmical prose flows from her deep feeling for her national idiom which she adapts closely to her emotion:

> Oh, my sisters in Christ!
> help me to beg just this from the Lord;
> for this purpose He has united you here;
> this is your real vocation;
> these have to be your occupations;
> these have to be your desires;

here is the place of your tears;
these are your specific petitions. (Chapter I, p. 235)

Teresa's second concern is to stress the need of radical poverty,
not only of the individual nuns but of the convent and the Order
as a whole. She might suppose that this crucial rule of poverty will
not easily be accepted by those of her nuns who are daughters of
well-to-do Spanish families. So she sweetens the bitter pill with a
long wordplay on *to fail.* The Lord of rents and of people of income (*señor de las rentas y de los renteros*) wanted the perfect
ones to live in complete poverty. The Carmelites came at His bid-
ding and He will not *fail* them; rather will Heaven and earth first
*fail.* But the sisters *fail,* if they are afraid He could *fail.* And if He
were to *fail,* then still it would be for the better, as the lives of the
Martyrs *failed,* too, when they died for the Lord. (II, p. 236)
Money and worldly honors are the archenemies of Holy Poverty,
which alone was honored by the Lord. Poverty is the Carmelite's
weapon; the house, the nun's garb, the speech, and the thought
have to be poor. A spacious convent is meaningless; there was not
much room in the crib or on the Cross. However, a garden within
the convent walls is justifiable, since the sisters are hermits and
need places of retreat for their prayers.

## II    *The Third Chapter*

The third chapter insists again on the nun's *central task,* that of
joining the Church in its great function of hindering schism and
heresy. Teresa does not accept the validity of any objection; her
nuns do exactly what soldiers and priests are doing outside the
cloister. Well, women do have a particular mission. If one does
not pray for one's own soul, the sisters may object, one will go to
Purgatory. All right, you may go to Purgatory, if you like, but in
any event do try to save other souls from Hell. One has to pray for
the king and the bishop; you say others do that sufficiently.
Maybe so, but the nun who does not dedicate her prayers, petitions, mortifications, and fasts to the public good has missed her
vocation.

## III    *Chapters Four Through Ten*

In the fourth chapter *charity is praised as the basis* of the entire
life in the convent; this charity must become evident from a great

love among the sisters. Teresa stresses her point by an anaphorical presentation reminiscent of the epistle of love written by St. Paul to the Corinthians, 1 Cor. 1–13: "All have to be friends, all have to care for one another, all have to love one another, all have to help one another." (IV, p. 242) This high praise of love is followed by two stern warnings: There must be no particular friendship among two sisters, no friendship with the confessor. Even if such friendships are harmless, they detract from the radical love of God.

Chapter five offers a footnote to the problem of the confessor. Every sister has to be free in choosing and changing her confessor. The latter should be under all conditions a learned man so as to understand the ascetic-mystical implications that have to do with nuns on the way to perfection. The local Bishop D. Alvaro de Mendoza is commended for his understanding of these problems and praised as a person friendly to each religious order and to sanctity, a servant of God from ancient noble stock and "very much in favor of this our own house." (V, p. 245)

Chapter six establishes the fundamental difference between *eros* and *agape*, mundane and divine love, with the remark that the sisters are supposed to know this difference anyway, even though only theoretically and not by experience. Teresa can help them to know through her own experience. The perfect lover of God has an intrinsic contempt for the world. (VI, p. 246)

Chapter seven gives some practical examples for training oneself in perfect love: one does unpleasant things with a pleasant face, attends recreation joyfully although one may not like it, does not call sisters by their pet names; and all this even though such renunciation may seem against female nature. But in the spiritual life the sisters have to be as strong as men, not weak women. (VII, p. 250) Radical detachment means not clinging to anything. Sisters who find consolation in seeing relatives are far from being detached. (VIII, p. 251) Perfect detachment erases earthly connections from the sister's memory, in order that she may embrace Christ all the more strongly. (IX, p. 252) And what else should detachment mean for sisters who came with the purpose of dying to the world? (X, p. 253)

### IV  *The Eleventh and Following Chapters*

It is Chapter XI that offers the most simple means of mortification, namely not complaining in suffering. Otherwise the sisters would have to be ashamed in front of unhappily married women, who feel obliged to hide their sufferings from their husbands. (XI, p. 255) In Chapter XII the Saint comes out with the real problem. A nun who always wants consolation is not a true Carmelite; for the latter comes to the cloister ready for death itself, and is willing to die this death slowly even though the martyrs did it in a single merciful moment. The detachment from the world by entering the Carmel was a first step only. Now comes the nun's voluntary consent to any difficult deed for Christ; and the decision not to be elated at any achievement of this kind. For this would be pride, and pride would deprive the action of any merit. Finally Teresa comes to her main point, which is the absolute need of perfection. This perfection has no limits. This house, she says, is a Heaven, if Heaven can exist on earth. (XIII, p. 259) The sister seemingly most despised is here the most happy. Humility is the mark of the perfect nun. At this point Teresa becomes quite emphatic, and exclaims in a well-rounded sentence:

My daughters, let us at least imitate somewhat the great humility of the Most Blessed Virgin whose habit we wear and whose nuns we call ourselves with confusion; because, however much we may seem to humiliate ourselves, we always fall short of being daughters of such a mother, and spouses of such a spouse. (XIII, p. 258)

A case in point is silence and resignation when wrongly accused of a fault. (XV) Humility again and again is a sign of love of God, of the way to perfection. Until now, Teresa has been austere but has said the expected things. Now she comes to a crucial point, that perfection in virtue correlates with perfection in prayer. The perfect prayer is, of course, contemplative rather than meditative. People misuse the terms. If somebody makes a serious examination of conscience every day, people say she is a contemplative, an angel, a saint. All this is nonsense. Contemplation is only given by God, not however as a compensation for holiness but as a stimulus to higher love, even in souls with venial sins. The important thing is to be aware of this offer and to cooperate.

Here comes in the much discussed passage of the chess game, about which the Mother Foundress certainly would not know anything if she had not been "sinful" enough to enjoy it in her youth. But she learned there that everything depends on capturing the king. This is the problem of prayer. Although the comparison is to the point, the chess game simile exists only in the autograph text of the Escorial. The Saint deleted it later in the autograph of Valladolid, perhaps as too "sinful." But what she kept is the panegyrical praise of the Love offered by the Maker to His nothingness, the creature. A sacred wordplay in antithesis and an ironic diminutive support Teresa's admonition to her sisters:

Look, what a beautiful exchange it is to give our love for His; consider that He is able to do everything and we here are incapable of anything except to do what He enables us to do. Now what is it that we *make* for You, Lord our *Maker?* It is as much as nothing, a shaky resolution (*determinacioncilla*). Thus, if His Majesty wishes that that which is *nothing* may merit the *All*, let us not be foolish. (XVI, p. 264)

But, continues Chapter XVII, it is a fact that the majority of sisters remain on the meditative level of prayer and in everyday activities. So what about them? Teresa has prepared her answer well. They have to take it in humility. Humility again is the way to perfection. Humility is the hallmark of sanctity. Martha is a saint as well as Mary and—Teresa adds with her imperturbable humor and pedagogical skill—it is very good this way, else our Lord would have gone hungry. And she has a second consolation for the non-contemplatives. They have less temptations and trials, and defend themselves like brave soldiers. The contemplatives are the ensigns who have to carry the banner without any possibility of self-defense when attacked, but the banner they carry is the banner of all the soldiers. (XVIII, p. 268) With humility everybody can be saved; without it the greatest ascetic will be condemned, if he acts like the hermit Heron, who, after a life of superhuman penance, was tempted by the devil to throw himself into a well in order to go to God by a treacherous kind of shortcut. (XIX, p. 273)

Chapter XX necessarily begins with a correction, as Teresa has said a bit too much in consoling those nuns who are perhaps too

active in what is after all a contemplative Order: "It seems that I
contradict myself." There are different ways to Heaven as there
are different mansions in the crystal palace of the soul. There are
different waters, streams, brooks, and pools of Divine water to
quench one's thirst. The pools are for children who would be
drowned in deeper water. But again Carmelite sisters are no children. They are obliged at least to try the highest way of perfection
and to leave it to God whether He will help them toward it or
whether He has chosen another path for them. He who buys a
rosary may use it more or less frequently, but he will not put it in
a drawer, otherwise it was foolish for him to buy it. Since Teresa
is convinced that every Carmelite can reach the first stage of contemplation (passive recollection), she now encourages all, in so
far as may be possible, to concentrate on prayer according to the
Carmelite Constitution, not with misgiving but with a determined
resolution to achieve contemplation. The Saint's humor is not lacking in the most serious and, for herself, slightly ambiguous discussion. There is a spiritual mob (*vulgo*), she says, and those belonging to it will say: "This is not for women, they only get illusions,"
and "better they would do some weaving," or "they do not need
such delicacies," or "the Paternoster and the Hail Mary are good
enough." (XXI, p. 275) This kind of criticism, she adds, will not
affect the humility of the nuns, for they know better.

Every prayer, even the vocal prayer, has to be mental, has to
absorb all the elements of love and attention and make one forget
the world. Teresa shows how a passage of the Paternoster is able
to draw her into delightful meditation. But the thought that nuns
are spouses of the Lord will also arouse their loving curiosity
about Him before whom the Angels are trembling. As his spouses,
they have a right to know about the qualities and possessions of
the Groom. (XXII) For the gifts received one gives something
out of love, not out of calculation, and the first gift is the resolution to make progress in prayer, never to look backwards, to act
bravely like the soldier who refuses to surrender even though he
knows that if made prisoner, he will be killed. (XXIII) Teresa
thus has laid an excellent foundation for progress in prayer: humility, resolution, concentration, and love. Concentration is para-
mount, no matter what theologians might previously have said
about this matter. She, Teresa, the Prioress, responsible for the
twelve Carmelites of St. Joseph's, is obliged to teach them to pray

in such a way that the nuns are aware to whom they are speaking
and who He who hears them is. (XXIV)

Having said this, Teresa dares a shortcut of the greatest pedagogical skill. If the vocal prayer, like the just-mentioned Paternoster, is said with mental participation and love, the turning point
toward contemplation is possible at any moment. Some crowded
participles seem to make such a discovery the most natural thing
in the world. The arguments, in the form of abridged clauses,
seem overwhelming:

> His Majesty, who listens to one who talks to Him, responds in His
> greatness by suspending the understanding, stopping the thinking and,
> as people say, taking, of the one who prays, the word from his mouth
> so that, even though one wanted to do so, he cannot speak. . . . The
> soul is consuming itself in love and does not understand how it loves.
> (XXV, p. 283)

The Saint adds that she is ashamed to avow that she has been
graced with this supernatural kind of prayer where God speaks
and the soul listens.

Surely it is up to the Lord to give others the same grace, and
one cannot do anything about it. But one may predispose oneself!
While praying orally we always must consider ourselves in the
presence of the Lord. At this point divine love overwhelms the
Santa, and one may imagine the convincing fascination, the hyp-
notizing of the sisters when she continues with imperatives and
rhetorical questions:

> Imagine with how much love and humility the Lord himself teaches
> you, and believe me, whenever you can, do not remain without such
> a good friend. If you get accustomed to drawing Him to your side
> and He sees that you are doing this with love . . . then you will not
> be able, as they say, to cast Him out. . . . Do you think that it is a
> small thing to have such a friend on your side? . . . Get accustomed,
> get accustomed! (XVI, p. 284)

A wife, to be well married, has to be sad if her husband is sad,
and if he is in good humor, she has to show herself full of glad-
ness, even though she really may never be glad. Now in case of
the spiritual spouses, the spouse lends himself, even subjects himself to their moods. If they are in good spirits they have only to

imagine the Lord in His glorious resurrection; when they are sad, they may recall Him as suffering in the garden, tied to the column, spat upon, betrayed by His friends, laden with the cross. Then He may look at them with His beautiful and compassionate eyes full of tears and forget His own pains to console them. Then the nuns will reciprocate in their real troubles. To all kinds of calumny they will be deaf, they will stumble, they will fall with the spouse, but not abandon His cross. Teresa imperceptibly has linked the life of prayer and the life of virtue, devotion and asceticism, both through and with Christ, the spouse.

## V  *The Seven Petitions*

In this mood of love, mortification, gratitude, Teresa enters her ascetic-mystical interpretation of the seven petitions in the Paternoster. If the Lord encourages us to call Him Father, we have to forget our earthly lineage, as noble as it may be, to consider ourselves as lowly as Peter, the fisherman who was raised by Christ to dignity; and as undeserving as the prodigal son, who was taken back lovingly despite his sins. Then we realize what it means to be accepted as daughters. Let us go out of the earth and be lifted up to Heaven, try to throw ourselves into His arms. And let us be good daughters so as not to be rejected. For who would not do everything in order not to lose such a good and loving Father? (XXVII)

At this point Teresa returns, with the aid of this first address to the Father in Heaven, to her mystical instruction. Where is Heaven? It is everywhere God is. St. Augustine was right in not looking for God outside man, and no doubt, as Teresa repeatedly said in other contexts, the pure soul is a Heaven because of the indwelling God. There are many ways to find God, but the shortest one certainly is to enclose oneself together with the Creator of Heaven and earth, who really already is there, in the small Heaven of our soul. The way to do this is not to look outside, where the exterior senses find their distractions. This way to the interior Heaven is an excellent way, says the Saint, because one covers a great distance in a short time. It is as it were a navigation by sea favored by a good wind which brings the traveller to his goal in a few days, while travellers by land will be much delayed. Then she introduces her later symbol of the interior palace occupied by the heavenly King. And she teases herself: womanish ideas, nonsense. And yet, she says, she was not aware of this palace for a long time when the vanities of the world blinded her interior eye. The place seems too small for the Heavenly Father, yes, but only so long as there are other idols occupying the space. Once they are got rid of, the room will grow for Him. This emptying of the space is active recollection. (XXVIII)

If all this appears difficult, one should keep in mind "that the favors of this world are all lies; they distract the soul from her attempt to go into herself . . ." But she can do this whenever she wishes to enter this paradise together with her God and shut the door behind her to everything worldly. "I say 'wishes,'" the Saint adds, "in order to make you understand that this is nothing supernatural but is dependent on our will." Teresa without any equivocation raises her voice here: nothing is learned without some painstaking. Active recollection is the foundation of the mystical life; in one year, even in half a year, it can be learned. (XXIX, p. 292)

The turn to contemplation—again a most ingenious educational "trick"—may occur as early as the first and second petition: "Hallowed be Thy name, Thy kingdom come." Why are these petitions put together? Because we cannot hallow the name of the Almighty, if His kingdom, his Heaven, is not first in ourselves to the point that we are not interested in things of the world but enjoy a quietness and a glory within. I almost seem to say, Teresa continues, that we have to be angels before we are able to petition the Lord for anything. Not quite so. This interior kingdom of quiet is for the non-perfect ones on earth before they have left the prison of the body. Therefore the quiet of the powers of the soul and the prayer of quiet are given only for brief moments as a sign and foretaste of the heavenly kingdom. Now pursuing this experimental instruction on the sudden coming of the kingdom, the Saint mentions a nun well known to her who complained about not being able to pray mentally or to contemplate. This nun hardly knew what happened to her, but while repeating the Paternoster she was literally raised and united to the Lord in mystical union. Thus the nuns only have to pray according to the instructions of Christ, i.e. to say "Our Father" with concentration and, precisely in that way, they may indeed be elevated even to the mystical union. (XXX)

Teresa uses one more chapter to persuade, nay to convince her sisters that the gift of passive contemplation, passive recollection, or the prayer of quiet is literally the inceptive stage of the kingdom of God in the soul. Simeon experienced this when he recognized the Messiah in the little child he held in his arms. He could by his own will not have this insight; it was given him. The baby at his mother's breast is not taking but is given the milk, to its delight. It does not know who gives the milk nor how the act of its feeding occurs, but it is in a state of enchantment. In comparable fashion the soul in loving quiet does not understand what happens to her, since the exterior senses are silenced. She is like a wanderer at the end of his travel, so near the refreshing fount that he almost feels that he is already drinking. Souls in quiet actually feel as though they were in the palace of the King to receive His kingdom. If now they tried to articulate the "Our Father," it would take them an hour. The coming of the kingdom is a supernatural gift. We cannot produce, shorten, or prolong it, just as we cannot hasten the daybreak or delay the nightfall. If the actual quiet has gone, we cannot by our own will do more about it than about reviving the flame of an extinguished candle; and were we to blow on it for more light while it is still burning, we simply would kill the flame. Therefore a warning: one must believe that he may retain this quiet kingdom by hasty prayer. For alas, some sisters, Teresa says in a masterfully constructed sentence of graded subordinations,

. . . are greatly delighted to talk and to recite many vocal prayers in a hurry, like somebody who just wants to finish his job, since they are obliged to recite them every day, so that, although, as I am saying, the Lord puts His kingdom into their hands, they do not admit Him with their kind of praying; they believe they do better, and so they get diverted, . . . (XXXI, p. 297–98)

diverted that is, from the kingdom that they prayed might come.

This negative final note is again pedagogically very valid: it is possible for one to refuse a gift. Nobody may say, even on the mystical level, that he has not received sufficient grace.

The third petition, "Thy will be done on earth as it is in Heaven," is applied by Teresa to the training in virtue. The earnestness of this petition depends on the earnestness and determination with which suffering is accepted. The one who suffers

most, loves God most; he who suffers less, loves Him less, meaning
by more and less the degree of glad acceptance. Now given the
fact that a soul seriously praying that the will of God be done is
already in the state of contemplation, she will, being closer to
Him, be treated with greater friendliness, favored with ecstasies.
If a response and reward are implied, they occur not because of
devotion, but because of the unselfish simplicity and humility
with respect to the will of God. (XXXII)

The fourth petition: "Give us this day our daily bread," for the
advanced souls in the cloister is the prayer for the Eucharist, a
prayer made with an enormous gratitude that the Father has not
sent His son only once, as Bread from Heaven, but continues to
send Him in the mystery of Holy Communion, where we actually
become one with Him by participation in Him as Bread. This consideration cannot but fill the hearts of the sisters with love and
make them understand that they are truly the brides of the
spouse. Out of gratitude this fourth petition should provoke an
ascetic reciprocation. No treasure would be great enough to buy
such a free act of love. It is to the highest possible degree that the
brides ought to give themselves as sacrifice; if they were capable
of doing this to perfection, then they would also mystically be one
with their spouse. (XXXIII)

The Bread is one of Christ's masks. Communion is an occasion
where Christ lifts his mask to His contemplative spouses and permits them sometimes to envision His mysteries and even His humanity, as Teresa experienced it. An aid to provoking such favors
may be induced by closing the corporeal eyes and opening the
eyes of the soul, but only if the desire to see Him face to face is
genuine and comes from an unquenchable love. The restrictions
show that Teresa is far from driving her nuns into hallucinations.
(XXXIV)

Even if for some reason the Bread from Heaven cannot be received at Mass, the sisters ought to receive it spiritually. The eucharistic Bread is the most precious thing we have. The "Lutherans" have desecrated it, destroyed the churches, killed so many
priests. Even these sinners are suffering from these outrageous
acts. The Church is in danger. "Save us, our Lord, we perish."
(XXXV) Amazing is the range from private mysticism to the Eucharist, from concentration on prayer to the needs of the Church
in danger, from the daily bread in the literal sense, for which Te-

resa thinks the folk at large ought to pray, (XXXVII, p. 310) to the Daily Bread in the center of the Church, the everliving Christ, the Church herself.

Teresa is aware of the immense implications of this most essential petition of all. But no one would be entitled to pray for it seriously, if he had not considered previously the human content of the fifth petition, "And forgive us our trespasses, as we forgive those who have trespassed against us." The Saint stresses that there is no escape to the form of the verb "that we will forgive"; no, without having forgotten radically the insults of those who have offended us, we simply cannot ask the same from God for ourselves. And here follows a long digression on the false honor, the *pundonor* under which Spain is reeling in all her social life; she, Teresa, the mother of Carmel, is not free of it, and she knows it lingers also in the convents. It is the poison for any kind of spiritual life. The Saint assures her sisters that contemplation is compatible with certain imperfections but never with the pride of honor, the lack of complete, loving forgiveness toward those who have trespassed against us. Self-concern and lack of forgiveness, since they are incompatible with humility and love of God, have to be stamped out. How is one to do this? The Saint becomes enthused when she prescribes the medicine in a most clear and limpid sentence:

Whenever . . . a great insult has caused pain, one should not have felt it profoundly before reason comes to the aid of the soul and raises its own banner and leaves that pain almost annihilated with the delight of seeing that the Lord has put into one's own hands a problem, namely that in one day one may gain before His Majesty more graces and favors for eternity, than one might gain in ten years by good works which one would like to choose by oneself. (XXXVI, p. 309)

Since Christ through "Our Father" taught all mankind forgiveness to personal enemies, this forgiveness may be more or less perfect. But for contemplative nuns it must be absolutely perfect. The slightest wavering here reminds us drastically of the sixth petition, "And lead us not into temptation but deliver us from evil." [1] (XXXVII) The Saint specifies that temptations and persecutions coming from earthly enemies, do not need to be feared by "the soldiers of Christ" favored by contemplation; what has to be feared as temptation is the ruse of the Devil, who as a disguised traitor makes the sisters proud of their virtues, thus destroying their humility. (XXXVIII) It seems paradoxical that Satan prefers to attack those who strive for perfection rather than those living in the world full of mediocrity. The Saint does not try to explain away this mystery, but brings one of her famous analogies with the *tertium comparationis* of the greater risk for the daring types. Whereas the onlookers at a bullfight in the amphitheatre are safe, the fighter on the horns of the bull is in the greatest danger. (XXXIX) What the nuns on the way to perfection have to pray for is the capacity to recognize especially the temptation of vanity. Against this temptation there exists only one remedy: the love of God. Teresa says it in an outburst of Paulinian enthusiasm:

Those who really love God, love also whatever is good, look for whatever is good, favor whatever is good, praise whatever is good, associate always with good people, favor and defend them, love nothing but truth and things worthy of love. (XX, p. 315)

And just as her great pupil John of the Cross says, "We shall be judged according to our love," so Teresa concludes that it will be a great thing to see in the hour of death that we shall be judged by Him whom we have loved more than anything else. It is actually the love of God which is the protecting force against all kinds of evil, hell and treacherous temptations.

The love of God cannot proceed, however, without the fear of God. The Saint is aware that she deviates here from her subject, but she feels she ought to speak about this necessary corollary which helps in avoiding even venial sins. These are always at hand, e.g., when criticizing gay persons as worldly, without knowing the circumstances and motives of their gaiety. Here is the danger that a sister may let her soul and mind be made small. This is not the way to sanctity but to many imperfections. (XLI) Repeating "But deliver us from evil" and adding "Amen," Teresa understands by evil the earthly life as such. And where is the great evil in this life? Not knowing for sure that one really loves God. And Teresa utters her doubts about this point in a final grandiose antithesis:

Oh, how different this life would be if we were not bound to desire death. How reluctantly does our will bend to the will of God. He wishes us to love Truth, we love the lie; He wishes us to love the eternal, we here bow before what is ephemeral; He wants us to love things great and sublime, we here love things low and terrestrial; He would like us to love only what is secure, we here love the doubtful. It would be ridiculous, my daughters, not to entreat God to deliver us from such dangers forever and to take us away from every evil. And if this desire on our part is not a perfect one, let us at least make an effort to plead for it with this petition. What does it cost to plead much, since we leave it up to His will, since we have given Him our own, and may His name be sanctified forever in Heaven and on earth . . . . (XLII, p. 321)

As always, Teresa gives God the glory; she has succeeded in making the prayer of the Lord more meaningful to her sisters, showing them the difficult way to contemplation and moral perfection.

*The Way of Perfection* is a literary document of love and enthusiasm, pedagogical skill, and stylistic perfection, although it is an early work, of 1562.

# CHAPTER 5

# *The Visions*

## I  *Their stylization*

TO attempt an explanation of Teresa's almost countless visions spread over different works, is a very large enterprise. Even the modern theologians, not to mention the psychologists, look at them with suspicion rather than with admiration.[1] Rather than Teresa's verbal translation into concrete visualizations and linguistically analyzable explanations, they prefer her statements of ineffability. The visualizations, however, have a curious precision and it seems evident to me that these descriptions have even influenced the art of El Greco in several concrete cases. Many arguments for these influences[2] have been accepted by competent critics of today, e.g., Gregorio Marañón. The interrelationship between Teresa and the visionary paintings of El Greco is also emphasized by Walter Nigg.[3] In this context we mean, of course, only these visions which Teresa herself calls imaginary visions, i.e. those affecting the imagination as mental pictures, not the intellect as intuitions, nor the corporeal eye as external apparitions; these, Teresa maintains, she had never experienced. Such imaginary visions occur in the *Life, The Interior Castle,* in the *Foundations,* and in her *Relaciones* (*Reports*) about the state of her soul, written for her confessors. It may be well to give first some examples from these condensed reports, where the Santa tells of the visions which occurred after 1558 or 1560.

A year rich in visions was 1570. On the second Sunday of Lent, after Communion, in her Malagón Convent of San José, the Lord appeared to her, Teresa reports, in the usual imaginary vision, (*Reports,* IX, p. 214) and looking at Him, the Saint was astonished that He wore not a crown of thorns but of resplendent gold. This was a consolation for her but nonetheless she could not help thinking of Christ's painful wounds. Christ, however, said to her that she should not worry about those old wounds but about the many wounds (sins) He is receiving now. We may derive from this example a certain pattern which Teresa applies to the reports on her visions. There is first given an exact date (here, the second Sunday in Lent); then the particular occasion (after Communion); third, the exact place (Convent of Malagón); fourth, the appearance of the Lord in an unusual guise, not with a crown of thorns but of gold; fifth, the thought provoked in her by the apparition; sixth, the Lord, knowing these thoughts, giving admonition.

Another apparition of the Lord she describes a bit less precisely with a slight variation of the pattern and stress on the locution, is the following: "A certain day (of 1571), I believe it was after Communion, our Lord resplendent, took His place beside me and began to console me . . . and told me . . . : Show me your hands, and it seemed to me He took them, put them into His side and said: Look at my wounds . . . From other things which He told me I understood that since His ascension to Heaven, He never came down to earth, except in the Blessed Sacrament, to communicate with anybody." (XV, p. 216) In this report the date is somewhat vague, the occasion again after Communion, as frequently, no church or convent is given, but the appearance of the Lord is dynamically extended; i.e. transfigured. He sits down beside her and repeats what He once said to the doubting apostle Thomas, putting at the same time her hands upon the wound in His side. Since He wants to console her in a state of bitter solitude, He tells her endearingly that He never communicated with anyone by actually descending from Heaven, and the vision dissolves into utterance. The Saint seems to be trying to make it clear that this vision is a mystical visitation and does not involve an actual descent of Christ from Heaven. Such clarifications protect her confessor against the Inquisition. But beyond this, Teresa seems to reconcile this revelation with the fact that she never has had a so-called corporeal vision and may doubt this type also for others. Further, her restriction "except in the Blessed Sacrament" hints at her extreme care to be correct in interpreting her individual mystical graces as admissible and logical from the viewpoint of the teachings of the Church.

Of another vision which transcends the eidetic and even haptic aspects, Santa Teresa stresses the absolute certainty without admitting of any illusion, although unaccustomed gustatory and olfactory elements are involved. It is the vision of the Precious

Blood. Mystics like St. Catherine of Siena or the French Ursuline Mary of the Incarnation claim to have had similar visions. But in the case of Santa Teresa the personal mysticism (as so often after Communion) develops from cult mysticism and the visionary element blends at once with tactile elements in the form of a spiritual hemorrhage. The blood of Christ is hot and tastes sweet. The modern reader may feel shocked. But the exactness of the Saint in details is amazing, and the most astonishing element is Christ's allusion to Teresa's gentle but foolish considerations made thirty years previously when she tried to protect Him against the cruelties of His enemies by inviting Him to her own miserable cell. She considers the vision as the Lord's reply to the earlier invitation:

> On Palm Sunday (1571) having just received Communion, I fell into such an ecstasy that I was not able to swallow the host and thus holding it in my mouth, it really seemed to me, when I returned somewhat to my senses, that my whole mouth had been filled with blood, and also my face and my whole body were covered with it, just as once the Lord himself shed it. It seems to me, it was hot and the sweetness which I felt was excessive and the Lord told me: Daughter, I wish that my blood may taste well to you and don't fear that my compassion may be lacking for you. . . . I want to return the invitation you extended to me the other day. (XXVI, p. 219)

Again the reader is struck by the familiarity between the Lord and the Saint, by the sureness of her affirmations, and yet also by the careful phrasing of the vision in so many "it seems" and "it seemed to me," finally by the effacing of the contours between an imaginary and a real hemorrhage.

## II  *Further Details*

The great visions of St. Teresa, as this one, start with an incident, e.g., she is not capable of swallowing the host, she is shocked to have to share the host with another sister, as in the following report which develops into the ratification of her mystical marriage. Again the date is given, quite precisely. Teresa is in her second year as Prioress of the Convent of the Incarnation in Avila; it is the octave of St. Martin, i.e., November 18, 1572. St. John of the Cross is officiating. There are not enough hosts. But since Teresa once had told St. John that she preferred large hosts, she believed he divided the host purposely to mortify her. The

Lord, however, starts talking to her, telling her that she ought not
to fear that any other person would be able to take Him from her.
Then in her deepest soul (*muy en lo interior*) He gave her His
right hand with the wound from the crucifixion and said:

Look at this nail which is a symbol that you will be my spouse from
today onwards. Until now you had not deserved it but from now on
you will not only care for my honor as Creator and as King and as
your God but as my true spouse. (XXXV, p. 222)

Teresa adds that she remained as though beside herself (*desati-
nada*) and that the whole day she was as though drunk, a comparison mystics often use to characterize the aftermath of an ecstasy.

What is striking here is not only the stress on the effect of the
superlative grace of the actual spiritual marriage, but also the
symbolization of this marriage, a symbolization not through a
wedding ring but through one of the nails of Christ's passion. We
have only to read Report XXXVI immediately and we get the
explanations: The Lord said in a new turn of phrase to Santa
Teresa: "Do you think, my daughter, that merit can consist of
delight? No, it consists of works, suffering and love." This, in passing, is a formula very reminiscent of the dialogue-adages of the
great Catalan mystic Ramon Lull, where the friend raises questions and the beloved answers. Lull has influenced the Saint considerably.[4] Now, the ring in contradistinction to the nail, becomes
the symbol of the *habitual* state of the mystical marriage.
Whether Santa Teresa is entirely conscious of this situation is not
certain. But one of her reports (XXXVIII, p. 233) leaves no doubt
about the implications: One day, she writes, she was in her new
convent in Beas (1575) and Our Lord told her, that since she was
now His spouse she might ask Him for whatever she wanted and
He promised her to grant it. And as a symbol and pledge (*señas*)
He gave her a beautiful ring with an amethyst-like stone and put
it on her finger, imitating the gesture of the groom. She apparently considers the amethyst as the symbol *par excellence* of a
spiritual marriage since the bishops wear amethysts in their rings
as symbols of their marriage with their diocese. But Teresa's envisioned ring is only *like* an amethyst, and as a supernatural ring has
a brilliance "very much different from the rings here below." This
expression is standardized with her for other visionary elements,

too. And she adds in her modesty that she writes all this to her own confusion, begs her sisters to commend her to God, and ends by saying: How can I write such absurd things? (*Esta bobería escribo . . .*), followed by suspensive points.

Santa Teresa's carefulness in relating her strange visions lies in the fact that she anticipates possible criticism of them, and herself declares them as madness from the merely human viewpoint. What to the believer is sanctity is to the agnostic madness, *Locura o Santidad* as Echegarray has called it in one of his dramas. On the other hand, Teresa stresses the supernatural and transcendental character of her vision even of things and colors as fundamentally different from earthly things, as we have just seen with the heavenly amethyst. One is reminded of Rudolf Otto's transcendental principle of "the utterly different" (*Das Ganz Andere*). What Teresa really considers beyond any criticism is the subject matter of her visions. The modern reader, e.g., would not be willing to see that God is particularly concerned with Teresa's choice of a spiritual director. However, in view of the great troubles caused to the Saint by some confessors who tried to contradict the (to her) irrefutable convictions coming from her visions, it is just this problem that is of importance. Even the great enlightened scientist Blaise Pascal believed that he heard Christ's voice telling him to listen to his confessor. Be this as it may, Teresa tells us of another vision experienced during the founding days of Beas, in which Christ appears to her together with Padre Gracián and decides on the latter's being her confessor always.

This vision is particularly colorful. Teresa starts again rather precisely. It was in the month of April, 1575, in Beas. Fray Jerónimo Gracián of the Mother of God had confessed her several times but not as director of her soul. Now, one day when she was eating, without any interior recollection, she felt she was going to be overwhelmed by a rapture, and with the quickness of lightning (*con la brevedad que es como un relámpago*) it seemed to her that Our Lord Jesus stood beside her in His usual majestic form. To His right was standing Master Gracián and to His left Teresa herself. Then Our Lord took their right hands, the Padre's and hers, and put them together. The Lord intimated that He wished Padre Gracián to take over His own place with Teresa for life, and that Padre Gracián and Teresa must submit to this decision. Despite her fear of hurting two other confessors involved in her guidance, she felt with the greatest certainty that God had decided, and a great peace came to her soul. This irresistible peace is here as elsewhere a reassurance for the Saint that neither the Devil nor her own imagination was deceiving her. (XI, p. 224)

But while this vision concerning Padre Gracián lasted only the instant of a lightning flash and brought peace, there was another vision that lasted an hour and a half (which Teresa herself found extraordinary) and the circumstances suggested to her pure and sincere soul that this vision might have been a satanic temptation, and she is afraid of it (*he habido miedo*). It needs recollection that Padre Gracián (1545–1614), who was thirty years younger than the sixty-year-old Saint, was treated by her with motherly love and admiration. She called him "my Elisha" (*mi Eliseo*), an allusion to the Old Testament prophet whom the Carmelites considered as the founder of their Order.

Now this long, strange, extraordinary, and almost literally Dantesque vision-temptation starts with an unusual feeling of emotional emptiness after Communion on the Vigil day of St. Laurentius (August 9, 1575). Teresa is absent-minded and envies the saints of the desert. A voice tells her: Patience, temptations are everywhere. And suddenly she feels recollected and illuminated. She is in another world, in a most delightful flowering garden which reminds her of a verse of the Canticle: May my beloved one come into his garden. And she saw there her Elisha not at all dark but white, with a strange beauty. Upon his head he wore a kind of wreath made of precious stones and many young women walked before him with branches in their hands and all of them sang hymns in praise of the Lord. Teresa tried to open her eyes, afraid of this vision, but she was not able to do so and heard now also a music of birds and angels. She tries to see whether there is still another man beside Padre Gracián. There is none, and she hears Christ's voice telling her to make haste to reach her confessor and collaborator, P. Gracián, in perfection. Teresa is perplexed, and she thinks the only lesson she may get out of this vision is a greater love for P. Gracián, and to imagine his presence for the future in transfigured beauty. (XLIV, p. 226) Since Teresa did not suppress this vision but revealed it to her own confusion as a possible temptation, it would be idle to seek more help from a modern psychologist than from herself for its elucidation. But the whole setting, reminiscent of Dante's earthly Paradise and the many unmentioned elements, give this vision all the character of a dream, a dream of great motherly love for her quasi-son and spiritual counsellor, Father Gracián.

### III  *The Repetition of the Visions. The Transfixion*

Teresa also had visions with great and clear consequences which were repeated during her life. She says so herself when she describes after its first occurrence the vision of the transfixion in the Convent of the Incarnation in 1562. This vision, mentioned above as her spiritual betrothal, was translated by Bernini (for Santa Maria della Vittoria in Rome) into his marble sculpture of Teresa's swoon after being pierced by the spear of the Cherub; for some, Bernini's interpretation is perhaps too "secularized." The Santa's own account of her vision reads as follows:

It was the wish of the Lord that I should see several times the following vision: I saw an angel beside me to my left in corporeal form, something I am not accustomed to see except by a miracle. Although angels present themselves to me many times, I do not actually see them. . . . But in this vision the Lord wished me to see it just that way. The angel was not large but small, very beautiful, his face so much aflame that he appeared to be one of the highest angels, who all seem to be burning from Love. He must have belonged to those called Cherubs. The names do not tell it, but I understand that in Heaven there is a difference between one angel and another . . . ; this I could not explain. I saw in his hands a long golden spear and at the end of its iron head it seemed to have some fire (*un poco de fuego*). The angel seemed to put the spear through my heart several times so that it reached my very innermost parts. As the spear was removed, it seemed to me that it took my entrails out with it and left me burning with a great love for God. The pain was so great that it caused me some moaning but the sweetness caused by this great pain was also so superlative that there was no desire to lose it, since the soul is not satisfied by anything less than God. This pain is not corporeal but spiritual, although the body cannot help participating in some manner and even a great deal. It is a loving communication (*requiebro*) so sweet between the soul and God that I entreat His bounty to give a taste of it to whoever may think I am not telling the truth. (*Life*, XXIX, p. 121)

This most famous vision had large repercussions. It led to the establishment of an Ecclesiastical Feast for Spain (The Feast of the Transfixion, August 27). As already mentioned, it inspired Bernini to translate the vision into the language of marble: an angel, not tall, as one would expect, but small, beautiful, his face inflamed with love (in Bernini's presentation, however, of a regrettable sensuality), standing somewhat elevated with a spear, starting to pierce Teresa's heart. The positive element in Bernini's interpretation is his translation of this vision as an ecstatic rapture into an *imaginary* vision, since not only the angel but also Teresa herself are "in the clouds"; these are portrayed in a painterly baroque fashion. Teresa's interpretation of the psycho-physical parallelism in suffering pain and bliss at the same time, is astounding; her sacredly humorous statement that she wishes this to all those who don't believe her is disarming in its naive candor; this is not to be found in Bernini's work.

Teresa's vision is presented without unessential details. There is no indication of the angel's clothing, and no color is mentioned except the gold of the spear. In a comparable vision of the Jesuit Bernard de Hoyos (1711–1735), as reported by his contemporary, Father John of Loyola, the angel appears as a young nobleman clad in white garments tinted with red, having reddish hair and carrying a cloth banner of crimson and white.[5] Santa Teresa's most original vision of a most original angel has influenced art in contradistinction, for instance, to Clemens Brentano's stylization of Anna Catherine Emmerick's vision of the Archangel Gabriel. Catherine's vision as rendered by Brentano presupposes a knowledge of pictures. Here the angel is of radiant youth with flowing yellow hair; he is coming down to the Virgin's room in an oblique line, surrounded by an effulgence of light that makes the lamp, burning in Mary's room, grow dim. He has his hands gently raised before his breast and words come from his mouth, visible like letters of glittering light.[6]

In the self-criticism of Santa Teresa there is still a point which disturbs her. She believed she saw the angel in bodily form, as a corporeal apparition; this contradicts her common experience and therefore seems to her a miracle. Her confessed lack of assurance does honor to her complete honesty. Her own "disciple," St. John of the Cross, constantly warned against this type of vision, and modern Catholic mystical theology does exactly the same, finding as suspect the too concrete "preternatural, extraordinary, miraculous" in the mystical life.[7]

Teresa's small but flaming cherub, with or without Bernini's interpretation, is different from all the angels we find in art history, be it the child-angels of Giovanni Bellini, the humble, youthful angels of Benozzo Gozzoli, the hieratic angels of Tintoretto, the passenger angels of Rembrandt, the lady-angels of Fray Angelico or the acolyte angels of Roger van der Weyden.[8] Teresa's visionary power gave the angel in Christian tradition a new dimension. In the context of her important vision, which means to her the ratification of her mystical betrothal, she might even have interpreted her imaginary representation as a bodily one so that what she considers exceptional and unheard of was only in her judgment and not in her perception.[9] Thus also this most important of all her visions would enter the normal structure and type of her imaginary visions. In these, for instance, any effort to determine the color of the eyes or the exact size of an envisioned heavenly person would end with the complete loss of the vision; (*Life*, XXIX, p. 117) this is another reason for her restraint in the recording of details.

## IV *Visions of Hell*

There are details, however, in Teresa's vision of Hell, which in their matter-of-factness may well compete with the grinning horrors of Hieronymus Bosch or Francisco Quevedo. The meaning of it is that God showed her the concrete, little, terrible place the demons had already prepared for her, not foreseeing the change of her life by the grace of God. In this vision (*Life*, XXXII, pp. 136–37) there is given almost the sense of St. Ignatius' *compositio loci*;[10] first the entrance is in the shape of a narrow but very long passage leading into a furnace, very low and dark, and causing anguish. The ground was covered with dirty, muddy water exhaling a pestilential stench and full of wicked toads. At the end was a concavity in a wall like an extremely narrow cupboard, and into this Teresa was set. The wall closed in, and in this narrowness and utter darkness she was unable to sit or to lie down. With a grim humor the Saint adds that all this, without any exaggeration, was pleasant compared to what she felt. She did not feel tortures which were inflicted on her from outside by devils, but she felt a destructive fire in the spirit of her soul. All the pains that she was accustomed to in her life, the paralysis and shrinking of her nerves which the doctors used to call unbearable, were nothing compared to those visionary pains which, as she understood, would never subside and which caused her a really intolerable oppression, suffocation, affliction, and despair. With nothing coming from outside, the soul tore itself to pieces, burning and dismembering itself at the same time.

Whatever Teresa might really have felt, it remains that her description of her experienced unbearable pain and despair is, in its literary aspects, a challenge to Dante, Bernanos and Sartre. Teresa describes a visionary dark night as Hell, comparable to St. Catherine of Genova who does the same for Purgatory. Again, as in the case of the transfixion, one would look in vain for models or patterns. With this vision of the "pietistic Renaissance" in Spain, as Marcel Bataillon would say, Teresa has outdated all the harrowings of Hell of the Middle Ages. On the other hand, Teresa is far from being a forerunner of those who doubted or minimized the horror of Hell by abstraction and symbolization.[11]

## V   *Other Visions*

Distinguishable details are also present in another vision which Teresa explains as the dangers of the world, which she specifies as honors, possessions, pleasures, tepid Christians, friends, relatives, and so-called good people, who do not understand and therefore obstruct the spiritual life. But what she envisions previous to her interpretation is the following: she finds herself alone in a large field, encircled by a great number of people. All have weapons in their hands to attack her; some have lances, some swords, some daggers, others very long rapiers. She is not able to break through without being killed, and there is nobody on her side to help her. In this plight she lifts up her eyes and sees Christ, not in Heaven, but high above her in the air, holding out His hand to her so that she is sure nothing would happen to her, and her enemies are indeed paralyzed in their planned attack upon her. This is a picture with only visual elements. Has she seen a painting of the kind depicting the capture of Christ? Or, has she inspired one? In El Greco's *Expolio* (1583) one has only to exchange the person of Christ with that of Santa Teresa and the main elements of her vision are there. (*Life*, XXXIX, p. 185).

The visions of the Blessed Virgin, patroness of the Carmelite Order, are presented with great dignity. Teresa pokes fun at a person who told a priest that Our Lady came often to her, sitting

on her bed and chatting for more than an hour with her. She calls
this "vision" madness, because there is no point to it. (*Foundations,* X, p. 494) But she would rule out madness for her own
visions whenever she feels able to give them a meaning. Now
when Santa Teresa became Prioress of the Convent of the Incarnation and feared her nuns would not like her as their superior,
she had recourse to a "trick." She put a statue of the Virgin in the
seat of the Prioress, and she herself was sitting on the floor, overwhelming her sisters by this act of self-humiliation. Did Teresa
feel that this act of humility might in Heaven be considered an act
of pride? Be it as it may, one day she envisioned the ratification of
her humility by the Blessed Virgin herself:

On the evening of the feast of St. Sebastian in the first year of my
duties as Prioress in the Incarnation, at the beginning of the *Salve* [a
liturgical devotion opening with the word: "Salve Regina"], I looked
at the seat of the Prioress where the statue of Our Lady had been
placed and I saw the Mother of God descend with a great number
of angels and put herself just here. [Carefully, with all kinds of restrictions, the Saint continues]: According to my impression I did not see
the statue in this moment but the aforesaid Lady. She seemed to me
to look somewhat like the picture I received as a gift from the countess
(Doña María de Velasco y Aragón). . . . The angels seemed to me
to sit on the back and the handrails [and now she startles the reader
by her continuation], although not in corporeal form since it was an
intellectual [sic!] vision. Our Lady was there during the whole Salve
and told me: "You have done the right thing in putting me there; thus
I shall be present at the praises you may give my son and I shall present them to Him." (*Reports,* XXV, p. 218)

As to the contents of this vision, one feels that Teresa is uneasy.
The psychologist has here a good case to show the visionary's reality (the statue) evaporating into an analogous apparition. The theologian is aware that Teresa is insecure in her interpretation and
that she calls an imaginary vision "an intellectual vision," which is
a revelation, a clarification, an insight, an intuition rather than a
vision. It seems out of the question that Teresa should lie, but she
does get confused. The real point is that she fears ecclesiastical
criticism and tries to maintain conformity with a terminology she
has not as yet completely digested. As to the literary presentation,
this vision is a charming moving picture with the naive implica-

tion that little angels are playing around the Prioress' chair and
that the Lady of the vision resembles the picture which the Saint
got from her noble lady friend. But the vision as such is a kind of
"Murillo," as Murillo will paint such concepts some time later.

In order not to overdo the sampling of Teresa's visions, we shall
add only two more concerning Our Lady. The first occurred on
August 15, 1561, in St. Thomas' Church in Avila. The Blessed Virgin appeared to Teresa together with St. Joseph to give her a
white habit and a golden collar, to attest her freedom from sin.
The beauty of Our Lady was extreme, but details of form were
not distinguishable except that her face as a whole was very lovely
and the white of her vestments of the greatest splendor, soft, however, and not dazzling. She appeared very young to Teresa and
stood with her a while, causing her a more glorious satisfaction
than she had ever experienced before. Teresa then saw her ascend
to Heaven with St. Joseph accompanied by a multitude of angels.
(*Life*, XXXIII, p. 147–48) On another Assumption Day Santa
Teresa envisioned a kind of continuation of the vision. "The
Queen of Angels and Our Lady" was shown to her by the grace of
Our Lord in her first ascent, or rather, assumption to Heaven,
together with the joy and solemnity of her reception in the place
where she habitually is. Teresa says she would not be able to give
any details. But seeing such a glory, Teresa's spirit was filled with
glory, too, and with a particular strength and desire to serve Our
Lady. (*Life*, XXXIX, p. 187)

Considering only the content of this type of vision, one may
find very little that is original. One would be tempted to say that
the Saint simply visualizes some dogmas of the Church, mostly in
connection with liturgical feasts related to them, feasts whose
prayers and readings were sufficient stimuli to develop the visions.
However, there is usually a particular element, variation, framing,
movement, or shift to extraordinary features which make them
different and surprising. For example: Christ appears wearing a
crown of gold, not of thorns. This does not confirm Teresa's belief
that His major wounds stem from His passion; rather, they reveal
to her that they result from the actual sins of men committed now.
This is the reason why He has to speak to her through a psycho-
acoustic locution, to strengthen Teresa in her own sacrificial
atonement. The visionary's repetition of the test of St. Thomas by
the wound in His side shows Christ not standing, but sitting be-

side her, and it is followed by the strange statement that His mystical appearance does not mean a concrete descent from Heaven. The vision of the Precious Blood is stylized as a reciprocation to Christ on Teresa's part to seek shelter under her roof. The mystical wedding vision contains two most striking elements, on the one hand the insight that she is not the only bride of Christ, as symbolized by the host shared with another sister; on the other hand that a spiritual marriage means suffering with and for Christ, symbolized by the nail as token of love and faithfulness. The later confirmation of the spiritual marriage by a ring may cause surprise by the stress on the amethyst, thus suggesting the ring which links the bishop by an institutional spiritual marriage to his diocese. All the other liturgical rings are different: that of the nuns in certain Orders is without stone, the cardinals have a sapphire, the Pope, as he chooses: a cameo, emerald, or ruby.

The ratification of Padre Gracián as the Santa's confessor by Christ's putting her hand in his, certainly does not lack originality. The curious vision of Padre Gracián in a procession of virgins in a strange garden resembled a page from Dante. But it is certain that Santa Teresa did not know any part of the *Divina Commedia,* taboo in post-medieval Spain. The transfixion in the form in which Santa Teresa presents it has no parallel either before or after her and had the very unusual consequence of establishing the Feast of the Transfixion (August 27). Teresa's vision of Hell seems rather conventional as to the details, but there are two original elements not traceable elsewhere: the very small cupboard in a wall in which the corporeally imagined soul can neither stand nor lie down and, secondly, the soul tearing herself to pieces by burning, grinding, triturating herself at the same time. If Teresa's vision of being surrounded by hangmen and torturers with sticks, lances, daggers, and swords is a reminiscence of a Passion picture she has seen, it does not do away with the originality of her personal substitution for Christ in this dangerous situation.

That a statue of Mary should come to life and change into the true and living Virgin would be simply a replica of the numberless medieval miracles of Our Lady, if in Santa Teresa's case the statue were not to remain too, and the descending Virgin did not have the features of a portrait given the Saint by a Spanish countess. Murillo-like angels are not lacking on and around the priorial armchair. The other Mary visions are original in her striking youth (again "Murillesque"), and by her appearance together with St. Joseph, of whose cult Teresa was one of the foremost promoters. There is also the Virgin's reception in Heaven vaguely but solemnly stressed while the pictorial tradition knows only her concrete coronation.

There is no doubt therefore that the stylization of the visions of Santa Teresa is no less original and individual than her symbols and comparisons. Her visions have, with all this personal touch and some surprises, a great restraint if compared to the visions of later, less responsible visionaries in Spain, particularly Sor María de Agreda (1602–1655) with her *Mystical City of God* (1670), which was called by the critics a sanctimonious novel. Santa Teresa, fortunately, could never receive such a label. Without the pressure of her superiors and confessors, perhaps she would never have revealed any of her visions; but she would have written of her free will and for the education of her nuns about her progress in prayer and asceticism, and her humbly received mystical graces crowning her spiritual human effort.

# CHAPTER 6

# *The Poetry*

**M**YSTICS have written poetry for different reasons. Some were born poets like St. John of the Cross, and the most normal thing for them was to entrust their lofty experiences first of all to the adequate language of poetry before expanding on them in prose commentaries. Others felt like crying out their mystical pain or bliss to the whole world in lyrical fashion like the Italian *laudesi,* particularly Fra Jacopone da Todi. Others again have poetically rendered the mystical experiences of others, not their own, by sheer empathy and speculation, such as the Spaniard Luis de León and the German Angelus Silesius. Finally there are mystics for whom poetry is a playful recreation. Santa Teresa certainly belongs to this last group, although some of her poems contain the most serious mystical considerations. Teresa wrote thirty-one *Poesías,* "poems." (*Obras* [*Works*], p. 641–54) Before interpreting some of them let us repeat that these poems are occasional rhymes written as relaxation. We know that Santa Teresa, despite her austere penances, ardent prayers, plans for foundations and reforms within her Order, was really able to relax. The sisters and particularly the novices used to sing a little ditty, saying that whenever Mother Foundress appears at their recreation, music, singing and dancing are assured.

One day at St. Joseph's Convent in Avila, to stress the austere discalced rule, the sisters, only in sandals, had changed their serge habits into costumes of coarse cloth. The sisters, however, and Teresa even more, given her personal cleanliness, were aware that this kind of cloth implied the danger of vermin. (Poem XXXI) Thus Teresa arranged a procession and provided the participants with a refrain (*estribillo*) which the sisters had to sing at the beginning and end of each strophe of the gloss (*glosa*) that the Saint improvised. The tenor of the refrain was this:

Since you give us a new habit
Heavenly King
Keep free from the known bad people
this coarse thing.

(*Pues nos dais vestido nuevo,*
*Rey celestial,*
*Librad de la mala gente*
*Este sayal.*)

The second half of this refrain then follows each of the three strophes and the whole refrain follows the third and last. The strophes say that the daughters of the Carmel in such a danger (*en trance tal*)—and Teresa uses the expression with tongue-in-cheek—should cast a glance at the cross and the Christ, their Light and Defender. This may suffice for a restless soul, supposing that the soul is well founded in prayer, with the heart lifted up to God in equanimity. Then follows the last strophe like a holy irony:

Since you have come here just to die (to the world)
Don't get dismayed
And of folk of such low condition (the insects)
Don't be afraid
It is in God that you will find your aid
In such a plight.

(*Pues vinisteis a morir*
*No desmayéis,*
*Y de gente tan civil*
*No temeréis*
*Remedio en Dios hallaréis*
*En tanto mal.*)

It is this occasional poetry which gives Teresa an opportunity to repeat her central teaching in a teasing admonition to her sisters. The poetical level of the song is low. One may compare it to an American hymn such as "Onward, Christian soldiers!" But like a hymn, it is catching.

Another song, with a structure still closer to a hymn, admonishes the nuns to follow the route to Heaven uncompromisingly and to take as examples the alleged Carmelites of the Old Testament: Elias and Elisha. (Poem X) This time the refrain has even the theme with variations of a hymn:

> Let us march to Heaven above
> Nuns of Carmel full of love.
>
> (*Caminemos para el cielo*
> *Monjas de Carmelo*).

The gloss consists of eight strophes in which the Saint describes the necessary attitude of the marcher: mortification, humility, self-contempt, deprivation of consolation, obedience, poverty. This is said to be the way up to the Lord, the way by which He Himself came down from Heaven. He loves us, He calls us; let us follow Him on His way back. To love us He came wrapped in human veil. We follow Him to share His wealth, we follow Elias imitating his strength and zeal, we follow Elisha renouncing our own wishes. Teresa uses the same refrain for another poem (XX) in which she tells her nuns to preserve most carefully their three vows of poverty, chastity and obedience. The poem ends thus:

> And if all this we do
> We shall vanquish our foe,
> And then after the "here below"
> Rest with Him who made Heaven above,
> Nuns of Carmel full of love.
>
> (*Y si así lo hacemos*
> *Los contrarios venceremos*
> *Y a la fin descansaremos*
> *Con el que hizo tierra y cielo,*
> *Monjas de Carmelo.*)

As in her processional songs, Teresa's playfulness in rhyming also appears in her *villancicos* (Christmas carols) in the form of pastoral eclogues of a rather primitive kind, always with refrains and in short lines with assonance rather than rhymes. Two shepherd lads converse, and one of them hears the angels' song, or they hear the Child crying, or they want to follow the three magi with their whole flock. Teresa has written seven of these poems.

(XI–XVI) We shall try to give an idea of the shortest and most archaic type, where the refrain itself is a shepherd's dialogue; the verses are trochaic octosyllables without any clean rhyme; "a" assonances and a naturalistic-rustic setting prevail, so that the one shepherd calls the other "boy, chum, or buddy" (*gallejo*):

> Buddy, *listen who is calling*
> —*Must be angels, morning's coming.*
> —I got such a ringing, tingling
> That it seemed a blow to me.
> Well, look Jack, the day's appearing,
> Let us go to see the lassie.
> Buddy, *listen who is calling.*
> —*Must be angels, morning's coming.*
> —Is she a relative of the mayor
> or who else is that young lady?
> —She is a daughter of God the Father,
> Shining like a real star.
> Buddy, *listen who is calling.*
> —*Must be angels, morning's coming.* (*Poem* XIV)

> (Mi gallejo, mira quién llama.
> —Angeles son, que ya viene el alba.
> —*Hame dado un gran zumbido*
> *Que parecía cantillana;*
> *Mira, Bras, que ya es de día,*
> *Vamos a ver la zagala.*
> Mi gallejo, mira quién llama.
> —Angeles son, que ya viene el alba.
> —*¿Es pariente del alcalde*
> *O quién es esta doncella?*
> —*Ella es hija de Dios Padre,*
> *Relumbra como una estrella.*
> Mi gallejo, mira quién llama.
> —Angeles son, que ya viene el alba.)

With these typically popular allusions, hints and suggestions, the primitive structure, the harmless ingenuity and artless approach to the Christmas message, Santa Teresa is in her very element. That is the way she feels: Bethlehem is not far from Ávila. Actually as genuine folk poetry the text contains only associations and connotations, no logical sequences, no denotations. The

angels of Bethlehem would rather sing at midnight, but here there
is a reminiscence of troubadour poetry "because the morning
dawn is coming"; the watchman's call for the separation of the
illicit lovers of the literary genre of the *Alba* (*Dawn Song*), has
found its way through popular songs to the sacred eclogue of
Santa Teresa. This heavenly song is conceived as very loud; therefore the shepherd's ears are tingling from it. It contains the message of the Virgin birth; therefore the abrupt conclusion: Let us
go to see the lassie. And this Virgin as Christ's mother is supposed
to be a highly-placed lady, probably the daughter of the village
mayor. Meanwhile the two lads have approached the crib, and
conclude from the halo of the Virgin that she is the "Morning
Star," at the same time mother and daughter of God, as a *culter-
anista* poet would not only hint at but explain at length. With this
vagueness Teresa has achieved a most genuine primitive Christmas play in Christmas carol form. The other Christmas *villancicos*
of Santa Teresa are more explicit, less "poetic," but also there it is
mostly the rustics Gil, Pascual, Llorente, Menga who discuss the
mystery.

For other ecclesiastical seasons and most of all for conventual
happenings like the veiling of the novices, Teresa has always a refrain ready which she will gloss appropriately. At Passiontide she
sings:

> On the Cross there is our life
> And consolation,
> Only the Cross is the right way
> To our salvation.
>
> (*En la cruz está la vida
> Y el consuelo,
> Y ella sola es el camino
> Para el cielo.*)

At the veiling of her nuns she develops an especially sacred
humor. On one occasion she makes a wordplay on *velar* (to
watch) and *velo* (the veil) which is inimitable in English, except
by an adaptation:

> Sister, you should be buried,
> Therefore you have received this veil.

> The way to Heaven you will not fail;
> Therefore you really should not worry. (Poem XV)

> (*Hermana, por que veléis,*
> *Os han dado hoy este velo,*
> *Y no os va menos que el cielo;*
> *Por eso no os descuidéis.*)

The poem repeats then the parable of the five prudent and the
five foolish virgins with the promise that the prudent watchers
will enter the palace together with the Bridegroom. For another
veiling the Saint starts from a still more exuberant, almost teasing
sacred refrain:

> Since our Bridegroom
> Loves our captivity,
> Up, take the wedding gown
> Of cloistered activity. (Poem XXX)

> (*Pues que nuestro Esposo*
> *Nos quiere en prisión,*
> *A la gala gala*
> *De la religión.*)

Of one veiling there has been left a dialogued refrain without a
developed gloss, reminiscent of that of the *villancico* quoted
above. The speakers of the dialogue are not mentioned but evidently they are the superior and the novice:

> —Who brought you here, young lady,
>    from the valley of sadness?
> —Almighty God and my fortunate gladness. (Poem XXIV)

> (—*¿Quién os trajo acá, doncella,*
>    *Del valle de la tristura?*
> —*Dios y mi buena ventura.*)

The most important poems of Santa Teresa are, of course, those
concerning her mysticism. But these also are "occasional" poems,
occasional in so far as they are linked to her mystical stages. They
are nonetheless playful. For this latter qualification there is even
documentary evidence in connection with one of her most beauti-

ful poems, the three *Quintetos* (five-line strophes) of "O Beauty
that dost well transcend/All beauties here below." (Poem VI) In
her letter of January 2, 1577, to her brother Lorenzo, Teresa says
she reconstructs and rewrites this for him so far as she remembers
it; that she made it once during a period of constant prayer, for
the sake of relaxation (*descansar*); she sends it to him for recreation (*recreación*). May God forgive him for making her waste her
time. Perhaps the poem may increase his devotion, but he should
not tell others about it. As to the terms relaxation and recreation,
the poem, very serious indeed, evidently is built around oxymo-
ronic contrasts and significant wordplays:

> O Beauty that dost far transcend
> All beauties here below,
> Thou without wounds dost pain no end
> And without pain dost ever quench
> The love of creatures low.

> O knot that wondrously dost bind
> Two things so different,
> Why has thou both us disentwined
> Since only bound we strength can find
> To hold the evils as God-sent!

> Though joinest who no being has
> With Being never ending,
> Endless thou dost perfection give,
> Not bound to love thou givest life
> And makest great thy nothingness. (Poem VI)

> (*¡O Hermosura que excedéis*
> *A todas las hermosuras!*
> *Sin herir dolor hacéis*
> *Y sin dolor deshacéis*
> *El amor de las criaturas!*

> *¡O nudo que así juntáis*
> *Dos cosas tan desiguales*
> *No sé por qué os desatáis*
> *Pues atado fuerza dais*
> *A tener por bien los males!*

> *Juntáis quien no tiene ser*
> *Con el ser que no se acaba;*
> *Sin acabar acabáis,*

*Sin tener que amar amáis*
*Engrandecéis vuestra nada.*)

In this serious poem the Saint gives her thought to technical scholastic theology. She starts from the love bond between Father and Son, the Holy Spirit (called *nudo,* "bond," "bow" in the second strophe) but addressed to Beauty, i.e. Divine Beauty, from the very first line of the first strophe. As the inner trinitarian bond of Love, the Holy Spirit extends His function also to mankind. In the creatures he can't produce the binding to Divine Love before first having detached the human souls from their love of earthly creatures. This is a painful process at the start, but a painless process at the end. (Strophe 1) In the second strophe the Saint wonders why this Loveknot, binding God and man together, is on earth an intermittant one, temptation and sin ever disappearing, but she wonders also that a lovebond between two such unequal partners as God and man should exist at all. She is aware that this bond may mean help in accepting evil and suffering as real goods for salvation. (Strophe 2) The third strophe is a philosophical speculation on being. Man who has no being by himself but only from God, is joined to the endless Being. This perfect Being that never ends, communicates from His being to human nothingness, thus giving it stature and grandeur, and proving at the same time His freely granted Love. The circle is closed: Beauty—bond of Love—Being deigns to take man as a partner in perfection—love —being. The fervor of this experienced mystical union is shining through the exclamations of this versified theology, and precisely thus makes poetry of it.

One of the most crucial stages in Teresa's mystical development was her so-called mystical betrothal, which produced a passive wish for death in the bride in order that she be united forever with the Bridegroom. The seriousness of the situation did not hinder the Saint's glossing of a popular refrain as a starting point. Her disciple St. John of the Cross has developed the same spiritual subject as a theme with variations, and there is no doubt that his version is poetically superior. It was thus an easy task for the philological critics to disentangle his and her strophes from a badly preserved, long and unwieldy poem in which both versions traditionally were mixed together. The Santa's refrain stems from Spanish popular love poetry where it has the following form:

*Vivo sin vivir en mí*
*Y de tal manera espero*
*Que muero porque no muero.* (Poem I, p. 641)

(I am living without life in me
And waiting thus in such a way
That, since I cannot really die
I end by dying every day.)

Glossing such a refrain which in the context of a metrical *villan-cico* is called "head" (*cabeza*) must have had for Teresa a great attraction, since a paradoxical mood had to receive comment by drawing content and form of the *cabeza* into the gloss. This process, however, has to take the idea of the third line also into the glossing strophe. With some slight liberty permitted between hep-tasyllabic and octosyllabic lines, the gloss, too, consists of two so-called *mudanzas* (variations), a *verso de enlace* (linking verse), a *vuelta* (return) which introduces the rhyme for the *represa* (re-prise) of the *cabeza*. Now, stressing these technical elements and marking the *cabeza* rhymes (*mí—espero—muero*) by ABB, the gloss shows in Spanish the following scheme ABBAABB:

My life's already out of me
Since I am dying from my Love;
And I am living in the Lord
Who wanted me always for Him.
When I deliver'd Him my heart
He wrote on it in such a way:
That since I cannot die at once,
I end by dying all the day.

(*Vivo ya fuera de mí*
*Después que muero de amor;*
*Porque vivo en el Señor,*
*Que me quiso para sí.*
*Cuando el corazón le di*
*Pasó en él este letrero:*
*Que muero porque no muero.*)

The second strophe of this poem says that Teresa lives in a prison of love (a medieval Spanish novel actually bears the title *The Prison of Love*) but in such a way that her heart is free and

God is her prisoner. The third strophe of this same poem *Vivo sin vivir en mí* intimates that given the length of a human life in earthly wasteland and iron fetters, waiting for the liberation causes severe pain; thus the fourth strophe says that because life where the Lord is not fully enjoyed is bitter, love is sweet, but waiting is a heavier burden than steel. In the fifth strophe Teresa praises a life with the hope of a death where true Life is acquired. In the sixth strophe Teresa explains that gaining life means losing it. The possible variations now seem exhausted but there is a seventh strophe which repeats in a more prosaic and direct form that Life in Heaven is the true life. The last strophe in turn restores the full paradox which may be quoted in full:

> Life, how can I give thee
> To my God who lives in me
> If not precisely losing thee
> In order to deserve to gain thee?
> Dying, I long to reach thee,
> Since I love my Beloved in such a way
> That, since I cannot die at once,
> I end by dying all the day.

> (*Vida ¿qué puedo yo darte*
> *A mi Dios, que vive en mí,*
> *Si no es el perderte a tí*
> *Para merecer ganarte?*
> *Quiero muriendo alcanzarte,*
> *Pues tanto a mi amado quiero,*
> *Que muero porque no muero.*)

Another paradoxically mystical poem arose from a challenge (*vejamen*) which Teresa proposed to the saintly layman Don Francisco de Salcedo, to the theologian Padre Julián de Avila, the mystic San Juan de la Cruz and to her own brother Lorenzo de Cepeda. All had to write about the phrase: "Look for yourself in Me." They all got from Teresa a rather sharp criticism and even teasing threats of appeal to the Inquisition for their interpretations. The Saint herself doubled the paradox and glossed five *quintillas* (five-line stanzas) around a refrain:

> Soul, you must look for yourself in Me
> And have to look for Me in thee. (Poem VIII, p. 644)

*(Alma, buscarte has en Mí*
*Y a Mí buscarme has en ti.)*

Then she develops the theme that the ideal picture of the soul
must be sought in the heart of God. But how to get there? Well,
the soul herself is the mansion of the indwelling God and therefore:

> And if by chance you would not know
> Where you could find precisely Me,
> Don't wander here and there quite free.
> But if you wish to find me, do it,
> And look for Me in thee. (Strophe 4)

> *(Y si acaso no supieres*
> *Dónde me hallarás a Mí,*
> *No andes de aquí para allí*
> *Sino, si hallarme quisieres*
> *A Mí, buscarme has en ti.)*

Let us close with another of the mystical poems of Santa
Teresa, namely a version of her Transfixion in a joyful metamorphosis where the Cherub with the arrow is the Sweet Hunter.
Again three lines of a long refrain are glossed in twice five verses
and reappear slightly varied after each of the *quintillas* so that the
rhyme scheme followed is ABAB cd cd db AB//ec ec cb AB.
Since we have developed a feeling for the technique of the Santa,
this poem will appear to us as typically Teresian:

> I totally surrendered and agreed
> And to this point I made a change
> That my Beloved is for me, indeed,
> And I for my Beloved rose in rank.

> When once the loving hunter sweet
> Shot and left me surrendered,
> It was His loving arms' embrace,
> That my dear soul had entered,
> And new life was here tendered
> And to this point I made a change
> That my Beloved is for me, indeed,
> And I for my Beloved rose in rank.

He shot me with an arrow
Burning with love so sweet
And my soul came quite narrow
To her Creator, freed;
I do not want another street
Since for my God I made the change
That my Beloved is for me, indeed,
And I for my Beloved rose in rank. (Poem III, p. 642)

*(Yo toda me entregué y di,*
*Y de tal suerte he trocado*
*Que mi Amado para mí*
*Y yo soy para mi Amado.*

*Cuando el dulce cazador*
*Me tiró y dejó rendida,*
*En los brazos del amor*
*Mi alma quedó caída,*
*Y cobrando nueva vida*
*De tal manera he trocado*
*Que mi Amado para mí*
*Y yo soy para mi Amado.*

*Tiróme con una flecha*
*Enarbolada de amor,*
*Y mi alma quedó hecha*
*Una cosa con su Criador;*
*Ya yo no quiero otro amor*
*Pues a mi Dios me he entregado*
*Y mi Amado para mí*
*Y yo soy para mi Amado.)*

Santa Teresa knows very well how to distinguish poetic from prose style. In the preceding poem the arrow has been provided with love, not with a symbolic flame of love. A distinction between temporary and permanent mystical union in poetry has not been made and the strongest formulation beyond all comparison has been used here in the Spanish text: "And my soul was made one with her Creator" (*Y mi alma quedó hecha/Una cosa con su Criador*). Teresa's poetic message, however, is the same as that of the prose metaphors: "The deification of the soul by granted participation of the Godhead." If one thinks of the first poem quoted above, the objurgation of the vermin to stay out of the sister's clothing, or the *villancicos* of the two shepherd lads hearing the angel's choir, and from these up to the last quoted poems of the mystical union between creator and creature, the dying from not dying, and the heavenly Hunter deifying the soul, one is astonished at the wide range of Teresa's relatively small amount of poetry and her sure distinction of poetic styles.

# CHAPTER 7

## *The Human Values in the Works of Santa Teresa:* The Letters

THE American readers of the works of Santa Teresa seldom will choose them for stylistic or historical reasons. Most non-Spanish readers are far enough removed from Teresa's spiritual message that they do not read her for religious edification. Why then do they read Santa Teresa's works as monuments of timeless value? The answer can be that the contemporary translations of her works into English, especially the classical translation of E. Allison Peers (see Bibliography) fill a desire of the English-speaking public to get acquainted with the Saint for her human values, for her mastering of life from a superior level, for her qualities as a woman and as a leader, for the warmth and endearment that radiate from her texts.

Therefore let us consider her works through certain characteristic texts from this viewpoint. We have explored from other angles the *Life* and the *Foundations* (Chapter 1), the *Interior Castle* (Chapter 3), the *Way of Perfection* (Chapter 4), the *Reports* (Chapter 5), the *Poetry* (Chapter 6). We have not mentioned until now her *Cartas* (*Letters*). It is in these 458 extant missives written over a period of twelve to fourteen years that the Saint reveals most directly her warm humanity, her wisdom, and her humor. These letters are not formally stylized nor made purposely attractive, and are therefore not comparable to the carefully wrought letters of Santa Teresa's French counterpart, Mother Mary of the Incarnation (Mme Martin). Teresa is not a "cloistered Mme de Sévigné." Her letters are written in a blunt, unvarnished, often obscure Spanish. Some of the allusions are no longer comprehensible. The main type of missive is the sober business letter. Teresa said of herself, "I am great in negotiations." (October 21, 1576) These business letters are written hastily, often late at night. Let us peruse them chronologically.

In her very first letter, July 6, 1541, directed to her aunt Doña

Elvira, Teresa expresses her dissatisfaction about convent business: her Convent of the Incarnation in Avila demanded from the
young novice an account of her heritage. In other letters from her
first years in the convent, she entreats one of the peasants on her
family property to take good care of the pigeons. In a letter of
November 9, 1561, to her sister Juana she speaks jokingly about
her favorite brother's prospering as a Spanish functionary in
America (Quito); she calls him His Excellency our Lord Brother
Don Lorenzo. One month later she already has her first foundation in mind, and thanks her brother for a large amount of money.
With this money she will buy the house. This will be done secretly
because of the opposition of the town and other religious Orders.
And in the sense of the legendary chaplain of World War II who
told his troops, "Praise the Lord and pass the ammunition!" Teresa adds that she prays for the enterprise to God and is already
hiring the workers, who will pretend to prepare a residence for
the still absent brother. And in her noble enthusiasm for the first
foundation she asks Lorenzo for more money if this should be
necessary. She concludes that, should he not be willing, God may
move him to spend the necessary amount nonetheless. (December
24, 1561)

In 1565 Teresa sends her *Life* to Father García de Toledo for
correction and begs him to send it on to Maestro Avila, but she
adds shrewdly it would be better to have a copy made so that no
one may recognize her handwriting (in view of the danger of the
Inquisition). Three years later she insists in a letter written from
Toledo to Gaspar Daza, the spiritual director of the nuns of San
José in Avila, that he should by all means forbid the nuns to speak
among themselves about their spiritual life, because, she adds,
surely with a twinkle, "each would contribute another piece of
nonsense." In a letter to one of her important sponsors, Doña
Luisa de la Cerda, (May 18, 1568) she expresses her embarrassment that Doña Luisa did not send greetings for the parish priest
but, Teresa adds, she gave them to him anyway. On another occasion, May 27, 1568, she tells Doña Luisa that she took a saddle
from her castle, that she knew her friend would approve, and it
would be nice anyway always to have a souvenir of Doña Luisa
with her. Teresa is so fond of Doña Luisa that she declares, June
9, 1568, that the Marchioness of Villena was very kind to her, but

it does not matter, since she needs only the kindness of Doña Luisa. Although all this certainly is true, one wonders what the Devil's Advocate would have been able to build up at the Santa's canonization with these shrewd and polite letters in hand. Having sent Doña Luisa the manuscript of her *Life,* and always afraid it might fall into the wrong hands, she writes: "Look, your ladyship, I have entrusted my soul to you; please send it back to me with all possible precaution as soon as possible." (June 23, 1568)

The letter to the pious gentleman and benefactor Don Francisco de Salcedo, who may be identified with El Greco's "Gentleman with the Hand upon His Chest," [1] in which Santa Teresa recommends to him San Juan de la Cruz, now twenty-six years old and on his way to Duruelo to take the vows of the reformed Order, is a sequence of gentle niceties:

Jesus be with you. Glory to God that after seven or eight absolutely necessary business letters I have a little time left to get some rest and drop you some lines so that you may see how much your letters delight me. And please don't think that writing me is a waste of time, since every now and then I need your letters, under one condition, however, that you don't tell me always that you are old. This really hurts me in all my being, as though in the life of the young there were a security against death. God give you life until I die myself and then, not to be in the other world without you, I have to do something so that Our Lord may take you soon, too.

Please have a talk with Father (Juan de la Cruz) and help him in his present undertaking, because although he is small of stature, he is, as I understand it, big in the sight of God. We certainly will miss him here badly because he is intelligent and fit for our kind of life, and therefore I believe Our Lord has called him for this work. There is not a single friar but speaks well of him. . . . It seems that God is leading him by His hand. Although we had in business matters some arguments and I, having been the cause of them, was sometimes angry at him, we never saw in him the slightest imperfection.

If you say you would pay six ducats for the possibility of seeing me, this seems an exaggerated sum, but I would give much more to see you. It is self-evident that you deserve a higher price. Who would appreciate a poor little nun? You who are able to distribute honey, wine, wafers, radishes, lettuce, who possess a garden and, as I know, are the errand-boy who used to bring us apples, you certainly are worth something more. . . . (September, 1568)

When Doña Inés Nieto loses her two sons in a battle in Flanders, Teresa does not begin to comfort the bereaved mother with religious considerations until she has told her that her own distress is so deep that she does not know how to comfort her. (November 10, 1568) In a similar gentleness she tells Luisa de la Cerda, during a period when she cannot see her, that although her love is always with her, she wishes that her body could be with her, too. (December 13, 1568) In March, 1569, Doña María de Mendoza y Pimentel, sister of the Bishop of Avila and Palencia, is lying ill in Valladolid, after having financed Teresa's foundation there; the Saint cheers her up by sending her from Toledo a kind of spiritual get-well card. She writes that she is pleased that Doña María's health has become much better, and that the way she is taking her trials is admirable. Even in Toledo everybody calls her a saint because she gives such a splendid example in suffering. This means, Teresa continues, that Doña María's fire of love, enkindled in her by Our Lord because of her sufferings, begins now to enkindle others, also. But Teresa's own trial comes through her Ladyship's absence and through the lack of constant news about her health. (March 28, 1569)

At the end of the same year news arrives that Teresa's brother Lorenzo will return from America. Teresa is delighted because she suffers from the separation, worried about the ups and downs of his political career and fears most of all that he might become a prey to greediness and moneymaking. She tells all this to her sister Juana de Ahumada and encloses a personal letter to her from their brother which, she says candidly, she was tempted to open but scruples hindered her; Juana, however, should send Teresa any news different from that in her brother's letter addressed to her. (October 19, 1569)

Writing to her brother Lorenzo himself, Teresa speaks about her foundations and the whole family, greets all her four brothers in America, rejoices in advance at Lorenzo's return as one of the few earthly pleasures in store for her. She explains that despite her hatred for money she has become an excellent business woman, who is delighted that she was able recently to receive one nun with eight thousand, another one with nine thousand ducats as a dowry, and that her niece made a rather good marriage. (January, 17, 1570) To Father Antonio de Segura, the Superior of the Franciscans of Cadalso, she writes that contempt of things earthly ought not to go so far that when he was in her neighborhood, he should forget that a certain Teresa of Jesus also existed. (Lent, 1570) There is no humor, however, in a letter to Don Diego Ortiz, executor of the founder's will for the Convent of Toledo. He had complained, probably in the name of the chaplain, that the nuns did not sing at the High Masses in that convent. With dignity she tells him that the nuns may sing or not sing as they please, and may he excuse her for not writing him a personal letter since she is too weak from bleedings and headaches. (August 15, 1570) How different this tone from the exuberant gratitude for butter and quince, expressed to her close friend Catalina Hurtado:

It seems you don't care for anything else but sending me presents. My care is to get your news and to know you are in good health. (October 31, 1570)

Even in her correspondence with the cantankerous Don Diego Ortiz, who continues to make difficulties for the Toledo foundation, Teresa finds her jesting mood again; she is writing teasingly and with a bit of poison in her pen:

I do not think to defend myself with reasons like people do when they have a bad case; I only shout into your ears that you are more obliged to favor your daughters who are orphans and minors than the chaplains. After all everything belongs to you, and how much more so as the convent and all those therein certainly belong to you rather than to those, as you say, who are only interested in rushing through their masses, and some even with very little devotion. . . . You may write me whatever you like and since I know the good will with which you are writing, only one thing causes me pain, namely that I am causing pain to you. . . . Your unworthy servant,

Teresa de Jesús.

Teresa's gentleness never is at odds with her sincerity. She tells Doña María de Mendoza she ought to scold the Dominican Provincial, Padre Alonso de Fontiveros, for not having visited her during his long stay in Salamanca, but she adds, "By the way, to tell you the truth, I don't like him particularly." (October, 1571) Teresa's youngest sister Juana has difficulties. Teresa combines the discussion of her spiritual needs with the physical necessities of

her own convent: "I beseech you for the love of God and of me:
Go frequently to Confession. . . . Send me turkeys, since you
have so many." (March, 1572) When she includes greetings to
Doña Juana's daughters, her own nieces, she calls them "my children" (*mis niños*). (August 27, September 27, etc., 1572) Teresa
consoles Doña Inés Nieto in her and her husband's troubles with
the King by a charming remark: "I feel so deeply for you and
your difficulties . . . that, if my sentiments could help you, the
troubles would all be over." (December 17, 1572) Even in very
serious and spiritual matters a certain shrewdness is not lacking in
her. She writes the King (Philip II) that her nuns are praying for
him; thus he may contribute to the expansion of the Order and
"the more the Order expands the greater will be the advantage to
your Majesty." (June 11, 1573)

Teresa is opposed to founding a girls' school with too many
pupils and, writing Padre Juan Ordóñez about it, she remarks: "I
know only too well what it means to have a great many women all
together. God save us." (July 27, 1573) After the unruly Princess
of Eboli has gotten the whimsical idea of becoming a Carmelite,
Teresa writes to Father Domingo Báñez in plain language: "The
Princess of Eboli as a nun is enough to make you weep." (January, 1574) No less blunt is her remark to the Bishop of Avila, that
his sister Doña María de Mendoza is not doing what she should
for the convent she founded: "Our Lady defends her daughters
better than Doña María protects her sponsored nuns." Then she
blames the Bishop for the scarcity of his letters to her and quips:
"As you have to deal with so many saints . . . you are forgetting
me. None the less, you will find in Heaven that you owe less to the
saints than to the sinner." (February, 1574)

To Mother María Bautista, her cousin, she writes about a letter
which Father Domingo Báñez apparently should not have seen,
but she will settle the affair by a little stratagem: "The letter in
Father Domingo's hand made me laugh a little; but don't say anything to him about it, since I am going to write him a very charming letter; perhaps he may show it to you." And Mother Bautista
who seemed to have aspirations for a super-hermit life gets no less
charmingly a piece of Teresa's mind: "My daughter, I think your
health would get worse . . . , I know your temperament . . .
and your desires for solitude are better for you than the solitude
itself." (May 14, 1574) This cousin-nun is a particular target of

her teasing. It is to her that Teresa writes: "I wish you the very best of health, let the other nuns be ill." (June, 1574) A whimsical consolation goes to this Prioress María Bautista: "Don't worry about not being able to see me. It may worry you more to see me so old and tired." (September 11, 1574)

A consolation for a member of the royal family of Portugal, Don Teutonio de Braganza, a chronic complainer, carries a chiding note: "If I were as clever in complaining as you, you would consider your own troubles as nothing at all." (June, 1574) There are people whom Teresa seems to consider as thinking a little too highly of their spiritual worth and this seems to be the case with Don Teutonio de Braganza as well as with the Prioress María Bautista. Therefore the Santa wishes a Happy New Year to Braganza with the words: "May the Holy Spirit . . . give you as many and as happy new years as I wish you, together with sanctity . . ." (January 6, 1575) If Teresa has a particular liking for a cousin, be she secular or nun, she does not hide her feelings. Therefore she writes to Mother Inés de Jesús (Tapia): "I love you more than others closely related to me." (May 12, 1575) She does not hesitate to write likewise to the General of the Carmelite Order in Rome: "All the sisters are eager to pray for you, since they realize how much I like you." (January 19, 1575) Again her preference for her favorite cousin Mother María Bautista: "It is surprising that almost everybody's letters make me tired but yours —and, of course, my confessor's; . . . actually receiving or answering your letters is refreshing to me." (August 28, 1575)

But when she sees intrigues and scandals she reports on them in the strongest terms to the Father General: "The whole body of the Discalced Fathers means nothing to me. . . . In broad daylight the police saw two Friars in a house of ill fame and . . . took them to prison. . . . I am not shocked at human frailty . . . but they ought to have considered the reputation of the Order." (June 18, 1575)

In the late seventies the mortal struggle between Calced and Discalced Carmelites forced Teresa to use pseudonyms and she did this with brio. She called herself *Laurencia*, thinking of her favorite brother Lorenzo. She called her beloved Padre Gracián *Eliseo*, since Gracián's baldness in relatively young years reminded her of the pictures she knew of the prophet Elisha. The learned San Juan de la Cruz was called *Seneca* because of his wisdom, and, because of his small stature, *Senequita.* The intolerant and harsh Father Baltasar de Jesús, the Calced Provincial, was called by her "the blessed one" with the Greek term *Macarios;* the Calced Carmelites on the whole were called cats. Now she was aware that Father Baltasar did not like to meet Father Gracián and she wrote to the latter: "I want to tell you that Macarios is terrible. . . . I wonder whether he wants to go back to his den in order to avoid a meeting with my Eliseo. I shall not be sorry at all if he does so until he becomes more reasonable." (September 27, 1575) Of Mother Ana de los Angeles, the Prioress of Toledo, Teresa writes to Padre Gracián: "Although she be friendly with the cats, she has many virtues." (October, 1575) Teresa tries to prevent her nephew's being sent to the wars in Italy and endeavors to place him as a page, although he is a bit too old and too stout. She adds disarmingly, as all the aunts of draft dodgers in the world would do, writing to the expectant Doña Inés Nieto: "If I thought he would serve the Lord well (as a soldier) I would not mind at all, but things in Italy are looking dangerous. May His Majesty keep the boy . . . and may he grant you a safe delivery." (October 31, 1575)

But in another story of a page, when P. Báñez wants to hire one for the children of Don Lorenzo back from America, Aunt Teresa is opposed to the project because a page would only spoil her nephews: "A page is absolutely unnecessary for the children." Thus she writes to her cousin Mother María Bautista. (December 30, 1575) In the same letter she jokes about the sudden sanctimoniousness of her brother Lorenzo who, having returned from America as a widower, wished to become a Carmelite himself. Teresa had dissuaded him from the idea, and she remarks: "The monkishness (*frailía*) of my brother ended in nothing." In another letter to her cousin-nun María Bautista, Teresa ridicules the spurious use of the title Don by members of her family and says: "I am awfully ashamed whenever I hear this term used by them," (April 29, 1576) and she explains that her brother Lorenzo with constant visits "has become a kind of embarrassment."

A buoyant letter was written to the saintly Fray Ambrosio Mariano de San Benito. She tells him that he spoils the Licentiate Padilla with his bad habits not to write letters or to send greetings to others. (May 9, 1576) With great liveliness Teresa describes to Father Gracián an adventure she had on her way to Malagón:

Oh my Father, what a mischief happened to me. Sitting on a heap
of hay near an inn, where there was no room for us, a big salamander
or lizard was creeping along my arms between the tunic and the skin,
and it was a grace of God that it was not in another part, because I
believe I would have died according to what I felt; but my brother
snatched it and threw it away. (June 15, 1576)

Teresa, having had trouble with the Prioress of Seville, Mother
María de San José, forgives her in a charming way, saying: "On
the supposition that you love me as I love you, I forgive you
everything, be it in the past or in the future." (July 2, 1576)
        Teresa found it very funny that her brother Lorenzo was re-
ceived by the housekeeper of Francisco de Salcedo with all kinds
of outlandish honors, so that Lorenzo himself had called her a
"master of ceremonies." Now Teresa writes her brother: "I was
tickled enough to laugh about the master of ceremonies. I really
was amused at it," but then she comes back to the educational
problem of Lorenzo's two boys. They need neither a page nor a
mule nor a pony, but they simply should walk to school, helping
one another, and learn something. (July 24, 1576)
        When the persecution of the Discalced Carmelites by the
Calced was in full swing, the letters of Santa Teresa really needed
a decoding key, so carefully chosen were her pseudonyms, even
one for God. He became *Joseph,* and she, *Angela,* as well as *Laurencia,* already mentioned earlier. Now wanting to inform Father
Gracián that God wished the Hieronymite Prior P. Yepes, her
later biographer, not to come any longer to visit her in her Toledo
convent, she writes: "When poor Angela was talking to Joseph, he
told her that he himself stopped his coming (to her convent)."
(December 5, 1576) To say "The nuncio Ormaneto is for separation of the Discalced from the Calced Carmelites," Teresa used
the code: "Methuselah is determined to comply with our desire to
be separated from the eagles." (September 6, 1576)
        In all these troubles Teresa remains the *charmeuse* writer, e.g.,
to the Prioress of Seville: "I don't know why I have such a particular love for your house and all those who live in it." (September 7,
1576) At the same time she maintains her extreme matter-of-
factness. Discussing with the Prioress of Seville the admission of a
nun with a somewhat disfigured face, she writes: "She has a kind
of mark on her face; if it disfigures her very much, don't take her."

(September 9, 1576) Meanwhile she continues her secret correspondence with Father Gracián and is jubilant about the "nepotis-
tic" opportunity offered by the fact that the Great Inquisitor Cardinal Quiroga has his own niece among the Discalced Carmelite
nuns. This message reads in her code: "The Great Angel is very
pleased to have a niece among the butterflies." (September 9,
1576) Or she teases him with a fit of unconscious jealousy with his
liking for Teresa's lady friend Doña Juana Dantisco: "I wonder
which of the two you love more, Doña Juana who, I thought, has
a husband and her children to love her, or poor Laurencia (herself) who has no one else in the world but you." (September 20,
1576) Such a sentimental feeling is quickly balanced by Teresa's
business-mindedness when she writes two days later to the Prioress of Seville, Mother María de San José "not to fill the convents
with nuns if they are not suited and not capable of helping to pay
expenses." (September 22, 1576) More concretely still: "Don't
take the daughter of that Portuguese . . . unless he first leaves a
deposit as security." (September 26, 1576) Thus Teresa thought
like the proverbial French bishop who said: "Let us pray for a
poor girl who is not rich enough to take the vow of poverty."

Teresa is shrewd not only in conducting on a high level the
complex discussions about the establishment of a separate branch
of the Discalced Carmelites; she is also shrewd in little things.
When she hears that even the Jesuits are opposed to the austerities of the Discalced nuns, she writes to the Prioress María de San
José: "It would be wise to arrange occasionally for a father of the
Company to hear the confessions of the nuns, who then would do
away with their misgivings." (October 5, 1576) Whenever anybody gives Santa Teresa titles, she becomes quite ironical, taking
it as an offense against her major effort toward religious reform
and simplicity. Thus she takes to task Padre Ambrosio Mariano:
"Since you are conferring the titles 'Reverend' and 'Señora' on
me, may God forgive you. People will think your own reverence
and myself have returned to the Calced." (October 15, 1576) And
when he makes bold to say that he could judge in a moment
whether a postulant is capable of becoming a good nun, she tells
him that women are more complicated, and she adds that even
"our confessors can judge us only according to what we tell them."
(October 21, 1576) She is not afraid to take her spiritual director,
Father Gracián, to task for technical mistakes: "You often make

no reference to things I have said, and you forget to put a date on
your answering letters." (October 23, 1576) She feigns to enjoy
food, as she writes to Mother María de San José: "We were sent
last week a tuna fish from Malagón. It was extremely good, . . .
delicious." (October 23, 1576)

Trying to avoid jealousy among her discalced brethren, she tells
Father Gracián disarmingly: "Please greet Fray Antonio [the Superior of Seville] very warmly for me, but if the greeting can be
avoided, it would be even better, since he ought not to know that
I am writing so often to your Paternity and so seldom to him."
(October 31, 1576) When Mother María Bautista in Valladolid
feels miserable after a bloodletting, Teresa scolds her and the
whole medical profession: "Did I not beg you the other day not to
let yourself be bled anymore? I don't know why you are so silly.
Don't pay any attention to what the doctor says." (November 2,
1576) About the irascible and hostile Prior of the Calced in Avila,
Teresa remarks boldly: "Our good Valdemoro, I think, means
what he says about being friendly to me, since for the time being
it seems advantageous to him"; (November 3, 1576) and more
bitingly: "What a wonderful friend I have in him. May God deliver us." (November 4, 1576) With the same unmasked sincerity,
she tells her brother how much she believed herself detached
from things earthly, but was nevertheless very much concerned
when Lorenzo was in danger of losing his property. "Well," she
adds, "we never really know ourselves." (November, 1576) When
Teresa hears that in Seville nuns are allowed to strike or pinch one
another for the purpose of mortification, she becomes furious and
writes to Mother María de San José, their Prioress: "Nuns are no
slaves. . . . These things cause me the greatest distress." (November 11, 1576)

When a too zealous visitor to her convents wants to add to the
rule some austerities to which he is canonically not entitled, she
frankly writes to Padre Gracián: "Our rule will not accept additions from boring people." (November 19, 1576) Then she tells
him still more frankly that she forbids her young nuns to have
with him the same familiarity as she has with him at sixty. And
since he knows the kind of love with which she is talking to him,
she begs him not to read her private letters to others, so little
would she like "any one to overhear my conversations with God."
(November, 1576) Teresa discovers in her beloved Prioress of Se-

ville a sin of pride, when the latter tries to insert in one of her letters a Latin sentence. She reproaches her and remarks: "God preserve my daughters from parading their Latin knowledge." (November, 1576)

But she tells her also about the rumors the Calced friars have spread about the aging foundress, namely that she would like to go to America to found Discalced convents there. "Well," says Teresa, "the best they can do is to say so many things about me that whatever they say will be believed by nobody." (November 26, 1576) When Father Gracián runs into trouble trying to convert a loose woman in Seville, Teresa shrewdly writes him: "Since the Devil has led her astray, he may do the same to your Paternity. . . . In my humble opinion you should keep out of the whole affair; there are others to win this soul. . . . What a malicious person I am." (November, 1576) Teresa in her matter-of-factness tells him that a still greater danger than women are the Calced brethren, whom she considers capable of poisoning him: "For the love of God, watch out as to what you eat in their houses!" (December 7, 1576) Then again she reports in a comic tone of Father Gracián's little sister, Isabel Dantisco, who as a child of eight years lives in the convent with Santa Teresa: "I gave Isabelita a piece of melon. She said melon is so cold that she feels thunderstruck in her throat. I tell you, she says the funniest things." (December, 1576)

In the dispute about whether the Discalced friars should wear sandals, Teresa insists that she always was for sandals, that going barefoot was meant only as a symbol of austerity, and that now the idea has been overdone by the young friars riding barefoot on mules: "I repeat that it does not look seemly that these young friars should go barefoot and yet ride on saddled mules . . . : there is too much going barefoot already." (December 12, 1576)

When she wants to make a gift to her friend Doña Luisa de la Cerda, she knows it has to be of the best quality. Therefore she writes to Mother María de San José: "On the condition that the sweets of which you speak are very good, it will be fine you send them to me." (December 27, 1576) Teresa is upset when the wealthy family of the Padillas wants to pay the dowry for little Casilda in installments, when they could have paid it easily in a lump sum. With her usual irony she writes to the Prioress of Malagón: "What an enormous expense for them!" (December,

1576) and in a letter to Mother María Bautista she gets quite angry about this matter: "As soon as self-interest is at stake, sanctity is forgotten. This makes me feel that I hate the whole business." (December, 1576)

Early in 1577 Teresa reminds Father Gracián of her particular vow of obedience to him in 1575, known also from an earlier mentioned vision as contained in *Report* 39, and in her purity daringly calls this vow a marriage. God was the marriage maker, she says, and "the knot was so tightly bound that only death can untie it." (January 9, 1577) With the same boldness she calls some naive Calced friars who were misused for intrigue against the Discalced "those simpletons." (To Fr. Ambrosio Mariano, January, 1577) At that time Teresa is in high spirits and teases Mother María de San José, since Mother María has to take care of two convents, as "a semi-Provincial" and tells her that she does not believe that the poems sent her were from all the nuns, but only made by herself. (January, 1577) Teresa's brother Lorenzo still wants to achieve visible progress in perfection, and tries to make on his part a vow of obedience to his saintly sister. Teresa tells him energetically: "I don't want any promise from you and, after all, I don't like such things." (*Quod licet Jovi, non licet bovi.*) To Lorenzo's idea that he feels an unusual sense of heat when he is praying, Teresa answers soberly: "This heat you mention will neither help nor damage your prayer, but it may do some harm to your health." (January 17, 1577) But Lorenzo goes on in his effort to become a saint, he scourges himself when saying the Our Father, he wears a hair shirt, he deprives himself of sleep. Teresa desperately tries to bring him to reason and remarks pointedly: "Consider that we middle-aged people ought to treat our bodies well in order not to ruin the spirit." (February 10, 1577)

The same human understanding combined with prudent energy is shown by the Saint also in business matters pertaining to religion. When Padre Ambrosio Mariano, trying to establish a Discalced monastery in Madrid, is living in a private house as are also four other friars, Teresa sees that this fact alone will ruin the whole project and she, as Mother foundress, figuratively gives him a real spanking; then at last she appeases him, appealing to his wish for perfection: "I am astonished at how much you can take without becoming angry." (March 15, 1577) She feels relieved when Padre Ambrosio finally stays with the Calced friars, but she

gives him further shrewd instructions to watch his words with
them and to please the Nuncio, since "obedience makes a good
impression." (April, 1577)

When the young nun Bernarda de San José died shortly after
her profession, and silly rumors about miracles or ecstasies were
spread by the nuns in Seville, Teresa intervened, writing to the
Prioress: "All those things are wild talk. Forget about them and
do not repeat them to anybody." (May 6, 1577) She opposes an
unjust taxation of the Sevillian nuns through a lawsuit and writes
Father Gracián: "You must give the procurator money—my
brother will send it—so that the suit may be expedited as effec-
tively as possible." (June 13, 1577) When Mother María de San
José wants to introduce two slave girls, helpers from America, to
the ascetical-mystical life, Teresa warns her: "The question is . . .
good service. . . . Do not make either of them depressed by
talking about perfection." (June 29, 1577) When this Prioress has
got more trouble than just the problem of those two girls, she
nevertheless sends Teresa a package of coconuts, whereupon Teresa writes: "The sisters were delighted with the coconuts and I,
too. . . . I am glad to see you have the courage to do such things
despite all the troubles you have. It is clear that the Lord knows
the right people to whom He may send crosses." (July 11, 1577)

Trials are considered normal by the Saint, but when she hears
about disobedient nuns like those of Malagón, she loses patience
and tells their chaplain: "You will see what happens to conten-
tious nuns. . . . Tell Beatrix . . . I do not even want to hear her
name." (July, 1577) Just as she can be stern with her nuns, she
can sulk charmingly as well when writing to the Bishop of Avila,
who has renounced his jurisdiction over the Convent of St. Joseph
and has commended himself to the prayers of the nuns: "During
all our life we never shall find anyone to show us more affection
than your Excellency. . . . We felt mortified to be told to commend you to our Lord. . . . We always are doing this. . . . We
feel quite offended." (August, 1577) When the Bishop is worried
that his very young niece has married an older man, Teresa is
ready with her consolation: "Not every thing can be perfect. It
would be much worse if the groom were very young. Women are
always better off when their husbands are mature." (September 6,
1577) As Teresa can handle the Bishop, she can handle the King,
when asking him to stop the scandalous accusations which the

Calced have raised against Padre Gracián: "Your Majesty, I am appalled at the wiles of the Devil and of the Calced Fathers. . . . What has given me courage to write . . . is the thought that as God our Lord endures my indiscreet complaints, your Majesty will do the same." (September 18, 1577)

Invited to present her complaint personally to the King, Teresa, the mystic, is no less excited than any other lady granted a royal audience in the Escorial: "Just think," she writes to Doña Inés Nieto, "what I, a poor woman, must have felt when I saw a great king before me. I was quite upset. . . . He commanded me to rise and made to this poor nun such a courtly bow as I had never seen before." (October, 1577) Teresa knows her weakness for enjoying such worldly honors, as when she is jubilant about the tax lawsuit that was finally won by the sisters of Seville. On that occasion she writes to the lawyer Don Alonso de Aranda: "The successful outcome of the lawsuit was a great satisfaction to me. . . . I am afraid it is no great perfection to take so much pleasure in temporal affairs . . . but I send you my congratulations." (November 10, 1577) In her decisive fight with the Calced for independence from them, she puts the problem before her powerful protectress, the Duchess of Alba. Using the strongest devotional language, she puts things almost topsy turvy, saying: "Your Excellency will keep in mind that this problem affects Our Lady, the Blessed Virgin, who at the present moment needs the help of persons like you in the war which the Devil is waging against her Order." (December 2, 1577)

The beginning of the year 1578 sees Santa Teresa in the danger of being forbidden to make new foundations in Spain. Shrewdly she makes some provisions to found convents in Portugal, and tries to use for this purpose her ancient correspondent Don Teutonio de Braganza, who meanwhile has become Bishop of Evora. Even in this letter of distress and emergency she warns him again not to use titles in writing her. (January 16, 1578) Teresa shows herself entirely on the defensive and in an unusual, complaining mood, when the Provincial of the Jesuits takes her to task for allegedly having lured Father Gaspar de Salazar into the Order of the Discalced Carmelites. No, she said, she did not do that at all; she had no pseudovisions, as the Provincial remarked, about this change of Order, and his accusations simply add to "the persecutions raining upon me, poor old woman." (February 10, 1578)

But her tone to the Jesuit rector of Avila is far from being lacry-mose, and she combines her usual energy with bitterness: the Fa-ther Provincial's letter shows "such a lack of sincerity and such a conviction that I have done something which never came to my mind that . . . it has hurt me." What should she write to a mem-ber of another Order? She suggests that perhaps she has had a "message from Heaven forbidding him to leave the Jesuits"; the Provincial, not she, must tell him what to do. (February, 1578) Teresa's very human indignation about this affair becomes evident from a letter to Father Gracián: " [The Provincial's letter] an-noyed me so much that I should have sent him a sharper reply. . . . I was extremely distressed. . . . To suppose that I per-suaded Father Salazar . . . would be an absolute lie . . . you see how silly it is . . ." (February 16, 1578)

What had enraged the Jesuit Provincial so much was a rather uncircumspect letter of Santa Teresa to Father Salazar in which she warned him "not to trust his brethren," with the suggestion that Joseph of the Old Testament had brethren, too. But Father Salazar found the retiring behavior of Santa Teresa "not very brave." In a second letter to Padre Gracián Teresa gives details from his letter: "He tells me I am like a mouse afraid of the cats." But Teresa knows of the threat of the Jesuits, that whosoever "takes Salazar into the Carmelite Order will be excommunicated." (March 2, 1578) To finish this most disagreeable story for Teresa, Father Salazar never joined the Carmelites, and maintained on his part the version that the Carmelites tried to conquer him for their Order. The truth seems to be that the Jesuits as the newest and most modern Order did not like any competition in austerity, the less so as constant "defections" to Carmelites and Franciscans took place.

In those years the establishment of a special Discalced Province was the main concern of the Saint. Like Cato's *Ceterum censeo*, Teresa would insert into her letters expressions like this: "God forgive those friars who are giving us such a bad time," (March 28, 1578) or she would think of peaceful means to reach her goal, e.g., an occasion to give a present to the Nuncio. (April 15, 1578) Or she would add to her usual warnings a witticism: "God deliver us from these times where we have to be afraid to do good be-cause we are looked upon with such an impassioned hatred." (April 17, 1578) When meanwhile in the inner circle Padre Ma-

riano shows himself hostile to Santa Teresa because of her preference for Padre Gracián, she does not mince her words, and feels
obliged to give Padre Gracián instructions of caution: "Tear up
this letter at once," or "I have opened this letter to cross out what
I said about Padre Mariano, in case the letter should go astray."
(May 8, 1578)

The circumstances of those years keep the usually amiable
foundress in an emotional turmoil. She feels outraged that the Prioress of Valladolid caters to the Calced and that she has asked
Fray Hernando de Medina, who had returned from the Discalced
to the Calced, for the ceremony of giving the religious habit to the
very sister of Father Gracián. (May 14, 1578) She declares herself
"distressed" about the heart ailment of Mother María de San José,
"distressed" about one of her trouble-making nuns for whom she
recommends the whip. (June 4, 1578) Likewise she complains to
Father Domingo Báñez of being destined to bear one cross after
another. (July 28, 1578) She asserts to Father Gracián that "the
Lord is permitting the devils and the world to attack with so great
a fury." (August, 1578) It is the time St. John of the Cross has
been imprisoned and mistreated by the Calced. Teresa, concerned
about his situation, writes letters throughout the night of August
18 about steps to be taken for his liberation, not knowing that he
was fortunate enough to have escaped already. Thus she closes
her letter to Padre Gracián: "They are ringing for Matins." (August 18, 1578) When Teresa finally hears from the escaped friar
what his Calced brethren had done to him, she is quite upset, calls
his suffering "a martyrdom" and entreats Father Gracián: "The
Nuncio ought to be informed of what those people (*ésos*) have
done to this innocent Saint." (August, 1578)

In all this trouble, when Teresa is vituperated as recalcitrant
and unruly, and considered a nuisance also by the Nuncio Sega, in
her energy she writes to an old influential Jesuit friend, Padre
Pablo Hernández asking him to tell the true story to the Nuncio's
confessor so that his conscience might be stirred toward truth and
equity. (October, 1578) Meanwhile, the General of the Carmelites died. Teresa had always wanted him to have an umpire in the
struggle between the Calced and the Discalced Carmelites, although Padre Gracián and Padre Mariano had been opposed. At
the news of the death Teresa is more than depressed. She writes
to Padre Gracián: "I wept the whole day, was not capable of do-

ing anything and felt terribly distressed . . . ; if we had approached him . . . , everything would have been straightened out." (October 15, 1578) In 1579 nothing has yet been straightened out. The nuns of Seville are intimidated and their Prioress María de San José removed from office. Teresa is horrified: "The Devil cannot stand the existence of Discalced friars and nuns." (January 31, 1579)

In the time of her own great troubles Teresa seems to console others in bothersome secular plights in a rhetorical way. When the secretary to the Duke of Alba, Juan de Albornoz, is imprisoned because he married his son to a royal lady-in-waiting without informing the King, Teresa writes to his wife Doña Inés Nieto: "I am convinced the time will come when he would prefer the days he wore the iron chains to all the chains of gold on earth." (February 4, 1579) But coming back to the rebellion against her in the Convent of Seville, Teresa's language drops all the golden-chain rhetoric: "This dismal Vicaress (*esta negra vicaria*) always invented calumnies. . . . O Jesus, how she has wounded me." (April 21, 1579) After a cooling-off period, however, Teresa is again St. Teresa when writing to the new Vicaress Mother Isabel de San Jerónimo in Seville: "Try to forget what has happened and think how you would like to be treated, if the temptation had occurred to you." (May 3, 1579) A month later she writes to Mother María Bautista in Valladolid: "You know, I don't govern now in the way I used to. Love does everything." (June, 1579) At that time Teresa calms down, and starts again to visit her convents, while in Rome the final regulation for peace between Calced and Discalced is discussed. Father Gracián has been forbidden by the Nuncio to speak publicly. Teresa, writing to him from Valladolid, alludes to this fact in her former humorous vein: "The Prioress here says she cannot write you, since although she likes to chat, she cannot talk to mute persons." (July 7, 1579) She teases him also about his "carelessness in telling the whole truth about everything." (July 18, 1579)

Great joy came to Santa Teresa again when the first small victory was won against the Calced by the reinstatement of her dear Mother José María as Prioress: "Praise be to God from whom comes every good and Who has brought your Reverence so victoriously out of the struggle." (July 22, 1579) The interdiction against Father Gracián's preaching is still taken lightly by her: "It makes me laugh that they have imposed a penance on you which gives you a rest." (July 25, 1579) Hoping that the division of the Order soon will be agreed on in Rome, Teresa remains in good spirits. When the sisters in Malagón in her presence move to a new house in solemn procession, she quips: "The nuns looked exactly like little lizards coming out into the sunshine." (December 12, 1579) This is one of the few similes occurring in her letters.

Another happy occasion is celebrated in a letter to the Prioress of Caravaca announcing that Teresa's holy and wise *Senequita,* San Juan de la Cruz, will arrive to counsel the nuns: "Treat him as though he were myself." (December, 1579) In a letter to Padre Nicolás Doria, the Prior of Pastrana, she jubilates: "Spiritually all is going extremely well," and in her jubilant mood she speaks of Father Gracián, who lived some time in the so-called Caves of St. Peter in Pastrana, as "the man of the cave." (January 13, 1580) She congratulates the newly professed nuns and novices of Seville, but jestingly takes to task one of the sisters who had called herself a dungheap: "I assume that her humility is not only a word problem." (January 13, 1580) But then comes the greatest joy of all: the prohibition of speech has been lifted for Father Gracián, and the nuns of Medina have helped in this matter by prayers and mortification: "Oh how Medina rejoiced when the nuns were told that you were no longer bound to keep silence! . . . There is a lay sister who gave herself the discipline a hundred times for your Paternity." (January 14, 1580) The Prioress of Beas, Mother María de Jesús Sandoval, is jestingly taken to task for her infrequent letters: "My daughter, if you were suffering from headaches like me . . . your charity might be excused for not writing me but as this is not so, I don't see why I should not complain about your charity." (February, 1580)

The situation of the Order having improved, troubles in Teresa's family find her better equipped than her brother Lorenzo to cope with them. Her other brother Don Pedro de Ahumada has become homesick for America, is cross with Don Lorenzo, suffers from loneliness and melancholia, has become restless and is bordering on insanity. Teresa sees that by staying in the house of Don Lorenzo, Pedro will ruin his own nerves and those of Don Lorenzo likewise. Thus she proposes that Lorenzo pay board and lodging for Pedro elsewhere. Then she specifies with a good business spirit: "If you give him anything, don't give it to him all at

once, but pay those who give him board by installments, since I
am convinced he will not stay in any place long." (April 10, 1580)
She rules out his staying with the friars of one of the priories. He
simply could not stand their frugality: "Even now, eating at an
inn, he refuses the meat if it is not well done and highly sea-
soned." (April 15, 1580)

Santa Teresa is "very glad" to hear from Rome that the brief
establishing a Discalced Province is assured; (May 5, 1580) actually the decision was made on April 14 and the brief published on
June 22. It is the moment when Philip II invades Portugal under
the pretext of his rights to the Portuguese throne. The Duke of
Alba becomes the commanding general of the invasion and is re-
leased from this purpose from prison. The shrewd Saint recognizes
the precarious situation of prayers for victory in what she considers an unjust war, and writes to the Duchess of Alba as follows:
"If I think of the pilgrimages and prayers with which your Excellency may now be busy, it must seem to you that life was more
peaceful in prison. God help me, how vain are the things of this
world!" (May 8, 1580) And yet Teresa's human attitude towards
her brother Lorenzo seems to take precedence over her spiritual
principles. One week before his death, Don Lorenzo writes his
sister that he feels his death is near. What does the Mother of
Carmel do, famous for her poem, "I die because I cannot die"?
She writes: "I fail to see why you have these ridiculous ideas and
feel oppressed by something that will not happen." (June 19,
1580) But it happens, and now she writes to Mother María de
San José in another key: "I am glad that he has left this miserable
life and is now saved. This is not only a manner of speaking."
(July 4, 1580)

Letters of condolence written by Teresa's hand generally are
full of sincerity. Thus she tells a widow who just lost her husband:
"You yourself have realized how unstable is this miserable life.
. . . I trust God will give you the light to understand what a
favor Our Lord is granting to a soul by taking it out of the world."
(August 6, 1580) At that time she consoles, in a most understanding way, her young niece, Sister Teresa de Jesús in Avila, whom a
nun had teased about her spiritual aridity: "These things have
nothing to do with perfection. . . . I wish that Sister were suffering herself from aridity . . . we may allow ourselves to wish her
that for her own good." (August 7, 1580)

Writing to Padre Gracián she raises an amusing "case of conscience." The small mule of the Padre is not good enough for him and endangers his dignity. Perhaps she could sell her brother's pony and buy a stronger mule with the money. But, after all, the small mule is safe, while the larger one may throw off his Paternity; so what to do? (October 4, 1580) Santa Teresa has to interfere in a doubt as to the occasions which permit raising the veil. She says never in presence of male persons except the closest family members, but surely in the presence of highly placed female persons like a duchess or a countess, because, she cleverly adds: "There is something to be gained and no risk run at all." (October, 1580) When her nephew Francisco de Cepeda, rather than taking perpetual vows, has left the monastery and married, Santa Teresa, shocked as a nun but understanding as an aunt, does not hide her feelings from Father Gracián: "I am afraid that he may get little happiness out of his marriage . . . but also that he may believe that I was annoyed at his decision." (November 20, 1580) To a group of girls in Avila who proposed to enter religion against the will of their parents, Teresa has this to say: "Under such conditions it is not so easy to take the veil. . . . I cannot imagine that you are so saintly that you will not be disturbed later, seeing that your father is unhappy because of you." (December, 1580)

Santa Teresa, realizing at last that her nephew Francisco has not made a mésalliance, almost forgets her misgivings as to his marriage when her usually hidden family pride lets her boast in a letter to her other nephew Lorenzo: "His bride is called Doña Orofrisia. . . . I should rather have said Doña Orofrisia de Mendoza y de Castilla. Her mother is a cousin of the Duke of Albuquerque and a niece of the Duke of El Infantazgo. Actually people say there is no one higher born in all Spain. . . . She is also a relative of the Marquis de Las Navas and of the Marquis of Velada." (December 28, 1580) The Saint seems to have forgotten for a moment her contempt for wordly honor, and the slip makes her, of course, all the more human, according to the adage that man is not a learned book but a being full of contradictions. To her sister she writes that the more she hears about Francisco's marriage and the fine character of Orofrisia, the more she has reason to be pleased. (January 13, 1581)

Santa Teresa, having drawn up the constitutions for her Order, thinks of some unwritten by-laws. Thus she beseeches Father

Gracián for the Carmel that he insist on clean table cloth and bed sheets "at whatever cost." (February, 1581) Her second concern after cleanliness is to do away with any scruples of the nuns about details. Thus she wants to delete from the draft of the constitution all kinds of detailed restrictions like the problem of stockings, or eggs at the collation. Third, seeing that her original ideal of no income for the Order will soon become impossible, she warns that this point be included in the rules; otherwise people soon would say that after a short time of reform the Carmelites have become "relaxed again." (February 21, 1581) The nuns of St. Joseph's in Avila do everything to distress Santa Teresa in asking for relaxations, the permission to eat meat and, whenever they do not feel well, to keep food in cells. They are vigorously rebuked. (February 27, 1581)

After the influenza epidemic of 1580 has killed so many of her friends, Teresa realizes at intervals how few of them are left; when, for example, her former confessor Fray Domingo Báñez triumphs in the competition for a famous chair in the University of Salamanca (March 4, 1581). Teresa's jubilation over the aristocratic marriage of her nephew Francisco with Orofrisia has quickly come to an end, too. The young couple is spending too much, their income is lower than was believed, the mother-in-law bothers Santa Teresa with all kinds of questions. Thus Teresa writes to Father Gracián: *Harto me querría apartar de todos ellos* ("I should like very much to get rid of all of them"). (March 12, 1581) Another concern of Santa Teresa is to get San Juan de la Cruz, for three years rector of the Discalced Carmelite college of Baeza, out of Andalusia, since "he cannot stand the people there." She thinks of a little trick: to persuade Padre Gracián as Provincial not to confirm his possible reelection. (March 24, 1581) But the scheming of the two Saints fails, as San Juan de la Cruz is elected Prior for Granada, and Padre Gracián feels bound in conscience to confirm the election. Teresa finds such interference *in sacris* not objectionable. There is a reliquary which the Marchioness of Alcañices has promised to Santa Teresa and which Santa Teresa apparently would like to have, and about which the Marchioness must have talked to a certain Doña María. So Teresa writes to the Marchioness: "Señora Doña María . . . will not feel at ease about the reliquary until you give it to me. . . . You have

a perfect right to keep it. . . . The Lord will intervene in this suit
and give the right judgment." (March, 1581)

When she realized that Father Gracián with whom she had
planned an inspection trip had advanced the date of his travel
without waiting for her, she really became sulky: "God deliver me
from people of haste." (May 24, 1581) The probability of Father
Gracián's absence at the inauguration of the new house in Palencia gives her pain, too: "Everything would be all right if my Father were coming, too; well, I don't know what to say." (May,
1581) Worried at that time again about the health of Mother
María de San José, she writes her the most endearing letter one
can imagine:

We do not want you to do penance, we wish you not to be ill, which
would inflict a penance on the whole community, but to be obedient,
not to be cause of my death. . . . I don't know why I love you so
dearly. (June 16, 1581)

One of the most dignified letters Teresa ever wrote concerns her
self-defense in a message to the King's chaplain who is also confessor to the Cardinal Primate; the letter is against the accusation
of having persuaded the Cardinal's niece Doña Elena de Quiroga,
a widow, to enter the Carmel. Far from accepting the charge and
begging the Cardinal's pardon, she rejects the accusation in her
splendid sincerity: "I have been against the idea . . . not because I thought His Eminence disliked it, but for fear there might
be a repetition of what occurred when another lady entered one
of our convents, abandoning her daughters." (June 30, 1581) This
is an allusion to a certain Ana Wastels de San Pedro. The rumor
that Doña Elena was rejected at the wish of the Cardinal was so
much against Santa Teresa's monastic integrity, that she entreated
Father Gracián with somewhat ambiguous words: "Let nobody
know that we refuse to take Doña Elena because of the Cardinal."
(July 14, 1581)

Shrewdness, kindness, diplomacy, discretion are the contradictory and yet converging qualities in the Saint's correspondence.
When she wants to look into the somewhat scandalous affair of
her niece Beatrix, and to meet her and her mother alone in Avila,
where they have to come from Alba de Tormes, she doesn't want

her brother-in-law Juan de Ovalle to join them. Therefore she writes with a delicate cleverness to her sister Juana: "Would it be too much to beg Señor Juan de Ovalle to be so kind as to permit you and your daughter to come although . . . he might be obliged to stay home and look after the house." (August 26, 1581) In Avila again, the sixty-six year old Foundress is tired and lonely. She feels her age, regrets her departed relatives and friends, and in a tone of resignation writes to Don Jerónimo Reinoso: "I feel very lonely here and have nobody to talk to for comfort. God help me—whilst I advance more in years, I know less where to look for comfort in this life." (September 9, 1581)

Teresa has one more year to live. Her travels become tiresome. The troubles of her administration do not decrease. The Cardinal's niece, Doña Elena, threatens to enter the Franciscan Order if Santa Teresa does not take her, and she, Teresa, has not received any reply from the Cardinal in this matter. The latter has called a bishop's conference for Toledo, where a decision will be made about Teresa's request for a foundation in Madrid, an application now pending for years. (September 13, 1581) The Mother Foundress is in a very awkward situation. Doña Elena actually is permitted to enter the Carmel within a month. But things in general become worse. A certain Casilda de Padilla, who had been allowed to enter the Order at sixteen, is quitting at twenty. Teresa is upset: "I do not know what devil has confounded her" and she has to fight the temptation to be glad that Casilda's sister has left the Dominicans at the same time: "This will prevent us from losing prestige—I mean with regard to the opinion of the world."

At the same time a Jesuit confessor takes sides in the disagreement between a Prioress and a Subprioress. Teresa is offended by such "trickery." She tells Father Gracián not to show any displeasure to the Jesuit Order, since the Jesuits send many novices, but that they should slowly get "disentangled from them" and replace those confessors by Discalced Friars. (September 17, 1581) But all these troubles are surpassed by the lost reputation of Teresa's niece, Beatrix Ovalle, who in the public opinion is believed to have committed adultery with Señor Ovalle's godson, Gonzalo González, so that the latter's wife has been granted a separation. Teresa is looking for advice from Don Sancho Dávila, brother of the rector of Salamanca on how to escape scandal, and speaks in this connection of "a great sorrow I have been bearing for almost a year." (October 9, 1581) In all this psychological turmoil Teresa says almost nothing in her letters about her innermost spiritual, mystical situation. But on one occasion she writes Padre Gracián that the "skeptical" priest-professor Dr. Castro y Nero, who "does not believe even in St. Bridget's revelation," would like to confess her, out of curiosity. Teresa remarks she would have liked this years ago, when she was not sure of herself, but now she does not like it "as I am at peace." (October 26, 1581) Likewise she tells Mother María de San José that she is experiencing the peace described in her seventh mansion. (November 8, 1581)

And yet, even in her last month of life as the overburdened Prioress of San José in Avila, she continues her exaggerated politeness to the Duchess of Alba, from whom she borrowed the copy of her *Life,* the original still being in the hands of the Inquisition. Since Teresa had no occasion to see the Duchess personally, she writes: "God knows how I feel about your Excellency's leaving on a journey without my having had the happiness to kiss your Excellency's hands. May He be blessed forever who wants me to have so little pleasure on earth." (November, 1581) She tells her even that her absence weighs more heavily on her than the affair of her niece Beatrix, while at the same time she urges her brother-in-law to go by all means with Beatrix to the country, ignoring Don Juan de Ovalle's opinion that a good conscience should not give in when confronted with slander. (November 14, 1581) Meanwhile she has come to grips with Dr. Castro y Nero, who read and criticized all her available works. She writes: "I kiss your hands an infinity of times." She wants to have him as confessor now, and we find it interesting that she is fascinated by the elegance (*galantía*) of his epistolary style. (November 19, 1581) But Teresa's dealings with the learned professor—and later bishop—did not always remain smooth. He did not like to confess the other nuns. As he also did not like to preach a solemn sermon at the profession of Ana de los Angeles, Teresa has to tell him that the nuns would rather miss the partridges at the festive meal than a sermon. (November, 1581) Finally Dr. Castro accepts, does splendidly, and Teresa, thanking him, tells him in her charming exaggeration, that if he does not promise her to become a great influence in the Church she would prefer never to have known him. (November 28, 1581)

Having got the permission for a foundation in Burgos, Teresa suggests to the Ovalles that they take Beatrix with them on their trip to get her out of town—"in vain, however." (November 29, 1581) They took instead their cloistered niece Teresita. (November 29, 1581) The aging Foundress, bothered by letters from Orofrisia's mother about the will of Don Lorenzo and the division of the heritage, (December, 1581) and also about her sister Juana and that brat (*moza*) Beatrix wishing to live in Avila, sighs under these burdens: "O Jesus, how little perfection exists in this life. How ridiculous everything is!" (December, 1581) Also in her congratulations to Don Lorenzo's son Lorenzo on his wedding—he emigrated in his turn to America—Teresa strikes a melancholy note. She would like to have him and his bride in Spain, nay, in her convent, but they would have there more trials than peace. But in the same letter the holy aunt, after taking the nephew to task for his sin against God in having had in Spain a natural child, bursts into her endearing language of love, saying: "The little girl looks so much like you that I cannot help taking her in my arms and caressing her very much. Since she is so tiny, it is strange how patient she is." (December 15, 1581) On the other hand, when she finally reports on the success of the Cardinal's niece as a nun, she says: "Her satisfaction is so great that she made me praise our Lord" and adds, *así ha engordado,* which a benevolent translator may render by "so much she has increased (in spirituality)"; but Edgar Allison Peers bluntly translates: "she has got fatter, too." (January 8, 1582) If this is the meaning of the clause, Teresa has not forgotten the troubles she once had over the qualifications of the young widow who is called Sister Elena de Jesús.

Teresa, at the beginning of the year which will be her last, shows herself extremely kind again, in one of her few letters of spiritual direction to individual nuns. Sister Leonor de la Misericordia, a short time after having taken the veil, complains about her lack of spiritual fervor. Teresa encourages her "dear daughter" Sister Leonor: "Don't worry. . . . Be proud to help our Lord carry the cross. . . . Only a hired soldier expects to be paid by the day." (January 15, 1582) Here exceptionally we hear the voice from the *Life* and the *Mansions*. A very kind letter goes also to the problem-niece Beatrix, who stays now with her uncle Perálvarez in Avila, far from the married woman whose jealousy brought her into trouble. Teresa calls her "freed from the past of the woman." (January, 1582) The Mother Foundress, after an attack of palsy

and at the height of her sanctity, has not given up her habit of
calling a spade a spade.

Despite colds and a sore throat during her difficult foundation
at Burgos, Teresa gives a piece of her mind to the Coadjutor Provincial Doria, telling him against his own convictions that the
young friars need not be learned but humble, nor need they boast
of their learning, which is small enough, and if they are lacking in
modesty, they would be better with no learning at all. (March,
1582) Despite this display of her old energy, she thinks of a successor as "Mother Foundress" and proposes this to María de San
José; "You know so much more . . . than I . . . old and of little
use." (March 17, 1582) What is still strong in her, however, is the
founding spirit. After the success of Burgos she wants to push the
difficult foundation of Madrid, writing to the rich business man
Pedro Juan de Casademonte: "I am very anxious for a foundation
in Madrid."

One of the gravest sorrows of the Foundress at the end of her
life is the quarrel of the Jesuits with the Discalced Carmelites, the
Jesuits whom Teresa had always rated so highly. Now "egotistic
interests" in doubtful donations and dissensions about the methods of prayer seem to her a plot of the Devil. (May 20, 1582)
Another trouble is the disobedience of the nuns in Granada who
took nuns from other convents to aggrandize their own establishment by a new foundation. The trembling voice of Teresa assumes the tone of the commander-in-chief, which she used to
avoid in lighter cases. Thus she writes to Ana de Jesús, Prioress of
Granada, who later will bring the first Discalced Carmelite nuns
to France: "In whatever concerns Discalced nuns I am the representative of our Father Provincial. In virtue of these powers I declare and command that, as soon as the necessary accommoda-
tions are provided, all the nuns from Beas have to return there
with the exception of the Mother Prioress Ana de Jesús, and this
even though they were to find a house of their own. . . . The
Devil is infecting this Order with his hellish principles. . . . My
head is not fit for writing more." (May 30, 1582) This letter is the
most severe Santa Teresa ever wrote, the more so as the sisters
involved have technically incurred excommunication. But it shows
also the sincere and circumspect leadership of the Saint.

A month later Teresa's ailment has progressed. She still
stays in Burgos and writes Father Gracián: "My throat is now

worse. . . . Do not worry . . . for it is in order . . . that I re-
pay His Majesty (God) . . . the favors He bestows on me each
day." (June 25, 1582) Worried about the many deaths in her
Order from the plague in Seville, the Saint still is "amused" about
the punctilious "obedience" of Mother Ana de Jesús, who sent her
nuns back to Beas on mules "so that God and the world could see
them" instead of using carriages which—so the Prioress had written—would have been objected to by "Our Mother" as too luxu-
rious. The first Prioress of Burgos still gets some written instructions from Santa Teresa occupied with many details for the new
convent, how the windows should be protected against the outside world, and how the laundry has to be done, but accompanied
by a new optimistic comment: "My throat seems better . . . my
room is nice and cool." (August 3, 1582) She even threatens the
troublemaking nuns in Alba de Tormes that she will come and
settle the affair herself. She knows the guilty ones who endanger
the reputation of the Order; the chaplain meanwhile ought to
punish them by restriction of their communions. (August 5, 1582)
    Teresa visits Valladolid and from there admonishes the Prioress
of Toledo to give the Bishop a worthy reception, announcing that
she herself will be back in Avila "by the end of the month." (August 26, 1582) Teresa remains her very self with all these little
cares and greater troubles, the worst of which is her real feud with
her nephew Francisco's mother-in-law, this strange woman who,
contesting Don Lorenzo's will, gives her "a terrible time." (September 1, 1582) Reassured by the chaplain that all has been set-
tled with the riotous nuns of Alba, Teresa calls them again "good
souls" and tells the chaplain that she will come soon. (September
5, 1582) Teresa's last letter is directed to the Prioress of Soria,
Mother Catalina de Cristo. On Teresa's mind then are further
foundation projects, at Madrid and Pamplona. The letter speaks
also of arrangements in the Convent of Soria, the place of kitchen
and refectory, novices and profession dates, but does not show the
slightest foreboding of Teresa's death, which will occur within a
month. (September 15, 1582)

    Since there has not existed up to now a chronological account of
the human aspects of Santa Teresa through her moods and
humor, this had been attempted in the preceding pages. The au-

thors who have written about the Saint have believed that showing her sanctity was their main task. As a result critics selected
their examples of humor to show "her quiet courage and self-
domination unaffected by adversities and oppositions on the
part of men." [2] The ups and downs revealed by our more systematic and objective sampling rather show the conquering, losing
and reconquering of these great human qualities. But the image
of Santa Teresa resulting from our dynamic presentation allows us
to draw a picture which is also in a static presentation more correct, and shows a Teresa confronted with the world and human
life and not only, as her other writings do (except the *Foundations*), in confrontation with God throughout her mystical life of
prayer.

Although living apart from the world, Teresa is an excellent
businesswoman, caring much for others, detached personally but
fighting with all admissible means for her Order, its reform, and
her foundations. She does this cheerfully and often humorously.
Teresa is always shrewd, magnanimous in less important matters
and on the whole extremely courteous with her correspondents.
She is unyielding, however, in struggles with her opponents, and
is justified by the fact that she generally has a greater clearsight-
edness. She is highly interested in her natural family, the well-
being of its members, in good marriages and worthy vocations. In
her understanding of family struggles, difficulties, sickness,
deaths, bequests, and legal entanglements, she shows an unusual
perspicacity. In argumentation she is both sincere and decisive.
But she softens her adversaries with witticism and compliments.
She pours water into the wine of fervent souls who do not recognize their spiritual limitations. In handling scandals she is fair and
open-minded; in hiding secrets she is ingenious (witness her
coded language during the long struggle between Calced and
Discalced Carmelites). She is interested in the welfare of all her
friends and wants them to be simple and free. Teresa likes to tell
anecdotes and to report *faits divers*. She is highly interested in the
best of everything, dislikes shoddiness in anything.

Writing to people she loves, her jests hardly keep her tender
feelings properly subdued, whereas in neutral letters she can show
a hard-headed matter-of-factness. She explores all possibilities toward advantage for her Order, and does not hesitate to rebuke

anyone she considers in error or in sin. She fights for the dignity of her nuns and for their treatment as respectable women. On the other hand she mentions her enjoyment of good food, shows contempt for physicians, is offended and jealous when not receiving letters from her correspondents. It is with the greatest frankness that she warns young confessors not to become too friendly with nuns or other women to whom they try to be of spiritual help. The Mother of Carmel is very fond of children and has much consideration for social custom and noble families, although disapproving of their cult of worldly honors and rich possessions. She does not shrink from calling names when she feels outraged, but generally calms excited persons by quiet words and commonsensical considerations.

Teresa gives words of warning when dangers are ahead, and is ready to meet them by a strategy of caution and even cunning. She is skeptical of the truth of silly rumors of miracles and ecstatic nuns; she thunders as a true superior and leader when she hears of movements of disobedience and signs of revolt in any of her convents. She is avowedly very happy over her successes, whether with the King, the Nuncio, or the State; she does not hesitate to enter into lawsuits for her Order. In her arguments about religious questions with other Orders, be it with the Calced or the Jesuits, she can become harsh and bitter. In her fight with the Calced opposition she even sometimes loses her poise and balance, is distressed and full of indignation.

Once more her calm self, however, Teresa seems to treat everybody with more love and charity than before. And with her increased charity, oddly enough, there comes also a heightened sense of humor. Teresa's feeling for the comic can be at times jubilant and even excessive. But in such a mood her practical sense in dealing with the "world" seems unequalled. When high policies are at stake, she steers a thoughtful course between her moral convictions and the ideas of her aristocratic friends. As a general rule her letters are adapted to the mentality of the recipients. This sometimes may appear like a surrender of her principles, but it is rather a proof of her great understanding of other people and the absence of any fanaticism in her. Asked questions of casuistry, Teresa never decides for the extreme, but for what is feasible. On certain points Teresa is very firm, however: she exhorts the uttermost cleanliness possible, permits not the slightest deviation from the fundamental rules of the Constitution of the Order, demands the eradication of an over-finicky scrupulosity. Teresa is herself astonishingly free from the minor scruples when she uses persuasion to get personal influence on elections and distribution of offices. To impose her will and express her displeasure she uses a whole battery of persuasive or domineering attitudes, whether endearing, sulking, sneering, or rebuking. In certain difficulties she may show both a flexible strategy and the finest discretion. She always seeks out sound and competent advice before making far-reaching decisions.

When Teresa admires someone or something, she may have recourse to exaggerations which at times may be ironical, occasionally in harmony with the style of the period, but which in another temperament than hers would jeopardize a remarkable straightforwardness. A great motherly love for her nuns, young friars, and particularly little children remains one of her notable qualities, helping her to overcome periods of melancholy and disappointments. Energy, however, is perhaps her most typical trait of character; this remains unchanged from her first decision to enter religion until the establishment of her last foundation. Leadership is her greatly distinguished feature in addition to unshakable faith and triumphant piety.

On the whole Santa Teresa lived and acted according to the sixty-nine *Avisos* ("Counsels") which she bequested to her nuns (to be read on pp. 629–31 of her *Complete Works*). The most remarkable rules in conformity with the *Constitutions* (pp. 605–28), i.e. rules for the Order in official form, are the following: To speak little in the presence of others; not to challenge others; to talk to everyone with a moderate joyfulness; not to poke fun at anyone; not to blame anyone without forethought, humility and self-restraint; never to excuse oneself if blamed, except in unusually important cases; never to say praiseworthy things about one's own knowledge, virtue or family except if it may be helpful to others; never to interfere with the problems of others unless requested to, and then only for charity's sake; not to say negative things about anyone except oneself.

We have to understand that all these principles represent not only a practical shrewdness but also the consequence of a mysticism whose central tenet was: "To die and to suffer must be our desire." This we read in a very short work of Teresa, the *Pensamientos y sentencias* (*Thoughts and Sentences*, p. 639 of the *O.C.* edition). Perusing only her letters, one may be tempted to forget what Teresa was first of all: a mystic. It is as a mystic that she has her large place in history.

# CHAPTER 8

# A Comparison of Santa Teresa with
# Other Mystical Writers

THE better poems of Santa Teresa have proved that whenever she felt strongly about something she tried to express herself even in poetry. The manneristic style of her times lent itself marvelously to the expression of her spiritual paradoxes. Nevertheless it would be out of place to compare her with spiritual poets of her times, especially with her great pupil San Juan de la Cruz (1542–1591) or with the first enthusiastic editor of her works, Fray Luis de León (1528–1591). What we admire in her as a writer is her use of prose.

## I  The Medieval Mystics

Mystical prose in the Western world throughout the Middle Ages was written in Latin. The medievalists still owe us evaluative statements as to its literary quality. The medieval mystics were partly experimental contemplatives like Santa Teresa herself, partly speculative theologians who wrote about the mystical way as a result of study. If they were vaguely known to our Saint, the knowledge was indirect, gained through her confessors as we see by an occasional mention in her readings. Referring in this context to a condensed history of Christian mysticism[1] and to a commendable anthology of it for more complete information,[2] we may set down here a historical mystico-literary sketch of the movement's evolution, mentioning only the greatest names and works. There is first of all St. Bernard of Clairvaux (1090–1153), who, commenting on Solomon's *Song*, changes the friends of the Lord into the spouses of the Lord and thus creates the nuptial love relation between God and the Soul on which Santa Teresa draws heavily. Richard of St. Victor (d. 1173) is the most outspoken teacher of the sharp distinction between active meditation and passive contemplation, according to the symbolic titles of his books *Benjamin Minor* and *Benjamin Major*. We know that this is the essence of what Teresa tried to teach her nuns, using more modern terms. The greatest mystical lover of Christ, however, was St. Francis of Assisi (1181–1228), who in his *Cantico del Sole* (*Hymn of the Sun*) praised all creatures in the Lord; we see this theme developed in Teresa's disciple John of the Cross rather than in Santa Teresa herself. In Teresa, however, we find the effort made by the Franciscan St. Bonaventure (1221–1274) to distinguish clear-cut mystical stages in the spiritual growth, as he did in his great work *Itinerarium mentis ad Deum* (*The Mind's Journey in God*).

Before continuing with the mystical theologians, let us recall once again that Teresa was a woman and that she wrote in the vernacular. In this particular context she had a long line of predecessors in the early German visionary and ecstatic Benedictine nuns whose writings Teresa, of course, did not know, but with whom she shares a great psychological and vital affinity. There is first of all Hildegard von Bingen (1098–1179), who as an abbess was also a foundress of convents and, like Teresa, corresponded with her sovereign. But she is famous most of all for her many strange visions to be found in the book *Scivias* (*Know the Ways*), probably written by her confessor in Latin but dictated to him in Middle High German. One may find in her doctrine quasi-"Teresian" concepts like the extreme stress on humility, out of which grow the wings of contemplation to make the soul fly to her inner tabernacle; the two images are reminiscent of Teresa's soulbutterfly and her interior castle. A century later general culture has developed to such a degree that Mechtild of Magdeburg (1210–1297), first a Beguine and then a Cistercian nun, is capable of her own penning, in classical Middle High German, of her mystical experiences. Her book is called *Das fliessende Licht der Gottheit* (*The Flowing Light of the Godhead*). It is considered by some an important source of Dante. Her affinity with Teresa lies in certain visions of the hereafter, Hell, Purgatory, and Heaven; in the Neoplatonic concept of the soul as prisoner of the body; her stress on beauty as far as the humanity of Christ is concerned; her devotion to the wounds of Christ and to His Passion in general; her abundant use of the terminology of courtly love in her boundless yearning for the absent groom; her concept of a peaceful sleep (of the senses and powers of the soul) and the delightful flight of ecstasy. Her stylistic alternation between prose and poetry, exposé and prayer, dialogue between Love and Soul, Creator and creature are reminiscent of similar devices in Santa Teresa.[3]

A third woman mystic of the thirteenth century was the Cistercian abbess St. Gertrude of Helfta (1256–1302). She, like Santa Teresa later, definitely knew the works of St. Augustine and of Gregory the Great, and she was even able to read them in Latin. Her ecstasies, like Teresa's, are provoked by liturgical occurrences and linked to the mysteries commemorated during the ecclesiastical year. She has a vision of "transfixions," less outspoken than Teresa's but at least with her heart pierced by the arrow of Divine Love; she registers many conversations with the Lord, she envisions Christ in different appearances and has also, like Teresa, the topographic notions of her standing to the right or to the left of Him.

There is still a fourth woman mystic of the thirteenth century, the Italian Angela di Foligno (1247–1309). Like Teresa, she comes at forty to a radical spiritual conversion. She dictated the account of her experiences in Italian to a confessor, who took them down in Latin. She suffers from an inexplainable illness and stresses the ascetical part of her spiritual evolution to the uttermost. Like Teresa, she preaches the embrace of the cross; like Teresa she considers sincere self-knowledge the key to the knowledge of God. She is thus the forerunner of what Robert Ricard has called—as far as Teresa is concerned—the Christian Socratism. Like Teresa, Angela di Foligno gives the Paternoster a mystical interpretation, like her she is aware of a rhythmical movement of heights and depths (sweet and bitter stages) which lead in seven steps to the mystical union; like her she sees her remaining imperfections in the higher stages as unbearable sins.

The fourteenth century, which is the epoch of speculative Dominican mysticism of the highest caliber, as witnessed by the great names of Master Eckhart (1260–1327), John Tauler (1300–1361), and Henry Suso (1296–1366), produced also the Dominican tertiary St. Catherine of Siena (1347–1380). She, like Teresa, progressed from a certain love of the world to the greatest austerities. She is the first to experience the Mystical Betrothal as a vision. This has been often reproduced in paintings where the Blessed Virgin takes Catherine's right hand and asks the Christ Child to accept her as a spouse, whereupon Jesus places a ring on her finger. One of the most famous examples is the picture of Lorenzo Lotto (1480–1556), an older contemporary of Teresa. These espousals have the power and virtue of changing Catherine's merely contemplative life into one of apostolic activities. Like Teresa she becomes an indefatigable letter writer in order to urge high-placed ecclesiastical and secular authorities to improve the state of the world. She finally goes in person to Avignon to persuade Gregory XI to return to Rome. In her main work, the *Dialogue*, she shows herself, like Teresa, a devotee of the Precious Blood. Actually Christ appears to her when she has accompanied a young Perugian, Niccolo Tuldo, to the scaffold and is standing there, bloodstained, holding the head of this youth in her hand. Christ receives this blood and in it her holy desire of love. The Lord shows her also, as Teresa developed later in her poem "O Beauty which transcends all beauties," that He alone is Being and she is nothingness.

Returning now to the great masculine—and more systematic—mystical tradition, we may first state that from all the mystics mentioned until now there is no clear-cut influence on Teresa; there is only a logically understandable analogy. But there are two streams of mystical literature in which not only conceptual but also structural and stylistical influences on Santa Teresa appear more tangible. The one stream comes from Arabic-Mohammedan mysticism, called Sufism, through the meditation of the Mallorcan Ramon Lull (1235–1316), writing in Catalan and continuing also the line of St. Bonaventure. The second stream comes from the North, where Tauler and Suso had as their most outstanding pupil the theoretical and experimental mystic Blessed Jan van Ruysbroek (1293–1381).

Ramon Lull, after a rather worldly life in his youth, became at the age of thirty a Franciscan tertiary, shaken by a vision of Christ on the cross, a vision he experienced five times. At forty he retired as a hermit to Mount Randa, where he wrote his famous *Ars Magna* (*Great Art*). Full of Arabic culture, he then made it his lifeplan to convert the Moslems; he died at eighty-one, a martyr in Tunis. Although he may have adapted his mystical writings (*The Book of Contemplation; The Book of the Friend and the Beloved*), as far as concept[4] and style[5] are concerned, to the patterns of Sufism, it seems nonetheless a long way from the Arabs to Ramon Lull, who was influenced considerably by early Franciscanism. Like St. Francis, Lull considers himself a singer and a fool of love. He places the mystical initiative in the will and the memory. These two powers first ascend the mount of contemplation; the understanding finally will join them. This looks somewhat Teresian and yet, despite the conviction of Sister Miriam Thérèse Olabarrieta,[6] it would be difficult to state whether patterns of affinity are due to a direct or an indirect influence.

## II  The Later Mystics

The predecessors of Santa Teresa, whom beyond any doubt she knew much better, and who also show Lullian traces, are first of all Francisco de Osuna (1497–1542). His *Tercer Abecedario* (*Third Spiritual Alphabet*), taught in its first part the meditation on the Passion of Christ, in the second part the ascetical discipline, and in the third the prayer of recollection. This *Third Alphabet* became, as we stated above in Teresa's biography, the decisive book for her spiritual life. It is bristling with all kinds of metaphors and comparisons, and even Santa Teresa was not able to outdo Osuna along these lines, although she refined some of them as she also enlarged his teaching. The second important predecessor was San Pedro de Alcántara (1499–1562). He is the saint whom Teresa admired as the greatest imaginable ascetic, and in whose book *Treatise of Prayer and Meditation* were to be found all the incentives for the Franciscan and Carmelite reform. A third forerunner was Bernardino de Laredo (1482–1540). He showed the royal way to mysticism, the way of perfection, by emphasizing the ascetical part in his work *Ascent of Mount Sion*. A fourth mystic is Blessed Alonso de Orozco (1500–1591), an Augustinian who in a very polished Castilian wrote two important books on the development of asceticism, the one called *Garden of Prayer and Mountain of Contemplation*, the other *The Spiritual Betrothal*.

It seems evident that Santa Teresa found in the one or the other of these authors certain literary "Lullian" motives which are not usual in the Western tradition of the Middle Ages. Such motifs are the laboring for the glory of the beloved, the binding *knot* of love, the beloved one's becoming the *prisoner* of the lover, the lover undergoing all tortures for the beloved, being put *in chains*, the *fetters* becoming tightened, *squeezed*, the prisoner being hanged, stifled, wounded by a spear, the lover being a *child* at the beloved's breast, *put to sleep*, the image of the unpolished *mirror* reflecting the imperfections, prayer as a *door* to contemplation, the *mansion* of the soul to be adorned, the soul's seeking for God, the continued serious wordplay on captivity as liberty and the greater love appearing as the greater suffering.

### III   *The Flemish Tradition*

These motifs from the Catalan tradition are different from the Flemish tradition reaching Spain through Latin translations. We suggested above that the main exponent of the Flemish influence is Jan van Ruysbroek (1293–1381). He was first a secular priest but retired as a hermit to Groenendael near Brussels, where he founded a group of contemplatives whose Prior he became after they adopted the rule of canons regular of St. Augustine. He simplified the ascetical stages but developed the mystical part to such a refinement that, had he not found a still more ingenious successor in St. John of the Cross, his books on the Spiritual Espousals and The Seven Steps of the Ladder of Spiritual Love would have become the epitome of mystical theology. Continuing the subtle speculations of Master Eckart, he worked out a mystical evolution of ever higher unions proceeding in the consciousness from Christ to Trinity. His teaching as a whole, where actually the soul "rises above" everything, was, as Teresa avows, no food for her. He has, however, some motifs which one may call "northern" and which did affect Teresa. There are, for instance, the common people *outside the castle* of the soul, the soul *sealed* with the image of God, the Divine Love *seeking* the soul, the *emptying* of the soul, the *jewels* for the bride ( *cierheit* ), *thunder* and *lightning* as symbols for the surprising rapture, the *absorption* of the soul by the sea of God and the mystical *death* for the spiritual union.

### IV   *Santa Teresa's Influence*

We turn now to an assessment of the influence of Santa Teresa on the mystical writers of the generation after her, and we are perhaps surprised at its relative lack. For while her doctrines played an important part in theological teaching and her system was considered classical, each of her followers offers his or her own system with particular stages, different metaphorical illustrations and varied stylistic devices. Let us mention only some very great names. First of all, her beloved but entirely independent pupil, St. John of the Cross. He became famous especially because of his emphasis on the bitter periods in the mystical life, which he calls with an unforgettable symbol *La noche oscura del alma* (*The Dark Night of the Soul*). He describes also a stage beyond the Mystical Marriage which he called *La llama de amor viva* (*The Living Flame of Love*). St. John doesn't mention visions, for he is opposed to all of them. His strength, does not lie in the showy metaphor, but in the definition and the technical terminology of his prose and a chosen archetypical symbolism in the poetry. A post-Teresian mystic, also Spanish but strongly influenced by the Flemish mystics, is Juan de los Angeles (1536–1609). His especial contribution was the elegance and presentation in his *Triumphs of the Love of God* (1590) and *The Spiritual Struggle* (1600).

The only mystic outside of Spain who notably followed Santa Teresa and made rather frequent reference to her is St. Francis de Sales (1567–1622). He knew the Santa's works thoroughly, thanks to his acquaintance with Madame Acarie, who introduced the Carmelite Order to France and, as a nun, adopted the name Mary of the Incarnation. The Carmelite rule was modified for the Visitandines, founded by St. Francis de Sales together with Madame Jeanne de Chantal. Francis de Sales in his *Treatise of the Love of God* actually developed Teresian ideas, e.g., her loving consideration of the humanity of Christ as the act of the Presence of God, her cult of extreme humility as holy indifference, her occasional concept of the child at the mother's breast, as a systematic allegory demonstrating the development of mystical love. De Sales also modified somewhat Teresa's concept of the wound of love. Essentially, however, he preserved her mystical stages.[7]

There still must be mentioned a great French woman mystic and Classical writer whom Bossuet called "our French Teresa," namely Madame Martin, who, as a young widow became an Ursuline under the name—like Mme Acarie—of Marie de l'Incarnation (1599–1672). She was mentioned above as sharing with Santa Teresa a vision of the Precious Blood. This Ursuline became famous because of her particularly advanced stages of mystical union and her missionary work in Canada. Outside of this, however, it is surprising that she has little in common with Santa Teresa, especially in the literary sense, since she tries to describe her stages by definition and description, not by metaphor, comparison, and simile; this, she says, would destroy the sublimity of her mystical experience. We shall compare the two mystics in a special chapter.

## V  A Literary Comparison

Now a literary comparison of Santa Teresa with these and other mystics[8] for an esthetic evaluation seems to me possible only through a consideration of the traits which all these mystical writers have in common. All of them want to express and to describe experiences by the most adequate similes to be found. In this "contest" it seems to me that Santa Teresa comes closest to a decisive clarification since she embraces many viewpoints at the same time and as a result, her metaphorical onomatology becomes most adequate to the phenomenon involved, as well as most pleasant in aesthetic presentation. The other mystical writers may sometimes surpass her in particular clarifications, but they appear less convincing on the whole. The principal difficulty they want to clarify is the difference between active meditation and passive contemplation. How do the pre-Teresian writers achieve this task? Padre de Alcántara says that to meditate is to strike the flint with the steel, to contemplate is to produce the spark of fire. Bernardino de Laredo provides Teresa the distinction between rowing with great effort and easy navigation in deep waters. The battery of metaphors and similes of Francisco de Osuna distinguishes the rough apprenticeship of a carpenter and the ease with which the master carpenter handles his art; or the slow ploughing of a tired ox left to himself and the rapid work of an ox urged on by the goad; or a wagon being drawn uphill and its moving over a plain with wheels greased. Osuna speaks also of playing on an instrument out of tune and on an instrument in tune; he distinguishes between a vase of clay and a vase of gold, between insipid water from the brook and fresh water from the spring.

What Teresa explains in the examples she imitates, varies and modifies with ease, is the *why* and the *how*. Why does she prefer the water illustration to the others? Because the soul is a garden and *needs* watering. How does the watering occur? Through complicated waterpipes from the far-distant spring or more simply at the spring itself, which never ceases to flow; (*Castle* IV, 2, p. 347) or by rain. What do servants of lower and higher rank mean to Santa Teresa (Osuna's meditating squire and contemplating knight)? They mean serving outside the castle far away from the King and serving inside the castle closer to his mansion. Teresa's comparisons are more to the point. She does not need oxen and wagons, vases and instruments, which are viewed in entirely different situations, but she chooses the continuum of an ugly caterpillar who spins his own cocoon to die therein and to rise out of it as a perfect winged butterfly. (*Castle* V, 2, p. 358)

Among the post-Teresian authors, her great disciple, Juan de la Cruz has ingenious comparisons which, however, do not quite match hers. To him meditation is a knocking at the door, contemplation is seeing the door opened; or the difference is that of cooking a meal and being allowed to eat it; it is to carve a wooden statue and simply to paint it; it is breaking the ground for sowing the seed and letting the seed grow; it is peeling a fruit and tasting its substance; it is an infant's spoonfeeding and an infant's full enjoyment of the milk from its mother's breast; it is a baby's clumsy attempt to walk and its being carried in its mother's arms. St. Francis de Sales stresses the difference as counting the details of a precious crown and enjoying its general aspect, as smelling each flower and smelling the bouquet. A pupil of St. Francis de Sales, Bishop Pierre Camus (1582–1653), in his treatise *La Théologie mystique* (*Mystical Theology*), takes up the traditional *row boat* and *sail boat* and Teresa's *bees* busy around the flowers and resting in the beehives. The famous quietist Miguel Molinos (1628–1696), in his *Guía espiritual* (*Spiritual Guide*), speaks about travelling with need of a constant recourse to a road guide and travelling with complete knowledge of the route. A Frenchman, Paul de Lagny, speaks about knowing a language by gramatical rules and knowing a language by practice. All the post-Teresian analogies, like the pre-Teresian ones, show interesting *proportions* between meditation and contemplation. None shows the *connection* between them. To have shown just this metamorphosis is the exclusive literary merit of Santa Teresa.

Let us make a similar test with the metaphysical striving to clarify the interior phenomenon of spiritual passive suffering and its *raison d'être*. Here Osuna already has good suggestions: God, the craftsman, puts his refined instruments to the statue after it has first been hewn out by the adze. Or he says that the vessel on the fire, thanks to the heat it receives, does not cease to drip hot water. The spinning top, wavering, will turn steadily after a blow of the whip. Thus Osuna gives an idea of the necessity of a painful refinement of the soul on the way to perfection which only God can achieve. Santa Teresa's comparisons, however, hint at still another aspect, namely at the quasi-despair on seeing imperfections more clearly in the all-revealing light of grace. The soul then feels like a woman who believes that she has the clearest water in a vessel, but as soon as a ray of the sun falls on the water, sees it full of small particles and then despairs of having water clean enough for her laundry. (*Life*, XX, p. 79)

This decisive element of quasi-despair when the slightest imperfections appear as serious sins to the advanced soul is lacking also in Santa Teresa's successors. St. John of the Cross stresses rather that these ineradicable spots on a piece of linen after a first laundering are taken out with a particularly strong soap and lye. But for the desperate feeling in this passive cleaning process, St. John of the Cross needs another image, that of a person who is conscious while being slowly devoured by a wild animal, reaching its dark stomach and being digested there. Juan de los Angeles only speaks comparatively of a sick man in bed who, not knowing where to turn to ease his pain, faces death or madness. The great French bishop and writer Fénelon chooses the image of being not only deprived of one's clothes, but flayed and skinned. This type of insistence on the degree of suffering is found very often. But Santa Teresa's simile of particles of dirt has only one parallel, that in the French Jesuit mystic Père François Guilloré (seventeenth century). He writes of the surface covering of a stagnant pool which, under the rays of the sun, breaks all of a sudden, and there issues from the apparently harmless water the exhalation of an unbearable stench. Also the famous political adviser of Cardinal Richelieu, the Capuchin Père Joseph, called the Gray Eminence (in whom Aldous Huxley was so much interested as an unbelievable case of mysticism), joins Santa Teresa in combining pain and purpose when he speaks of the young eagle trembling between the claws of his mother who is carrying him to the highest cliff in order to teach him to face the sun.

## VI  *The Teresian Symbolism and Other Mystics*

How finally does Santa Teresa compare with other mystics in her symbolizing of the mystical union? In Francisco de Osuna,

Santa Teresa's preferred author, *ecstasis* and final mystical union are not as yet clearly distinguishable. Osuna speaks about the heron who soars after the eagle, which finally takes the heron. Osuna explains that the eagle yields to loving desire as the Beloved, conquered in Solomon's *Song*, follows the bride to her house and to her bed. He uses also the simile of the diver who plunges to the depth of the water, and the comparison of the sponge filled with the water into which it was thrown. For Santa Teresa, we remember, ecstasies were quickly-passing comets, soundless thunders, piercing whistles; (*Castle*, VI, 2, p. 372) the intermittent union was the felt presence of a beloved person in a darkened room, (*ibid.*, VII, 1, p. 410) the Betrothal the union of the flames of two candles, the Marriage the unified light in a room coming through two windows, the rain falling into the sea, the rivers absorbed by the sea. (*ibid.*, VII, 7, p. 412)

Even a St. John of the Cross cannot do better, seeing the soul in rapture inundated by all the rivers of the world and overwhelmed by the mightiest thunderbolts. His exaggerated eloquence falls short of Teresa's visualization. Again, his presentation of the mystical union may be more correct but less captivating, when he says that the same fire which transforms the wood into flames has first disposed it to become fire, or that the light of the star is joined to the light of the sun, which first enabled the star to shine. The same problem concerns Luis de León, who in his book *Los nombres de Cristo* (*The Names of Christ*) more cautiously still compares the mystical union to a glowing iron, saying, "The iron which gets inflamed, although in its essence is iron and not fire, in its appearance is fire and not iron." Fray Juan de los Angeles uses the same comparison and, theologically still more sophisticated, adds that the glowing iron is fire by participation. St. Francis de Sales changes Teresa's simile of two persons in a room into two spouses who enjoy their mutual presence in tranquility without discussing it; and her simile of the rain falling into the ocean appears as a drop of ordinary water falling into a sea of naphtha, wherewith the theologian underscores an absorption which is not a destruction but an absorption enjoyed. Francis adds the less distinguishable drop of perfume penetrating the cotton wool.

If concretization of the highest mystical experiences is the goal of all of the mystical writers, if condensation and brevity are the most adequate means for making such demonstrations convincing and attractive, Teresa has achieved this goal with the greatest stylistic skill. The other mystics before and after her have nothing to offer that could compare with Santa Teresa in originality or fascination. The role of Teresa among the mystical writers would be outstanding for this reason alone.

# CHAPTER 9

## Santa Teresa and Secular Spanish Literature

SANTA Teresa is a proper exponent of Spanish literature because of her spontaneous, natural art of writing, which is lexically rich and syntactically rebellious, thanks to her unusual imagination and her psychological perspicacity. These are reasons enough to grant her a central place in Spanish literature, and she represents as a spiritual writer an almost unique case in literary history.[1] Although she was to a degree an untaught literary genius in her own right and not a genius through having known much of secular Spanish literature existing before her, this literature nonetheless prepared the instrument which she was able to use for the expression of her thoughts and feelings. The question is not what she acquired consciously of this literature, but how well she fitted into its evolutionary stream. We are certain that she knew one or another of the chivalrous novels. She had read all the works of Fray Luis de Granada (1504–1588), the representative and defender of the best classical Castilian prose. Curiously, she was likewise interested in the great stylistic experimenter and source of English euphuism, Fray Antonio de Guevara (1480–1545). Although apparently not especially attracted by his culteranism, nevertheless his paradoxes, antithesis of adjectives and excess in certain kinds of word formation seem to have impressed her.[2]

Those who have tried to characterize what is typical in a Spanish writer came to the conclusion that his attributes are sobriety, spontaneity, improvisation, pragmatism, moral austerity, closeness to life,[3] but he also reveals a curious introspection, an attitude of conflict and agony.[4] Teresa shares with the oldest epics like the *Poema del Cid*, and with the Chronicles, the interest in details of daily occupations and behavior. In the ancient literature one also finds her type of energy and austerity combined with tenderness and human understanding: The Cid, the implacable scourge of the Moors, treats his wife and daughters with affection and considerateness. In the old Spanish epics, in contradistinction to the French ones, exterior miracles are lacking, while the contact with the other world, as later in Santa Teresa, is maintained by imaginary visions within meaningful dreams. Teresa's anarchic, irregular syntax appears very Spanish if placed between the irregular versifiction of the *Cid* and the irregular dramatic form of the great Spanish *Comedias* of the seventeenth century (Lope, Tirso and others), fully ignoring the Aristotelian rules.

Listening to the lamentations of Santa Teresa over the bitterly felt absence of the Beloved, one cannot help thinking of the oldest songs of yearning love, in which the girl expresses her longing for the far-away lover on a crusade or elsewhere. These were Galician songs known under the name of the songs for the friend, *cantigas de amigo*. One of them by Pao Meozo (1250) reads:

> O hinds of the mountains, I came to ask you a question:
> My friend has gone and if he stays with you,
> What shall I do?

> (*Ay cervas do monte, vin-vos preguntar*
> *Foy-ss'o meu Amigo, e se alá tardar,*
> *Que farey?*)

These *cantigas* are also the cradle of Teresa's glossed refrains. What she does with the popular love poetry, turning it into the realm of the divine (*a lo divino*), the great King Alfonso X, the Wise (1221–1284) did long before her in his *Cantigas de Santa María* (*Songs in Honor of the Virgin*). The oldest *villancicos* which Teresa imitated so well were recited by the singer (*juglar*) and joined by the choral song and dance of the listeners, as Teresa's *estribillos* preceding and following her glosses were sung and danced by her nuns. As for the strong opposition between body and soul in Santa Teresa, this is certainly less Neoplatonic than it is anchored in the tradition of the *dispute between soul and body,* reaching back to the twelfth century, where body and soul are mutually accusing one another for the sins committed. Teresa's concept of dying from the absence of the beloved partner is a motif of one of the oldest Spanish poems, the *Razón de amor* (*Reason of Love*). Gonzalo de Berceo in the thirteenth century is the first Spaniard who writes about spiritual problems not in Latin but, as he says at the beginning of his *Life of St. Dominic of Silos,* in the language "in which the man in the street is accustomed to speak to his neighbor." His is a truly Teresian program, which is enhanced by an eidetic and picturesque power, a rustic phraseology, ironical remarks and humble self-criticism.

The creation of a pure Castilian prose capable of expressing everything as well as Latin or even better, was the enormous merit of King Alfonso el Sabio, mentioned above. Without him Teresa would have lacked the instrument on which to play. The great variety of subjects treated at this King's inspiration in translations from Arabic and Latin provided a wealth of vocabulary and facilitated syntactical choices. The King's interest in law and order, as demonstrated in the codification of Visigothic and Roman law in *Las Siete Partidas* (*The Seven Divisions*) is still living, on a minor scale, in Teresa's *Constitutions* drawn and written by her, and accepted for the whole Order.

The first really great and individual work of Spanish literature is *El Libro de Buen Amor* (*The Book of Good Love*) by Juan Ruiz, the Archpriest of Hita (d. 1360). It is a somewhat veiled life story with many inserted episodes and reflexions, and thus despite its quite different content it is technically comparable to Teresa's *Life*. Like Teresa the Archpriest often stresses his lack of information and education, although with a grain of salt. Like her, he surrounds his narration with moral and ascetical digressions. But he is also inexhaustible in similes, comparisons and images. He has an optimistic sense of humor and an extraordinary gift of observation. Sharing so much with Santa Teresa in detail, the Archpriest shares with her in general the typical Spanish character, the way of looking at things, and of translating observations into the purest (*castizo*) idiom. The qualities of the Archpriest let us recognize why Santa Teresa was called *la Santa de la raza* (the Saint of the Spanish race), who, in quite another sense than the heroine of the Archpriest, is as Foundress a jealous, reforming, and austere *Trotaconventos* (Go-between, going from one convent to another).

The greatest prose writer of the fourteenth century, Don Juan Manuel, the nephew of King Alfonso the Wise, founded the Monastery of Peñafiel and retired there as a Dominican in his later years. He has in common with Teresa a great interest in education and guidance, shown in the pedagogical treatise he wrote for his son. His interest in his own life and his family made him write an autobiography; however it is not one of humility but of pride, *El libro de las armas* (*The Book of Weaponry*), a primer of deeds of chivalry through heraldic interpretations. If Santa Teresa is fond of anecdotes, Don Juan Manuel certainly is her forerunner in *El Conde Lucanor* (*Count Lucenor*), 1335. He is her greatest predecessor in a moralism and didacticism of literary excellence. He, like her, is under the influence of Ramon Lull, and is much concerned with the salvation of souls. None of the stories of *Count Lucanor* deals with carnal love. Instead there are, as in Teresa, constant examinations of the author's own conscience in the sense of whether he could be sure of not going to Hell.

A trembling observer of the schism of his time, as Teresa will be of the Reformation in hers, was the Chancellor Pero López de Ayala, who complained about it bitterly in his main work, the *Rimado de Palacio* (*Palace Poetry*). Ayala is the third artist after Juan Ruiz and Don Juan Manuel to handle Castilian style well nigh perfectly. Without his translation of the *Moralia* of St. Gregory the Great, Teresa would have been unable to read this work. Ayala's writings, like Teresa's, offer a practical wisdom, stressing the dangers which wealth may bring to the soul. Ayala knows the art of throwing, against a grey backdrop, a sharp light on outstanding persons of his *Crónica*, like King Pedro I and King Juan I, just as Teresa detaches certain spiritual leaders like St. John of the Cross and Padre Gracián, from the many pale background figures she mentions in her *Life* and in her *Foundations*.

The tone of desperate love in the most passionate sense had to enter Castilian literature before it could be modulated *a lo divino* by Santa Teresa. Evocation of passionate love was due to the "Catalan Petrarch" Macías, whose poems found a wide echo and were responsible for the many "Hells of Love" in the fifteenth century. If Santa Teresa's poetry was called an "occasional" poetry or poetry rising from specific circumstances, the first master in this domain was Alfonso Alvárez de Villasandino. And if there was any imitator of Dante in the fifteenth century who aroused the taste for symbols and allegories, visions and transcendental landscapes, it was Micer Francisco Imperial who had also a liking for wordplay and strange concepts much like that of Santa Teresa a century later.

It is in the fifteenth century that Teresa's main theme *Todo es nada* ("Everything is nothing") is already audible in the poets who sing about the *vanitas vanitatum,* like Ferrant Sánchez de Talavera in his *Decir de las vanidades* (*Exposition of the Vanities*). And yet, these poets are also the first Spanish humanists, among whom the Marques of Santillana excels. He stresses the importance of the learned man (*docto*) as Teresa will do particularly in view of choosing an intelligent confessor who has to be a *letrado,* an educated man. Like her, Santillana prefers to gloss and comment, e.g., on his own collected proverbs. As in Teresa's vision of Hell, in Santillana's *Infierno de los enamorados* (*Hell of Lovers*) there is absolute darkness and the fire is in the very breast of the damned. A far-away echo of the architecture in Dante's *Commedia* and a not too far-away and very Hispanic foretaste of Teresa's seven mansions is Juan de Mena's *El Laberinto* (*The Labyrinth*) where Fortune's wheels of past, present and future have the seven sacred divisions. If at the beginning of this chapter we said Teresa enjoyed the style of Antonio de Guevara, we may add Juan de Mena certainly as his stylistic forerunner in hyperbaton, circumlocutions and strong syntactical subordination.

Teresa's philosophy of life, her devaluation of it, and her desire for death is present even to the poetical form in the great lyrical poet Jorge Manrique (1440–1478). One actually seems to hear a strophe from Teresa's famous *Vivo sin vivir en mí,* when reading in Jorge Manrique:

> Do not delay, o Death, my dying,
> Come, let me live with thee,
> Love me who in love is vying
> With thee, and for thy coming trying
> To end all struggle in me.

> (*No tardes, Muerte, que muero;*
> *Ven porque viva contigo;*
> *Quiéreme, pues que te quiero,*
> *Que con tu venida espero*
> *No tener guerra conmigo.*) [5]

One finds Teresa's famous image of the mystical union of the human rivers flowing into the Divine sea well sketched in Jorge Manrique's no less famous *Coplas a la muerte de su padre* (*Verse of Jorge Manrique on the Death of his Father*):

Our lives are the rivers
Which are flowing into the sea,
Which is death.

(*Nuestras vidas son los ríos*
*Que van a dar en la mar,*
*Que es el morir.*)

"Teresian" here also is the half-verse "Que es el morir"; Spaniards call it the *pie quebrado* (broken foot) and it is applied to serious subject matter, although created for lighter topics. Teresa's forerunner in glossing popular-spiritual refrains is Alvaro Gato who shares with her also the humorous approach, saying certain things somewhat tongue-in-cheek.

The diabolic monsters, toads, and serpents threatening and punishing people, which Teresa is constantly envisioning, make a typical appearance in the *romances* (ballads) of the last Visigoth king, Don Rodrigo, seducer of la Cava, daughter of Count Julian who, avenging her, calls the Moors to Spain, according to the legend. As penance a hermit buries Don Rodrigo in a grave together with a two-headed serpent which begins to devour him. And if we conceive of some of Teresa's visions as Spanish literary motifs, the *ballads,* among many other motifs offer the foreboding of death of Roland at Ronceval. Or they show the dead appearing to the living as in the ballad *En la ermita de San Jorge/una sombre oscura vi* ("In the hermitage of St. George/I saw a dark shadow)." many ballads the epic narrative is interrupted by a lyrical exclamation to introduce a startling fact. This is the way Teresa interrupts her reports, and with the same purpose of establishing the marvelous; the old formula *¡Ay, Dios!* and similar expressions introduce the new lyrical notes.

If Santa Teresa met the Devil quite normally to fight him, the famous Don Enrique de Villena (1384–1434) is said to have met him for making a pact with him to learn the magical arts. He shared with Santa Teresa the fate of seeing his books confiscated, he as an alleged necromancer, she as an alleged *alumbrada,* that is, as a heretic of extravagant beliefs repudiated by the Church.

Vanity and love of the world were denounced in a perfect literary form a century before Teresa, not, however, with her detachment and contempt, but rather with a certain degree of approval by Alfonso Martínez de Toledo, the Archpriest of Talavera (1398–1470) in his *Corbacho* (*The Whip*). A greater link between the two is the familiar, elliptic, conversational, realistic, savory style full of popular expressions, never used in earlier prose. The divine love analyzed by Santa Teresa in its yearnings, sufferings, and torments, as well as her concept of the Beloved as prisoner of the lover might have been impossible without another tradition, that of human love, idealized, by the way, and offered for the first time with an exact love psychology in the short novel *Cárcel de amor* (*Prison of Love*) by Diego de San Pedro, the "Werther" of the fifteenth century. This book made such an impression on Spanish readers that it reached the climax of twenty-five editions and was still a "best seller" in the times of Santa Teresa. The hero Leriano, for whom the beautiful Laureola is unattainable, is fasting to the point of death, not being able to endure the absence of his beloved: Teresa-like, he dies from not dying. But Teresa seemed particularly impressed by the combination of love and heroism which she found in the novels of knight-errantry. These fascinated her when she was quite young and it was even believed, without too serious a foundation however, that the youthful Teresa had written a chivalrous novel herself.[6] Be that as it may, we know of Teresa as well as of St. Ignatius of Loyola that they not only read works like the *Amadís de Gaula* but got out of them a sense of adventure, generosity, perseverance, invincibility; in short, a chivalrous attitude which became with them a spirit of ascetic renunciation and apostolic energy.

If Teresa was preceded in her way of tracing physio-psychological portraits (e.g., that of her father, or of Francisco de Salcedo, or of San Pedro de Alcántara) then certainly it was by the earlier portraitists Fernán Pérez de Guzmán (1376–1460) and Hernando de Pulgar (1436–1493). And in his three eclogues or embryonic Christmas plays, the first great Spanish dramatist, Juan del Encina (1468–1529), inserts much that could be called pre-Teresian, particularly the realistic dialogue within the lyrical *villancico* and the spirit of humor combined with a thoroughgoing realism. In Encina's secular play *The Triumph of Love,* a shepherd is told about the "dying from not dying" of love in the form of an *agudeza* (witticism):

Watch out, shepherd, and heed
That love is of such a kind
That of all the agonies of the mind
With which it threatens thee
The worst is, it will no killer be.

(*Mira bien, pastor, e cata
Qu'el Amor es de tal suerte
Que de mil males de muerte
Que nos trata,
El peor es que no mata.*)

The strong lyrical dialogue of many plays of Encina was apropos, since the performances took place in a drawing room of the noble Alba family with which later on Teresa entertained friendly relations.

In contradistinction to St. John of the Cross, Santa Teresa was not particularly interested in the lyrical poets of her time. But she appreciated the poem "Come, death, so secretly" by the Comendador Escrivá, the Ambassador of Charles V to the Holy See. Teresa wished this poem to be read to the dying. Another of her older contemporaries was Fernando de Rojas, whose outstanding dramatic novel *La Celestina* is as little classifiable as to genre as Teresa's *Interior Castle*. Both are masterpieces of a new introspection. If in *La Celestina* one reads the lament of Pleberio over the suicide of his daughter Melibea, one imagines he hears the *exclamaciones* of Santa Teresa: "O Life, full of adversities, accompanied by miseries . . . you seem to me a labyrinth of errors, a horrible desert, a place for wild animals!" But while in the *exclamaciones* of Pleberio there is more than a little of Renaissance and pagan humanism, in Santa Teresa's *exclamaciones* there is a fundamental sense of the Divine, of a Providence within the world.

Santa Teresa was convinced of her mission as a call to hinder the pagan Renaissance in Spain. Hence there is no link with Boscán or Garcilaso, or with Torres Naharro or with the "progressives" of the time of her youth, the Erasmians and the brothers Valdés. These writers introduced a new spirit into literature, an anti-ascetic compromise with life. This spirit is what Santa Teresa, like St. Ignatius Loyola, hated most. Her contempt for life, however, is, we should add, not absent from secular literature. The great secular version of the *Todo es nada* ("All things are nothing"), may be found in the first picaresque novel, *Lazarillo de Tormes*. The *Lazarillo* has in common with Teresa's *Life* the literary autobiographical character steeped in the same *contemptus mundi*, in spite of Teresa's piety and Lazarillo's cynicism. And both autobiographies hide the author behind the picaro and Teresa's self-styled *ruin persona* in self-revealing humility; both make a sincere and unembellished examination of conscience; both reveal also true sorrow and true suffering, true rejection of wealth and honor, ambition and pride. Seen from outside, the borderline between the social nihilism of Lazarillo and the "Christian nihilism" of Santa Teresa thus appears very tenuous. Seen from inside, the ascete and the picaro are characteristic exponents of the Spanish style of life, restless and never satisfied with this world, and craving something better. Santa Teresa's works and the *Lazarillo* therefore were both avidly read from the day of their publication.

Santa Teresa's writings were submerged, so far as literary importance is concerned, by the rising flood of works during the Golden Age culminating in Cervantes' *Don Quijote*. Thus it would be difficult to establish any traceable influence of her particular concepts and style on secular Spanish literature. But so far as secular poets are concerned, they seemed to be more interested in Santa Teresa's personality than in her writings. At the relatively early date of her beatification and canonization (1622) and the festivities arranged on this occasion in Madrid, the most famous poets of the time like Lope de Vega, Juan de Jáuregui, Luis de Góngora, and others contributed to her homage in a poetic competition provided for this purpose. And similar tributes occurred at each centenary.[7] Lope de Vega wrote two dramas dealing with the Saint, one called *The Blessed Mother Teresa de Jesus*, the other *Life and Death of Santa Teresa de Jesus*. Another Teresian drama was written later in the century by Juan Bautista Diamante (1674). The topic "Life is a dream" taken up by Calderón de la Barca may be called Teresian in substance. Outside of Spain, Santa Teresa inspired the English metaphysical poet Richard Crashaw to three long poems of which the best known is *The Flaming Heart*. In his *Hymn to the Name and Honour of the Admirable Saint Teresa*, Crashaw achieves a sketch of the mystical life and works of Santa Teresa in a few lines:

How kindly will thy gentle heart
Kisse the sweetly-killing dart!
And close in his embraces keep
Those delicious Wounds, that weep
Balsam to heal themselves with. Thus
When these thy Deaths, so numerous,
Shall all at last dy into one,
And melt thy Soul's sweet mansion:
Like a soft lump of incense, hasted
By too hott a fire and wasted
Into perfuming clouds, so fast
Shalt thou exhale to Heaven at last
In a resolving sigh.

In France, Teresian dramas appeared very late, one by Catulle
Mendès, *La Vierge d'Avila* (*The Virgin of Avila*), 1906, and one
by the priest-dramatist François Ducaud-Bourget, *Thérèse qui
mourut d'amour* (*Teresa Who Died of Love*), 1955. Scholars tried
to construct other influences of the Saint's psychological insights
on Descartes, on Bergson, on Kafka. But these remain doubtful.
Santa Teresa's literary influence was bound to remain limited
even as her practical influence on the spiritual life within the
Church had become considerable. One of her latest visible influences was her conscientious imitator, the Carmelite Edith Stein,
who not only wrote about the *Kreuzeswissenschaft* (*Science of
the Cross*), but died a quasi-martyr.

# CHAPTER 10

# Santa Teresa and Mary of the Incarnation

•

IN Chapter Eight we mentioned the great French Mystic Mary of the Incarnation whom Bossuet called "the Teresa of our days." (*Instructions Concerning the States of Prayer,* Book IX, Ch. 3) I have made a close comparative study of the two "Teresas" in my book on Spanish Mysticism.[1] Here I offer this comparison in another form, but refer to my book for the quotations according to editions, works, chapters and pages which I do not repeat here.[2]

The reason for this comparison between two varieties of feminine mysticism is this: in the two Teresas we have exceptional cases which translate in entirely different ways the same experiences that are considered ineffable. We know that Santa Teresa relies almost exclusively on analogy, allegory, symbol, and metaphor; Mary of the Incarnation, as we shall see, depends on definition and circumlocution. But before we confront Teresa's metaphors with Mary's metonymies, the question ought to be raised why these fundamental differences occur despite the same subject matter and the same motives. There is even more implied. The highest imaginable spiritual experiences are handled with a different, but in either case, truly linguistic and stylistic virtuosity.

This virtuosity, different in kind, is all the more surprising as both women are deprived of the tools of technical theology. They do not know Latin and have no access to the writings of the schoolmen and the mystics who wrote in Latin. Both women are restrained, critical and yet inebriated in their divine love. They speak different languages, belong to different cultures, experience entirely different conditions of life, belong to different centuries, possess a quite different education, read different books, and come in contact with quite different people. It is known that Mary of the Incarnation (1599–1672) has read the works of Santa Teresa (1515–1582), and yet does not show the slightest traceable influence of the fact.

As a Spanish woman, Santa Teresa is of a visualizing type; as a French woman, Mary of the Incarnation is of an abstracting type. The realistic Spaniard, practical and antiphilosophical, knows and sees the concrete details of his environment; the abstract Frenchman speculates on general problems and prefers thought and logical conclusions to any experimental seeing, hearing, or touching. Accordingly, the psychological and metaphysical domain offers itself to the Spaniard in images of the exterior world; his theatre is action, gesture, movement. To the Frenchman interiorization gives the most important value; his theatre is a struggle of ideas and ideologies, his action an endless word-dialogue which arises among heroes who are carriers of problems and theses concerning the abstracted man, always and everywhere valid. The Spanish language accordingly is fanciful and full of imagery: the chandelier is compared to a spider and called *araña;* the seat of the coachman with his whip is compared to an angler and called *pescante;* a gang of urchins is compared to loose grapes and called *granujas.* The French language is so abstract that even very concrete things are called by abstract terms; therefore a wedding ring is called *alliance,* a married couple a household (*ménage*), a small seat in the cathedral choir for the canons to lean on when they are supposed to stand is called "compassion" (*miséricorde*).

Thus the speech of the two mystics is predetermined by the character and frame of their idiom. Santa Teresa follows the metaphors of her language when she sees white columns as made of sugar; white friars in a meadow are flowers, and the emaciated body of Pedro de Alcántara is the roots of a tree. While Teresa can think only through such analogies, Mary of the Incarnation either is unable to find them, or, having found them, immediately rejects them. Thus she says either: "I do not think whether I might find some comparisons, for really I don't find any which are helpful to my purpose," or "if I had wished to make comparisons, I would have vitiated the purity of such things as do not tolerate any admixture."

If Teresa's Hispanic imagination is of the same type as the mental pictures aroused in the *Spiritual Exercises* of St. Ignatius and the fancies in the inexhaustible visual interpretations of Don Quijote, Mary's critical analysis follows the Cartesian principle

*Cogito ergo sum,* and her own soul does not admit of anything but direct and exact statements about psychological and spiritual experiences. Santa Teresa as a *conquistadora* in the spiritual realm systematically conquers her soul and believes she defends herself in an interminable struggle with the Devil who besieges her castle; she undergoes constantly a psychomachy in the literal sense. Mary of the Incarnation scrutinizes herself with a kind of depth-psychology as do the Racinian heroines; she participates like Pascal in the subtle unsolvable distinctions between grace and free will. Therefore she makes less clear-cut statements about what she is doing and what happens to her. Whilst Santa Teresa ponders on the structure of the progress of her soul under the device of a watered garden, a silkworm becoming a butterfly, an interior castle with demons outside walls and God in the inner-most apartment, Mary of the Incarnation simply tries to discover the essence of pure love, sacrifice, reversibility and bliss.

The biographical circumstances may be called up, too, to explain fundamental differences that cannot be covered by slogans like extraversion and introversion. According to the life events of the two women, one would expect just the opposite. Teresa is the well-protected child of a noble family from Ávila; Mary, with her family name Marie Guyard, is a commoner, the daughter of a baker in Tours, exposed to all the difficulties of life. But strangely enough, while the young Teresa is impressed by novels and adventures, young Mary is enthused by the ecclesiastical ceremonies and the liturgical ritual. She has already a mystical dream-vision at the age of seven. While young Teresa, flirting with her cousins at the grill of her convent school, does not at all like the cloistered life as a possibility for her, young Mary beseeches her mother in vain to give her permission to enter the religious life. While, however, Teresa overcomes her original reluctance and enters the Carmel at twenty-one, Mary out of obedience gets married at seventeen to the silkworker Claude Martin. While Teresa, sickly and undecided, spends twenty years in her convent without any extraordinary event, Mary loses her husband after two years, is left with a child six months old, is carried during ten years to the highest mystical graces, has an unquenchable desire finally to join the convent but has to remain outside to educate her son and to earn her livelihood as a kind of clerk in her brother-in-law's business office. While Santa Teresa at forty has her first great vision,

Mary at twenty-six has already reached the stage which the mystics call the mystical marriage, and all this still in her civilian life. At last she enters the Ursuline convent in Tours at thirty-two. Both mystics develop a comparable apostolic activity. While Teresa at forty-seven starts the reform of the Carmel and begins the foundations of her sixteen convents, Mary at forty goes to the missions in Canada, founds a great convent and school for the education of the children of the French colonists and young Indians. She learns the Algonquin language, writes a famous catechism and a dictionary, but like Teresa, undermines her health by overwork. Both mystics die approximately at the same age, Teresa at sixty-seven, Mary at seventy-three.

As to her literary readings, Santa Teresa, as we know, got her second-hand theology from saints' legends, books of edification, sermons, St. Gregory the Great, St. Augustine, Laredo, Alcántara, and Osuna. Mary of the Incarnation is supposed to have read the much more sophisticated French Oratorians, Cardinal Bérulle, and other authors of the so-called French school. Both learned much from their confessors, and their writings reveal quite different attitudes toward mystical phenomena. Santa Teresa under a strong Franciscan tradition concentrates on the presence of God in the soul; Mary of the Incarnation, following a contemporary French trend, concentrates on the adherence to God under the concept of the Sacred Heart.

But what seems so sublime in the Teresian and so devotional in Mary's concept develops according to the premises discussed above, again in opposite directions. Whatever Teresa experiences, she believes she sees. She sees Christ in the Passion and Resurrection; she sees as distinct parts of His Body His hands and His head; she sees the Holy Spirit as a Dove; she even sees the three Divine persons, and she declares: "I saw with the eyes of the soul more clearly than I could have seen with the eyes of the body." Mary of the Incarnation spurns such visions purposely to rely only on intellectual interpretations: "Whenever I underwent a kind of vision, this was effaced at once by an abstraction of the spirit entirely detached from the imagination." In her central vision, the transfixion, Teresa sees the Cherub piercing her heart and she feels a pain not only in the soul but in her very body. Mary of the Incarnation's experience of the exchange of her heart with that of Jesus is a dream. She reports thus: "I sensed that my

heart was carried away and enclosed in another heart. I did not
feel any pain."

We remember Teresa's vision of Hell where she is surrounded
by reptiles and stifled by a pestilential stench. Mary believes she
once perceived a great flame coming from an airhole and timidly
adds: "It seemed to me the mouth of Hell." Teresa's participation
in the Trinitarian life is for us an almost shocking visualization:
The Heavenly Father receives the Body of Christ in her soul.
Mary expresses the same experience by saying: "My soul was
blessed with caresses which could never be expressed in human
language." Of course, Teresa, too, would mention sometimes that
what she has to say is ineffable, but only after having tried all
kinds of visualizations and comparisons. She would even criticize
her attempts as inadequate, but she would try hard before giving
up. Mary, as far as visualization is concerned, gives up from the
outset because she insists in her intellectuality that "impressions
without form or figure" cannot be translated into something else.
Teresa's concern is communication, Mary's an adequate precision.

The most difficult problem to be translated into language is for
both mystics the growth in contemplation from which are derived
the seven stages of Teresa and the thirteen stages of Mary. Teresa
simplifies this growth by considering only the passivity, the the-
opathy, the undergoing (*padecer*) of God's activity in the soul;
Mary maintains the always present minimum of activity in the
passive soul and speaks of a *laisser faire*. The soul, as one remembers, before all the powers are unified, is to Teresa a goat attached
to a pole but free to move in a certain space of her pasture, then a
little donkey with closed eyes going round and round to move the
wheel of the well, then a baby instinctively drinking at his
mother's breast, finally a wax on which the Lord puts the seal.
These precious images apparently always cover only one aspect of
the spiritual situation. Mary of the Incarnation stresses in all
stages of passivity the degree of the soul's acquiescence and adherence. She remarks that in each single case of passive prayer she
was aware whether the will or the understanding was first bound.
Her activity, of course, is a supernatural activity. Therefore she is
able to say: "I always have caressed Him up to the end of the
prayer and He, on His part, made me appreciate how much He is
Love." Or she would say: "I followed the operation of Him who
worked in me." Or: "My soul put by a Power into a passive state,

talked to God in great privacy." Or she would say paradoxically:
"Oh, if I had only been able to talk in my amorous activity!" Here,
I would say, the Cartesian mind of Mary throws a more refined
spiritual light on the didactic and entertaining imagery of Santa
Teresa.

Almost all of the occidental mystics speak of the intermittent
contact of the soul with God as of the spiritual Betrothal and of
the more permanent contact as of the spiritual Marriage. Santa
Teresa and Mary of the Incarnation make evident how different
the approach to these concepts and expressions can be.

Santa Teresa uses the term betrothal (*desposorio*) but seems
not to understand the archetypal meaning of the symbol. It is true
that the soul is a bride-to-be, wounded by the love of the Spouse
who comes to give the soul certitude, security and strength, and
leaves her again to cause her nostalgia, desire, despair. But this
nostalgia for the absent Spouse is used by analogy with the bride
of the *Song of Solomon*. Teresa's own interpretation is that the
Lord comes from time to time as a lightning, a thunderclap, a
comet, a fragrance, a shrill whistle, a giant tossing the soul like a
straw, or like a small craft on a high wave, but then again she is
left alone as though hanging or crucified between heaven and
earth. In her plight she does cry out for the permanent possession
of the Spouse; she seeks a liberation from her desire through
death and prays: "Oh poor me, poor little butterfly, fettered with
so many chains that you are not allowed to fly whereto you would
wish. Have mercy, my God." Here are implied two problems: first,
the existential problem to the effect that the nun and virgin Teresa
has small interest in the relationship between spiritual and human
betrothals; second, the stylistic problem that Teresa, as always,
splits up a central image into a number of secondary, more
clarifying images. Here they do not clarify, however, the original
symbol, they make clear only a psychological situation for the
understanding of which the first symbol, that of betrothal, was
introduced on the same level as all the later pedagogical metaphors.

The young widow and mother Mary of the Incarnation, however, understands clearly through life experience the analogy
which escapes Santa Teresa, since Mary knew both earthly and
divine love. She interprets afterwards as a mystic her earthly marriage as "a condition opposed to the Spirit" and as a temporary

"captivity," but she applies all the more surely the whole erotic terminology to her mystical life. Her spiritual betrothal was hallowed by a childhood dream in which Christ gives her a kiss. From this moment on she desires another "holy communication," out of an "amorous gratitude." Christ tells her that He is Love and she responds with a "sigh for her Divine Object." One has to know that the beloved one in the language of the *précieuses* of Mary's century was called "the Object that has wounded me." Mary's sighs do not involve death not because of unbearable suffering but because of the clear desire for the mystical marriage: "Oh, my Love, when will marriage be achieved?" or "Oh my chaste Love, I do not want only a part of you; I want to have you entirely." In the state of betrothal which Mary calls the "sweetness of a saintly familiarity," "the soul," she says as a genuine *précieuse*, "seems to have internal arms which are continually outstretched for the embrace." For, in view of all the graces granted by the "Divine Lover" in this state, the soul declares that she is content but not satisfied, "since the marriage has not been consummated." The bride-to-be recognizes that her great sufferings are just the "preparations for marriage," since to "accommodate the respect, the awe of the bride, to her love, love is able to make room for privacy." It is noteworthy that Mary of the Incarnation develops the betrothal symbol with an unequivocal logic without any metaphorical deviation from the central symbol.

After the treatment of the betrothal, it is not difficult to guess how the two mystics will handle the spiritual marriage. Santa Teresa again breaks away from the symbol. She stresses marriage as the conscious presence of the whole Trinity in the soul, as an enduring possession. Even at times of trial and darkness the soul is sure of God's presence just as one is sure in a dark room that the beloved persons whom one has seen before the shutters were closed are present. Or, she says: The spirit of the soul becomes transformed into and united with God just as the rain does with the fount into which it falls, the river in the estuary with the sea, or two streams of light coming through two windows within the same room. Such is, says Teresa, this "sublime matrimony," "this heavenly union with the uncreated Spirit," a union which she also calls, however, the "brotherhood with this great God." The mystical marriage "where only He and the soul enjoy one another in the greatest silence" is for Teresa the undisturbed peace of the soul as

fitting in with biblical images: The thirsty deer has reached the
source; Noah's dove has returned with the olive branch; and—on
the same level without any qualitative distinction—the Bride of
Solomon's *Song* has received the long desired kiss. Teresa adds
revealingly: "Oh that one might know all the many examples
which Scripture has to make understandable this peace of the
soul!" Our statement at the outset of this book that Teresa's mystical language is erotic although only slightly so will still appear as
an exaggeration if we check on what Mary of the Incarnation has
to say about the mystical marriage in truly erotic language.

Mary announces her spiritual marriage in language entirely
suitable to the subject matter: "This adorable Person (God) took
possession of my soul and embraced her with an unexplainable
love, united her to Him and took her as His spouse." Her transformation into Him is a kind of spiritual procreation due to "penetra-
tions of Him into me and by a wonderful kind of reciprocation of
me to Him so that, lost to myself, I did not see myself anymore,
since I had become a part of Him." She refuses to make this mysterious wedding clearer by comparisons: "Earthly comparisons for
this I simply cannot find"; but she continues instead: "The Divine
Word who takes the place of the Spouse" grants the soul "the
status of a bride. . . . He fills her by the kisses of His Divine
mouth with His Spirit" and enables "the return of the soul's embraces to her beloved Spouse." Knowing exactly what she is saying in plain direct language, Mary of the Incarnation adds this: "It
is the Holy Spirit who makes the soul act that way with the Divine Word. It would be impossible to a limited and restricted
creature to have such a boldness as to deal in this manner with its
God." Mary's is the language of a spiritual directness which leaves
the concept of the mystical marriage in its archetypal environment as a fulfillment of loving and desiring by embracing and
interpenetration, while Santa Teresa with her many metaphorical
reinterpretations of the concept leaves us with an encounter, a
touch, a union with God, even a transformation into God, but at
the expense of the clarity of the central symbol.

A relationship of such spiritual magnitude between Creator and
creature leaves in the soul, of course, a feeling of unworthiness,
humility, shortcoming, and failure on the part of the human
spouse. Santa Teresa tries in vain to find a name for this ontologi-
cally conditioned failure. She enlarges her imperfections into sins

and therefore calls herself constantly a mean, vile, despicable person, a bad creature and miserable thing. She would find an "excuse (*disculpa*), if she had not so much guilt (*culpas*)." She explains that "the sorrow of one's sins grows even as one receives more from our God." Or in a still clearer fashion: "When I see that I receive graces continuously and pay so badly for those which I have received, this is a terrible torment to me." She still remarks: "A soul understands clearly that she does not possess any good thing by herself, and sees herself ashamed before such a great King because she pays so little back to Him for the many things she owes Him."

If one may sometimes think that Teresa's language is emotionally exaggerated, the poised Mary of the Incarnation with her French restraint still outdoes Santa Teresa in this matter. Mary calls herself "the lowest and vilest creature under the sky." She declares she "committed sins enough to deserve the punishment of a million of hells." She calls herself "nothing but dirt" and explains: "If I had acted in accordance with the immense mercies of God, I would have made a quite different progress in sanctity, but my infidelities make me fear for many reasons."

Santa Teresa clarifies the situation by her usual mode of comparison: Apparently clear water in a glass bottle appears full of dust when the rays of the sun fall upon it; some specks of dust in a room suddenly seem cobwebs under the same condition, that is, when the sun shines upon them. But Teresa does not tell us with all her visualization exactly what the guilt of the spouse consists of except that she is not always thinking of the Divine Groom. Again Mary has the decisive word: "Infidelity," and with a self-coined term "incorrespondance." This insight, she says, comes from God Himself as "an inexorable censor"; or in more detail: "The Groom wants impartially to scrutinize the soul in the light of the secret fire of His Divine justice and thus reduces her to the nothingness of an unspeakable humiliation." Teresa knows this reduction to nothingness, too; she has even a name for it, *anonadamiento*, but she lacks the sophistication of her French counterpart to explain it.

If Teresa and Mary are as different from one another as metaphorical exemplification and direct definition are, they yet have much in common within their different approaches: verbal sincerity, convincing clarity, natural simplicity, elegance and facility, freshness and gracefulness, colloquial naturalness with literary shadings whenever necessary. Their methods of presentation ought not to be judged as necessarily superior or inferior. Whenever Teresa tries to use Mary's manner of definition and terminology she disappoints us. Why does she call self-made consolations "sweetnesses" (*ternuritas*) and granted consolations "tastes" (*gustos*)? But if she puts the same problem before her readers as the allegory of the ignorant herdsman who is more impressed by the embroidered garment of the king than by the king himself, her didactic skill is overwhelming. Then she certainly competes successfully with Mary's philosophical but somewhat pale explanation of the same problem: "Bliss is not the sensibility which cries out, but the force and vigor of the spirit which enraptures." Mary may have smiled at Teresa's idea of the presence of God in the seventh apartment of the soul. Teresa would have been baffled at Mary's statement that "that grace of His holy presence comes with a great purity to the understanding and the will in spiritual terms." This rather would have been another occasion for her famous outbursts against philosophical language: "Understanding or thought or imagination: I do not know what that is."

Teresa delights in paradox, pointing out that any formulation of the ineffable has to be a "glorious nonsense" or "celestial madness." Accordingly she says, "All things are nothing," "Life, how can you go on, absent from your life?" "I am dying because I do not die." This is no fare for Mary of the Incarnation. She translates these very paradoxes into the clarity of French Classicism to which she belongs. She speaks to God: "You are pleased by my torment. You can deliver me from it by death. Well, why do You not do it?" Or she stammers: "O my Love, I cannot stand it any longer." Thus paradox and matter-of-factness are another distinguishing feature of the two mystics.

Santa Teresa uses the Spanish language with sovereign liberty for her metaphorical purposes; she makes it her servant. Mary considers herself as the servant of the French language against whose sovereignty she never would try to rebel. This springs from the way in which Teresa and Mary try to interpret biblical passages. For Teresa they are an occasion to give free rein to her imagination and arbitrary associations; for Mary, to undertake a careful checking on parallel passages. We remember Santa Teresa's explanation of the petition: "Give us this day our daily bread." The literal meaning, she thinks, is good enough for the people in the world, but not for Carmelite nuns. They pray for the bread of the doctrine of the gospel, for the bread of virtue, for the sacramental bread of the Eucharist, for any bread that sustains the spiritual life. But the bread of the Eucharist is Christ, who also uses this bread as the good shepherd. The shepherd offers bread to his sheep by whistling for the lost ones, by throwing his staff between the legs of the fleeing ones, by protecting the good sheep against poisonous plants. But being the Bread Himself, He is also a Lamb Himself, a lamb which was roasted on the cross for our food. Actually Teresa takes us into a metaphorical maze of confusing language; she makes the reader dizzy and overwhelms him with this particular kind of "sacred madness."

Mary of the Incarnation has a more objective approach. She unfortunately has not commented on the "Our Father" so that we might have a close antithesis. She interpreted, however, John 15, 16: "I have chosen you . . . that Ye should go and bring forth fruit." Mary ponders on this purpose and sees it realized in the Blessed Virgin. That makes her understand the use of the term "fruit" in the angelic salutation: "Blessed is the fruit of thy womb." She thinks the choice of the word has a bearing on Christ as the eucharistic fruit where He is the wheat. Suddenly also a passage of Zechariah, "The wheat of the chosen," makes sense to her. She thinks of the inseparability of bread and wine in the Eucharist and finds in the same passage from Zechariah that Our Lord is the wine that brings forth virgins. This, Mary concludes, is meant for the religious souls, for the Ursulines whose principle it is to bring forth fruit in Christ.

The difference between the two procedures is clear. Even if there is in both cases a procedure by associations, Teresa's are the associations of words, Mary's the association of facts. Attitudes of language are attitudes of life. Actually in trying to translate the ineffable of the mystical process, we remember that Teresa with her Socratic introspection wants to know *how* these mysterious things happen to her soul. Exactly this introspection is what Mary of the Incarnation does not like: "I have an aversion against it since I fear it is sheer curiosity." Mary, rather, is eager to know *what* occurs to her metaphysically and how it can be put into harmony with theological lore, Scripture and Christian tradition. In this point Teresa is less interested, and she knows how dangerous such statements can be for an unlearned woman surrounded by the watchdogs of the Inquisition. Pressed to make such statements, she would say: "What this actually is, I cannot explain; this is all expounded in mystical theology."

# CHAPTER 11

# Santa Teresa and St. John of the Cross

ALTHOUGH St. John of the Cross will be treated in a volume of his own in Twayne's World Authors Series, it is necessary to deal with him here as a disciple and collaborator of Santa Teresa and to show the likenesses and diversities between him and the Mother of the Carmel. In order not to disparage the greatness of Santa Teresa, this parallel has to take in account the consideration that Teresa is an unlearned, self-made writer, striving for expression, San Juan de la Cruz the Thomistic theologian and scriptual scholar with the great linguistic resources.[1]

As to their mystical writings, it is surprising that both authors do not quote any text but the Scriptures. As far as Patristic literature is concerned, they rely only on St. Augustine and St. Gregory the Great.[2] All critics know that the influence of Santa Teresa on San Juan de la Cruz (1542–1591) was paralleled by the influence of the younger disciple on her, and nothing is more difficult than to pinpoint these mutual spiritual inspirations between the *Santa* and the *Santo* as the Spaniards used to call the two.

But in contradistinction to all other mystics in Spain and abroad, Teresa and John have in common a basically fourfold approach to the mystical development, namely, active recollection, passive recollection, intermittent union and constant union. The subtleties of the subdivisions are less important, however, than the variant accents put on those main divisions in a different way by either of these authors. Teresa speaks, as we have seen earlier, in didactic fashion of the four ways of watering the garden; she writes of the metamorphosis of the caterpillar into a butterfly, or of the apartments of the interior castle. These comparisons occur, however, in quite different works and are not all central symbols. San Juan de la Cruz has grouped his four great works around four central symbols: (1) the difficult ascension of a mountain: *La Subida del Monte Carmelo* (*The Ascent of Mount Carmel*); (2)

the dark night of Faith: *La Noche oscura del alma* (*The Dark Night of the Soul*); (3) the Nuptial Song of the Soul: *El Cántico Espiritual* (*The Spiritual Canticle*), and (4) the living flame of Love: *La Llama de amor viva* (*The Living Flame of Love*). The rest of San Juan's work is less important: *Avisos* (*Advices*), *Consejos* (*Counsels*), *Cautelas* (*Cautions*), *Cartas* (*Letters*), and *Poesías* (*Poems*).

The first two great works, *Subida* and *Noche*, are also conceived as one long night of ascetic purgation and mystical trials. The Saint actually presents two parallel nights, one of meditation and one of contemplation; these he subdivides accordingly into the active purgation of the senses and the active purgation of the spirit; and again, the passive purgation of the senses and the passive purgation of the spirit. Thus what Teresa does in a more general way finds an awesome explication in Juan's four subdivisions. The active purgation of the senses signifies a complete mortification of sensuality, that of the spirit, much more clearly than in Santa Teresa, the gradual reduction of the powers of the soul for supernatural purposes. Whilst Santa Teresa is not so clear about the active or passive participation of the soul in this process which, according to her, leads to the unification of these powers as the *conditio sine qua non* for contemplation, San Juan the theologian with the active purgation of the spirit wants to make the field free for the full operation of the infused virtues of faith, hope, and charity. The indifference to the discursive and critical use of the human understanding makes the soul rely exclusively on an unshakable faith. The maximum elimination of the imagination and its re-evoking of the past creates the best condition for the invasion of Hope, thus replacing the interest in the past by an interest in the future, i.e. in the beyond. With the complete elimination of all desires of the will for earthly bonds of love, all barriers against the infusion of Charity are removed. This is for St. John of the Cross the difficult ascent of Mount Carmel or the active Night of the Soul. Santa Teresa would not tell her doves and butterflies, as she calls her nuns, that their active effort has to be of such a crucial kind.

The *passive* dark night of the senses and the spirit is for San Juan the exposure of the actively purified soul to the direct and very necessary illumination by God. Teresa here would first stress the joy of having at least some bliss from the presence of God. San

Juan, however, would maintain that the senses and the spirit are not purified enough as yet to feel this presence. The reason is that this presence is a light which cannot pierce as yet the still prevailing darkness, and a warming fire which still burns and hurts the soul not ready for it. The light at this stage consequently means a painful communication of wisdom and insight with divine mysteries, the fire an unquenchable thirst of love for a more palpable presence of God. At this point of the mystical development, Teresa, without entering into San Juan's details, would declare that she is dying from not dying. The mystical betrothal of Santa Teresa is for San Juan the morning dawn after the passive Dark Night of the Soul.

While, however, as we have seen in Chapter 10, Santa Teresa pays a kind of lip service to the spiritual betrothal and the marriage concepts, San Juan starts his third work, *The Spiritual Canticle*, with a most literal, profound, and beautiful interpretation of these two mystical phenomena. In his presentation he follows Solomon's *Song* rather closely but, in retrospect, keeps also in contact with his preceding works, and so he says in strophe 15: "My Beloved is a night full of rest towards the rise of dawn." The bride was looking for the groom in woods, meadows, and pastures and finally has found Him for an inseparable union of mystical conjugal bliss. This involves a poetic elaboration in forty strophes with long commentaries of what Teresa tells us in the sixth and seventh mansions of her *Interior Castle*. San Juan presents us in his *Living Flame of Love* with a still higher type of transforming union which, as an experienced phenomenon remained unknown to Santa Teresa.

Thus San Juan de la Cruz not only supplements but transcends the mystical writings of Santa Teresa. His empirical mysticism has the advantage of being supported by speculations which would have been impossible for Santa Teresa's greater simplicity. Nor would she have wanted them. San Juan makes clear that only a thin veil separates him from the direct vision of the Lord and that Death will take away this veil. Santa Teresa never made a similar statement.

The way of Santa Teresa leads through many ecstasies, visions, and exemplifying images; San Juan's way is based on one great symbol, but his experiences are imageless. We said in our last chapter that Santa Teresa never asks what actually happens, only how something unknown happens to her. San Juan has solved the theological question of what happened to the mystic: Faith in its essence becomes transparent and a certitude through love. Teresa might have felt that, but only her pupil was capable of formulating it.

As different as the systems of the two Saints are, their ideas, with certain differences of nuance, are very similar. Both authors praise adversities and hardships as wholesome and necessary. "I do not believe it to be an evil that God sends an adversity, since in this way He has elevated all His chosen ones"; (Teresa: *Letters*, 615) and "In all instances, no matter how hurtful they may be, we have to be joyful rather than depressed." (Juan: *Ascent*, III, 4) Both Saints see in the slightest affection for the world the greatest danger for their spirituality. Teresa says: "When I wanted to stay with God, my affection for the world made me restless"; (*Life*, 8) and San Juan: "The light of Divine union cannot take hold of a soul, if not all her affections are first driven out." (*Ascent*, I, 4) Pleasure in things earthly develops greed for them, and this is a spiritual impediment since greed is unquenchable. Says St. John of the Cross: "From the enjoyment of visible things can come immediately inordinate greed." (*Ascent*, III, 25) Teresa exclaims: "How can anybody not have a great thirst, if he is burning in the living flame of the greed for the miserable things of the earth." (*Exclamations*, 9)

Any kind of suffering has to be a subject of joy. Teresa states: "Blessed are those who in the fearful moment of death are joyful." (*Exclamations*, III, 2) San Juan affirms: "The Bride who in this life is cleansed from all imperfections feels like enjoying a new spring in liberty and restraint and joyfulness of spirit." (*Canticle*, XXXIX, 8) This divine joy can never come from human comfort; this has to be avoided: "It would be vulgar to look for comfort in pains which Our Lord has granted" (Teresa: *Foundations*, 12) and, "Besides the Beloved the soul does not receive comfort from anyone." (*Canticle*, I, 14) Therefore friends and relatives have to be excluded and God has to be considered the only friend: "The true friend to whom we have to be responsible is God," (Teresa: *Letters*, 179) or, "Take only God for Spouse and friend." (Juan: *Advices*, I, 65) Friendship with God is the essence of any mystical relationship before and after mystical experiences. Teresa emphasizes: "Mental prayer is nothing else but dealing with God in friendship" (*Life*, 8) and San Juan says that the soul after the dark night "feels and enjoys a great sweetness of peace and amorous friendship with God." (*Night*, II, 7)

Discussing endlessly the love of God, both mystics stress its unselfishness as the motivation for all acts: "Those who really love God love everything good, do not love anything but truth." (Teresa: *Way*, 49) Perhaps we do not know what "to love" does mean. "It does not consist of the greatest satisfaction for us but of the greatest determination to want to satisfy God in everything." (*Castle*, IV, 1) San Juan would say on his part: "A Christian has to ask, not whether he is performing good acts but whether he is performing them only out of the love of God. . . . He has to take care that the value of his good works may not so much be based on quantity as on the love of God, and that they will be worthy in the degree in which they are done with pure and complete love of God." (*Ascent*, III, 27) The love of one's neighbor is, of course, included in the love of God, and this to such a degree that Teresa insists that "what matters in order to reach union with God is the love of one's neighbor"; (*Castle*, V, 3) and St. John of the Cross: "The more the love of God increases the more also the love of one's neighbor." (*Ascent*, III, 23) Neighborly love is in these Saints a natural attitude. Santa Teresa states: "When we see a person in trouble it is our very nature which invites us to compassion." (*Life*, 32) San Juan remarks of a person beset by the trials of the dark night: "We must have great compassion for a soul that God puts into such a stormy and horrendous night." (*Night*, II, 7) On the other hand a conscious love of self is an impediment to the love of God. It is difficult but completely necessary to exterminate it. Says Santa Teresa: "This separation from ourselves and being against ourselves is a difficult affair because we love ourselves very much." (*Way*, 10) Stronger still San Juan: "The love of self is what in the most subtle way is wont to deceive and obstruct the conduct of spiritual people." (*Ascent*, II, 6)

Divine love as anxiety for the absent Spouse is so strong in both mystics that it seems hurtful to their bodily health. Santa Teresa's desire for God coincides therefore with the death wish: "The soul is left with a very great anxiety to die." (*Castle*, VI, 6) San Juan with a clinical precision remarks: "The anxieties for God are so strong in the soul that it seems as though from this thirst the bones are drying out." (*Night*, I, 11) Visions as a response from God to

this anxiety seem to Teresa normal, while Juan rejects the idea
and the visions themselves with it. He only accepts the biblical
theophanies. It follows that Teresa believes that her visions have
contributed to her spiritual progress, (*Report*, 1) while this progress for San Juan comes only from the greatest patience in suffering and in the renunciation of consolations. (*Advices*, I, 75) Both
Saints insist on the only weapon against the world, the flesh, and
the Devil: The cross of Christ. (Teresa: *Castle*, II, 1) (Juan:
*Canticle*, XIII, 9)

The world means shackles for a soul that strives to be free for
God; the world is the soul's prison, her indulging in things earthly
a captivity. Therefore Teresa exclaims: "O great liberty to consider the obligation to love and not to act according to the laws of
the world, a sort of captivity." (*Life*, 16) San Juan turns the formula around without changing the meaning: "If the soul is pas-
sionately affected with anything, the will is imprisoned and freedom is lost." (*Night*, II, 13) This captivity is also a blindness
caused according to Teresa by the Devil, according to St. John by
an inordinate appetite: "In many things the Devil has put blindness"; (*Foundations*, 29) and "An inordinate appetite causes
blindness." (*Ascent*, I, 12) Too great a zeal for perfection at the
expense of others is, however, also blindness and seems to both of
the saints the work of the devil: "The Devil infiltrates into a soul
a very great zeal for perfection so that the slightest failing of the
sisters appears to her a great imperfection—and sometimes it may
occur that she does not see her own faults because of her supposed
great zeal for religion"; (*Castle*, I, 11) and, "If you wish to find
fault with something, even though you live among angels, many
things will not appear good to you, and if you don't take care,
whatever good purpose and zeal you have, the Devil will catch
you up in one way or another." (*Cautions*)

It is a good thing to be weary of the world. Santa Teresa cannot
understand why anybody should love this life on earth: "We see
how weary Jesus was of this life and yet today those who have
lived a hundred years do not get tired of it." (*Way*, 42) San Juan
agrees: "All the wealth of the world must be taken as filth and
vanity and weariness." (*Letter*, 10) The virtue which delivers one
from the love of the world is charity. Says Santa Teresa: "The
King established in me His charity in such a way that the love I
had for the world was destroyed." (*Concepts*, 6) San Juan formu-

lates: "Charity voids and annihilates the affections and appetites for anything that is not God." (*Night,* II, 21)

The world, of course, is mainly the flesh. The formulations concerning the power of the flesh do not avoid exaggeration. Teresa affirms: "The good Jesus says in His prayer of the garden: The flesh is weak. . . . Well, if this divine flesh is weak, how can we expect ours to be so strong?" (*Concepts,* 3) San Juan says: "Since the flesh keeps the spirit bridled, it is the flesh that holds the reins and curbs the mouth of that swift horse called the spirit." (*Flame,* II, 13) A symbol of being interested in one's flesh is eating meat. Both Saints are averse to it. Teresa has the principle: "One never should eat meat without necessity." (*Life,* 36) St. John explains: "Only because the sons of Israel kept an affection for and memory of the meat and meals of Egypt, they were not allowed to taste of the delicate bread of the angels in the desert." (*Night,* II, 9) Not daring to follow the difficult road is for both authors cowardice. Says Santa Teresa: "It means making the soul a coward if one thinks it is not capable of doing great good." (*Life,* 10) St. John puts it even more positively: "The soul loves God indeed if no obstacle makes her cowardly to the end that she may do and suffer whatsoever is necessary in His service." (*Canticle,* II, 5) From avoiding meat both Saints go on to the advice to eat as little as possible and to abstain from the enjoyment of food. Santa Teresa, who admired the Franciscan friar San Pedro de Alcántara for eating only once a week, exclaims: "O what a poor soul it is that wastes the time only in sleeping and eating." (*Life,* 21) San Juan de la Cruz gives reasons for abstinence: "From the pleasure of the taste of choice morsels of food springs directly gluttony, intoxication, lack of charity for one's neighbors and for the poor." (*Ascent,* III, 25) What is true in the case of food pertains also to any kind of bodily comfort; it was the rejection of this that was the very *raison d'être* for the reform of the Carmelite Order. Santa Teresa has experienced that "There is more spiritual and internal joy if the body does not have its comfort." (*Foundations,* 14) San Juan declares: "The true spiritual man never cares whether his place for prayer has any kind of comfort." (*Ascent,* III, 39) •

Solitude with God does not admit of any human companionship. On this point both reformers are adamant. Teresa thinks that "Desert and solitude are better than any company in the world," (*Life,* 20) San Juan that the soul "has to be a friend of solitude and silence so that she may not tolerate the company of another creature." (*Advices*, II, 42) Teresa hears Christ's voice telling her: "From now on I want you to have no conversation with men, but only with angels." (*Life*, 24) San Juan warns: "For those who enter into only the smallest bit of conversation and friendship the spirit will be lost at once." (*Ascent*, I, 11) Hence Santa Teresa prays: "God deliver us from the need of earthly creatures," (*Letters*, 133) and San Juan insists: "Affection for God and affection for human creatures are contradictory." (*Ascent*, I, 6)

A small imperfection or bad habit may eventually ruin the soul, or at least make her incapable of union with God. "If we were aware what great damage might result from starting a bad habit we should prefer to die," (Teresa: *Way*, 13) and "The habit of voluntary imperfections hinders the divine union, e.g., the habit of much talking." (Juan: *Advices*, II, 43) One of the greatest attractions of world and the flesh is money. "With how much charity would one treat another, if the interest in money were lacking," (Teresa: *Life*, 20) and "The soul that has made money her god has consciously put her heart, which she ought to place in God, on money." (Juan: *Ascent*, III, 19) Another great trap, according to both Saints, is the craving for worldly honors.

Fighting temptations in the cloister is traditionally done by the whip called "discipline," i.e. scourging oneself. On this point Teresa is less "progressive" than San Juan. She prescribes the whip for Lent and Advent every weekday, for the rest of the year on Monday, Wednesday and Friday. (*Constitutions*, 58) San Juan forbids the three-day scourging. (*Letters*, 5) Conversely, as to the problem of absentmindedness in prayer, Teresa is lenient and ascribes it to the weakness of the head. (*Ibid.*, 381) San Juan is severe and ascribes it to "the enjoyment of things visible which lead right away to vanity of the spirit and distraction of the mind." (*Ascent*, III, 25) The two Saints differ also as to the temptation of doubt in religious matters. Teresa declares disarmingly: "The demon had never the strength to tempt me so far as to make me have doubts in any matter of faith," (*Life*, 19) while St. John admits: "The doubts and suspicions which beset the soul never subside." (*Night*, II, 9)

As a result our Saints see the relationship between faith and miracle in a different way. Santa Teresa asks: "How can one doubt that Jesus, so deeply within our innermost being, will work miracles, if we have faith?" (*Way*, 34) while San Juan thinks, "The more God is believed and served without signs and miracles, the more He is exalted by the soul." (*Ascent*, II, 32)

As long as the soul remains in the body she is exposed to the attacks of the demons. Teresa wonders that "The Devil seems to have in each apartment of the soul many legions of demons to fight her" (*Castle*, I, 2) and San Juan gets excited over the fact that "The malicious demons attack the soul with fears and spiritual horrors which sometimes mean a terrible torture." (*Canticle*, XVI, 6) Therefore the battle against "the dragon" has to be fierce and relentless. Teresa considers this the situation of all the saints: "The great saints who lived in the desert fought big battles against the demon and against themselves"; (*Report*, 36) and San Juan warns his disciples: "It is a great pity that many who enter the spiritual battle against the (many-headed) beast may not even be capable of cutting off its first head." (*Ascent*, II, 11) "But love and fear of God are the two strongholds for the war against world and demons." (Teresa: *Way*, 40) "The demons get strength from the other foes, the world, and the flesh, to wage war against the soul." (*Canticle*, III, 9) Epitomizing, the two Saints warn: "The demons go about playing ball with the soul," (Teresa: *Life*, 30) and "Never are demons lacking for trying to overthrow the saints." (Juan: *Cautions*, 9) The only effective weapon against them is an ironclad will, an unbreakable determination. "The demon," says Teresa, "has a great fear of determined souls." But if he sees that they do not have a strong resolution to persevere he will not leave them alone by day or by night. (*Way*, 23) San Juan stresses likewise the importance of a strong determination. "The soul has to go on breaking all difficulties and overcoming with the strength and determination of the spirit all sensuous appetites and natural affections." (*Canticle*, III, 10)

Heroic suffering is the only way to escape the almost inevitable purgatory. Says Santa Teresa: "I understand that of all the souls I have envisioned none was spared Purgatory with the exception of . . . the holy Father Pedro de Alcántara," (*Life*, 38) and San Juan: "Those who because of the need of great purification do not enter Purgatory, are few." (*Night*, II, 20) Hell is as vivid a reality for both Saints as is the Devil. Santa Teresa exclaims: "What will a soul feel immediately after dying when she sees herself surrounded by that monstrous company, put into that fetid lake full

of serpents, in that miserable darkness where there will be seen
only things that provide torture and pain?" (*Exclamations,* 11)
San Juan says less picturesquely but no less seriously: "Sometimes
the soul seems to see Hell open so vividly and sense her own per-
dition that she descends literally to Hell alive." (*Night,* II, 6)

The explanation of the Christian pessimism of both Saints is
their absolute theocentricism in the sense that everything short of
the union with God appears as a mockery (*burla*). Teresa declares: "Whatever I see with the eyes of the body seems to me a
dream and a mockery." (*Life,* 38) St. John goes even further and
includes here everything that is not direct contact with God. He
addresses the Lord, saying "What you communicate by indirect
means is like a communication by mockery." (*Canticle,* VI, 6) In
view of so lofty a goal the soul has to watch out carefully by way
of asceticism not to be tempted into imperfections. Says Teresa:
"The true way not to fall is to have a grip on the cross." (*Report,*
3) More radically still, San Juan remarks: "The affections and appetites of the soul, if they are not mortified, make her fall every
day." (*Ascent,* I, 9) Both Saints refer to the fact that the friends
of Christ must be able to drink the bitter cup with Him: "The
Lord wishes to test his lovers to know whether they will be able to
drink from His cup." (Teresa: *Life,* 11) "The two disciples who
asked Him for a place at His right and His left were offered the
cup He would have to drink." (*Ascent,* II, 7)

Everything, however, is possible with the help of the warmth of
the divine love. Says Teresa: "The Divine Sun gives warmth to
our works," (*Castle,* I, 2) and San Juan: "The third step of the
ladder of love energizes the soul and gives her strength not to
fail." (*Night,* II, 19) Both Saints use still another drink-metaphor
of their own: What the soul needs as a refreshing drink is the
Word of God and Prayer. Teresa says: "Praised be He who invites
us to come to drink from His gospel," (*Way,* 31) and St. John: "In
setting herself to prayer the soul will drink wisdom and love."
(*Ascent,* II, 14) Both authors emphasize their gratitude to God,
first for their being and sustenance and then for all spiritual benefits: "Let us never forget that we have received from God our
being, our sustenance and all the other benefits," (*Life,* 10) and,
"Realizing the great debt to God for having created her, and for
thousands of other benefits, the soul feels obligated to God."
(*Canticle,* I, 1)

As regards humility, both authors recommend suffering every-thing and keeping silence. "It is a sign of great humility," says Teresa, "to see oneself condemned without any guilt and to keep silence," (*Way*, 15) and San Juan formulates: "It is a sign of great wisdom to know how to keep silence and not to judge the re-marks, deeds, and lives of others." (*Advices*, 2) In a somewhat different way the two Saints comment on the biblical narrow gate and the straight path that leads to Heaven. Teresa is aware of following the straight path herself, but being humble and wishing to encourage others, she pretends it is a rather wide street: "I cannot see, my Lord, and do not understand why the way leading to You, should be narrow; I rather see that it is a royal highway and not a path, and that whoever puts his foot on it determinedly will walk with a greater security." (*Life*, 35) San Juan, on the contrary, stresses the dreadful narrowness of the path and ex-plains that "There are very few who are able to enter it and to persevere in the straight way which leads to life eternal. . . . This narrow way is the night of the spirit, a way so straight, dark, and terrible that very, very few are those who walk in it." (*Night*, I, 11)

Given their fundamental tendency to look into the interior of things, Teresa and John are equally cool towards stress on ecclesi-astical ceremonies. Santa Teresa decrees: "It is only a slight fault if a sister undervalues or fails strictly to observe genuflexions, bowings of the head, or other ceremonies." (*Constitutions*, 49) San Juan warns: "The great reliance which some persons have on many kinds of ceremonies introduced by unlearned people lack-ing in the simplicity of faith is unbearable." (*Ascent*, III, 43) As to the "interiority," however, the two saints differ somewhat. What Teresa feels as a contact with God is for her an unshakable certainty: "How is it possible that what we do not see, remains in us with such a certainty? If anyone were not left with His cer-tainty, I would say that there was no union." (*Castle*, V, 1) San Juan is more circumspect and cautious: "Words and visions of God can be true and certain, but we may deceive ourselves with them nevertheless." (*Ascent*, II, 19) Heaven or the beatific vision is graded according to the spiritual level reached on earth by which all degrees of mysticism have their merits. Thus Santa Te-resa states: "I would be satisfied to be in Heaven although it be in the lowest place." (*Life*, 37) St. John of the Cross makes the general statement: "In Heaven some see more, others less; however all see God and all are satisfied." (*Ascent*, II, 5)

Purity of conscience is the most important thing, praised by the two authors above everything else: "Who serves the Lord with the greatest purity of conscience will also be the holiest," (Teresa: *Castle*, VI, 8) and "God prefers from you rather the lowest degree of purity of conscience than whatever good work you may perform." (Juan: *Advices*, I, 12) This purity of conscience comes basically from frequent and sincere confessions in which it is necessary that the confessor of advanced souls be learned (*letrado*), as Teresa puts it, (*Foundations*, 19) or mature (*maduro*), as St. John has it. (*Ascent*, II, 30)

The two Saints know very well that the proof of a pure conscience is conformity with the will of God. Teresa says: "The aim of whoever starts a life of prayer is to conform his will to the will of God." (*Castle*, II, 1) And San Juan: "One has to try always to take trials and temptations with patience and in conformity with the will of God." (*Counsel*, 4) The struggle for this conformity is helped by the knowledge of self which reveals one's own sinful insufficiency. This is Teresa's famous Christian Socratism, as professor Ricard calls it. Teresa actually says: "It is well understood that God gives us the insight to know that we all by ourselves do not possess anything that is good." (*Life*, 15) San Juan makes it still stronger: "The soul sees more clearly than daylight that she is full of evil and sin, because God gives her this light of knowledge." (*Ascent*, Prologue) Conformity for our two mystics is most of all confidence in God's guidance toward passive contemplation and in using or not using active meditation at the appropriate time. In this sense Teresa consoles her sisters: "I know," she says, "that many persons using vocal prayer are raised by God to sublime contemplation." (*Way*, 30) Conversely, San Juan warns: "The progressing worshipper who starts entering the state of contemplation must time and again help himself with natural discourse and the work of the natural powers." (*Ascent*, II, 15) The central idea is to please only God in everything. Teresa insists: "What do I care for kings and lords and to please them, if I were to have in the slightest to displease God for them?" (*Way*, 2) And St. John: "One has to preserve the spirit of poverty and contempt of everything if one wishes to please God alone." (*Letter*, 15) At the same time one has to be generous. Teresa thinks that one has

to be eager to give much more than one receives. (*Way*, 6) San
Juan believes that "losing oneself to the advantages of all others is
a sign of valiant souls and generous hearts." (*Advices*, II, 50)

As we have seen above, it is the mystical union that causes in
both Saints a radical depreciation of the body. In view of her
ecstasies, Santa Teresa complains: "Oh what a soul it is that sees
herself compelled to return to waste her time with the body! At
this point she feels in truth the captivity we have in our bodies."
(*Life*, 21) San Juan comments: "As long as the soul is within the
body, she is, as it were, in a dark dungeon." (*Ascent*, I, 3)

What we may call infused prayer is, in good mystical tradition,
compared by either Saint to a spark which develops into the flame
of divine love: "This type of prayer is a small spark kindled by the
Lord in the soul with His true love. This spark kindled by God,
small as it may be, makes great noise"; (*Life*, 15) and, "This divine little spark leaves the soul burning and consuming herself in
love." (*Canticle*, XXV, 8) Both Saints share also the image of the
soul as wax receiving the seal of the divine impression. (*Castle*, V,
2 and *Canticle*, XII, 1) Infused wisdom makes human science appear ridiculous. Says Santa Teresa: "The Lord makes perhaps a
poor old woman much wiser in spiritual wisdom than the great
scholars." (*Life*, 34) San Juan specifies: "The highest science consists in a most excellent perception of the divine Essence."
(*Poems*, 4)

How do the two mystics explain their *raptures?* For Teresa it is
as though the soul would leave the body temporarily. (*Life*, 38
and *Castle*, V, 7) For San Juan it is a visit of the Holy Spirit who
communicates with the spirit of the soul. (*Canticle*, XIII, 6) Both
Saints have experienced raptures; both resent their occurrence in
public. The public would understand them as little as the daring
language of familiarity and intimacy of the advanced souls with
God. (Teresa: *Concepts*, I, 11 and San Juan: *Night*, II, 20) Teresa and Juan are well aware—and that is one of the reasons for
their writings—that in such delicate matters the advice of experience is absolutely necessary. Therefore both insist, as already
mentioned, on learned and circumspect confessors and directors
of souls: "It is very important to look always for advice," says
Santa Teresa. (*Way*, 38) San Juan de la Cruz finds it fitting "to
advise the souls that, when God comes to them with His delicate
unctions, they should take care what they will do and in whose

hands they put themselves in order not to go backwards." (*Flame*, III, 27) Planning the ascetico-mystical life with the best counselling is nevertheless the minor part in the process; God alone takes care of the decisive development. The formulas of the two Saints in this respect are revealing. Santa Teresa thinks: "The Lord helps so much on His part that for the same reason as we sacrifice our will and our reason to Him, He makes us rulers of these." (*Foundations*, V, 12) San Juan echoes: "It is God who has to put the soul into the supernatural state but the soul has to dispose herself for it with the help that God gives her." (*Ascent*, III, 2)

Both mystical souls desire and receive God's highest response of love in the spiritual "kisses of His mouth"; (*Song of Solomon*, I, 2) Teresa's soul craves for the kiss of the Lord: "Lord, I do not beg Thee anything else in this life but that you kiss me with the kiss of Thy mouth." (*Concepts*, 3) St. John's soul even craves for the grace to be able to respond to the Lord's spiritual embrace: "I alone would embrace Thee alone, and this is only possible in the spiritual marriage which is the soul's kissing of God." (*Canticle*, XXII, 7) For this bliss, comparable only to the final heavenly reward, the contempt and renunciation of all earthly good seems a small sacrifice to both Saints.

The ascetical detachment from visible things does not curtail the faculty of their observation, evocation and description. Actually, Santa Teresa and St. John of the Cross are excellent observers. Their allusions to Nature are remarkable. Santa Teresa is an enthusiast of water: "Water," she says, "has three qualities: It refreshes, cleanses and quenches the thirst," (*Way*, 19) or "I am such a friend of this element that I always looked at it with more attention than at other things." (*Castle*, IV, 2) "If there were no water with which to cleanse, what would become of the world?" (*Way*, 19) Hedgehog and turtle serve her to explain the retreating into ourselves. (*Castle*, IV, 3) Teresa loves fields and gardens, wheat and flowers, plants, trees and fruits, carnations, roses, cornflowers, plums, nuts, oranges, quinces, mellons. She observes oxen, doves, peacocks, butterflies, bees, flies, worms, ants, newts, fish, caterpillars, toads, serpents, vipers, lizards, beetles, cats, rats, and shrewmice. She speaks of products like potatoes and bread, butter, honey, marmalade, sugar, lozenges; silver and gold, feathers, linen, wool, silk, serge, bedsheets and blankets, cushions and tunics, veils and coifs. San Juan de la Cruz can not observe nature enough as is seen in his *Spiritual Canticle,* and especially water, air, deer, foxes, wolves, sheep, birds, doves, nightingales, mountains, valleys, caverns, rocks, groves, hills, sheepcotes, woods, rivers, wine, pomegranates, flowers like roses and lilies.

Both Saints seem to look at nature with the same eyes. They are struck by the industrious bee. Teresa says: Whatever the hardworking bee eats is converted to honey, (*Foundations,* VIII, 3) and Juan: "The bee sucks the pollen from the flowers she finds." (*Canticle,* XXVII, 8) The spider is for Santa Teresa something ugly and poisonous, (*Foundations,* VIII, 3) for St. John something beautiful because of her delicate web. (*Flame,* I, 32) Thus the reaction to the same objects may be quite different, too, in both authors. To earthly beauty Teresa seems instinctively more open than San Juan de la Cruz despite his symbolic poetry of nature. Due to her visions, Teresa imagines the souls in Heaven, like Dante, as glorified beautiful bodies: "If there were nothing else in Heaven for the delight of the eye but the great beauty of the glorified bodies, that is already a very great glory." (*Life,* 28) San Juan, despite his preserving the beauty of the bride of the *Song of Solomon,* for symbolical reasons does not trust natural beauty at all and insists "for all beauty I shall not get lost." (*Divine Gloss*).

Metaphors and comparisons based on nature seem to both authors absolutely necessary for their purpose. Says Santa Teresa: "The comparisons do not concern what happens, but out of them come many other things." (*Castle,* III, 2) San Juan remarks: "It is with figures, comparisons, and similitudes that the souls overflow from what they are feeling." (*Canticle,* Prologue)

Our comparison of Santa Teresa and San Juan de la Cruz ought to consider also the two mystics as poets. But since San Juan is considered one of the greatest, if not *the* greatest poet of Spain, the comparison would turn out detrimental to the poetic limitations of Santa Teresa which we know from Chapter 6. Since also the choice of poems of Teresa would be very difficult, we renounce this doubtful enterprise, remaining, however, with the impression that the unlearned mystic Santa Teresa can well cope with her most learned pupil in the "science transcending all sciences."

# CHAPTER 12

# *Summation*

SANTA Teresa was born during the short-lived Spanish Humanism and wrote under the pressures of the evolving Counter-Reformation. But despite her difficulties with confessors and inquisitors, she shared the ideals of those who created difficulties for her: the desire to destroy Renaissance paganism, undo the Protestant Reformation, re-catholicize the world and strengthen the missionary conquest of the New World. As a precondition of such a task she was convinced of the need of reforming the individual as well as the religious Orders. Within this framework she became the great mystic as well as the reformer of the Carmel.

This nun with clear ideas and a will of steel was very gifted as a writer. In a conversational tone with hundreds of digressions she often says more about mysticism than the treatises of the theologians with all their scholastic terminology. The reason is that she handles with equal mastery the analysis of psychological experiences and their expression through an adequate language, using the most astonishingly original and fitting comparisons and metaphors.

Her *Life,* by the analysis of which this book began, combines the external and internal events of her life in an unusual blend, and offers a serious biography as well as a hagiographical novel without, however, the slightest purpose on the part of the author to do more than give her confessor an insight into her soul and its spiritual development. The insertion of the great allegory of the watering of the garden qualifies Santa Teresa as a spiritual educator with a rare pedagogical skill to teach the difficulties, the relapses, progress, and glory of prayer from the stage of oral stammering to the raptures of love. After this more personal book of her life, Santa Teresa, pouring out in a new grandiose imagery her fundamental concept of the progress in the spiritual life, dared to formulate a systematic presentation of the mystical stages in the manner of the theologians. She did it in her classical work, *The Interior Castle* or *The Mansions*, where the Soul is presented as a global diamond-fortress in whose center is the dwelling place of the Lord Himself, the Lord who attracts more and more the spiritually progressing spouse-to-be in order finally to unite Himself most intimately with her.

Desiring for her Carmelite nuns their capacity to follow this way of perfection as far as they could achieve it, she writes her stylistically most moderate book as a matter-of-fact guide for them, *The Way of Perfection*. The psychologist, the pedagogue and mystagogue in her is equalled by Teresa the visionary. Compared to other visionaries in the history of piety, she appears moderate despite her eidetic propensities to which we owe also her rich imagery elsewhere. Teresa's attempt to translate her visions into a language which should make them appear as non-earthly is unique, and seems to have influenced even certain paintings of El Greco. Teresa was not a born poet. But her love of the language occasionally made her also try some poems which have the character of improvised productions; they refer mostly to her internal life, but often also to external events. In the latter case they are even pleasant and humorous. Humor and many other human qualities show up in all of her works, but most of all in her extensive correspondence (*Letters*) with her family, with dignitaries of Church and State, members of her Order and plain people. In all the letters she shows herself the resourceful, competent, loving but determined woman that she was. Her place in the history of piety and in the history of Spanish letters is equally important. In her comparison with great mystic writers like the French Ursuline Mary of the Incarnation, who is more precise in terminology but pale as to picturesqueness, or with San Juan de la Cruz, who also is superior to her in theological exactness and in poetical beauty but lacks her humor and humanity, Teresa will always show herself a worthy competitor.

# Notes and References

## Preface

1. See Denis de Rougemont, "Courtly Rhetoric in Spanish Mysticism," in *Love in the Western World* (New York: Pantheon, 1956), pp. 159–66.

2. Louis Bertrand, *Sainte Thérèse* (Paris: Fayard, 1927).

3. Henri Delacroix, "Sainte Thérèse," in *Les Grand Mystiques Chrétiens*. Nouvelle Edition (Paris: Alcan, 1938, pp. 1–117).

4. René Fülöp-Miller, *The Saints that Moved the World* (New York: Crowell, 1945), p. 417.

## Chapter Two

1. Luis A. Moscoso Vegas, "Aportaciones para un estudio español en Santa Teresa de Avila," in *Casa de Cultura Ecuatoriana. Homenaje Cuadricentenario* (Cuenca, 1962), pp. 173–96.

2. Guido Mancini Giancarlo, *Expressioni letterarie dell' Insegnamento di Santa Teresa de Avila* (Modena: ETM, 1955), pp. 117–29.

3. Helmut Hatzfeld, *Estudios literarios sobre mística española* (Madrid: Gredos, 1955, 1968).

4. A synthesis without a literary stress on the imagery, in Sebastian V. Ramage, OCD, *An Introduction to the Writings of Saint Teresa* (Chicago: Regnery, 1963), pp. 54–70.

5. This interpretation is Leo Spitzer's in his article "No me mueve, mi Dios," *Nueva Revista de Filología Hispánica*, 7 (1946), 608–17.

6. Henri Delacroix, *Les Grands Mystiques Chrétiens*. Nouvelle Edition (Paris: Alcan, 1938), XVI.

7. Marcel Lépée, *Sainte Thérèse mystique* (Paris: Desclée de Brouwer, 1951), p. 284.

## Chapter Three

1. The high rank of this work among the many Spanish mystical treatises of the sixteenth century becomes evident from *Corrientes Espirituales en la España del Siglo XVI. Trabajos del II Congreso de Espiritualidad* (Barcelona: Flors, 1963).

2. P. Quercy, *L'Hallucination* (Paris, 1930).

3. Josefina Alvárez de Cánovas, *Psicopedagogía de Santa Teresa* (Madrid: Studium, 1961), pp. 103–9.

4. E. Allison Peers, *Mother of Carmel* (New York: Morehouse, 1946), p. 158.

5. Eduardo Juliá Martínez, *La Cultura de Santa Teresa y su obra literaria* (Castellón: Armengot, 1922), p. 18.

6. Father Thomas, ODC, and Father Gabriel, ODC, *St. Teresa of Avila* (Westminster, Maryland: The Newman Press, 1963).

7. See Bernardino de Pantorba, *Santa Teresa de Jesús* (Madrid: Compañía bibliográfica, 1962), p. 121.

8. Gaston Etchegoyen, *L'Amour divin* (Paris: Boccard, 1923), pp. 333–36.

9. Images and doctrine become complicated here. See P. Alejandro de San Juan de la Cruz, "Un comento al 'Castello Interiore,'" *Vita Carmelitana* (1941), pp. 13–51.

10. Fray Luis de San José, ODC, *Concordancias de las obras y escritos de Santa Teresa de Jesús* (Burgos, Monte Carmelo, 1945), p. 1.

11. P. Crisógono de Jesús, *Doctrina de Santa Teresa* (Avila: Imprenta Católica, 1940), pp. 55–57.

12. P. Martín de Jesús María, "El concepto del alma humana en las *Moradas* de Santa Teresa," *Espiritualidad:* 1 (1941–1942), 203–14.

13. P. Marcelo del Niño Jesús, "Paralelismo entre las *Moradas* Teresianas y las *Noches* Sanjuanistas," *El Monte Carmelo:* 43 (1942), 289 ff.

14. Fidèle de Ros, "La 'Palomica' des *Moradas*. Papillon ou colombe?" in his book *Un Inspirateur de Sainte Thérèse. Le frère Bernardin de Laredo* (Paris, 1948).

15. Irene Behn, *Spanische Mystik* (Düsseldorf: Patmos, 1957), p. 760.

16. Also St. Bernard, instructing his monks, cautions them against erotic interpretations: "Take heed that you bring chaste ears to this discourse of love; and when you think of these two lovers, remember always that not a man and a woman are to be thought of, but the Word of God and a soul." Quoted in Dom Cuthbert Butler, *Western Mysticism. The Teaching of SS. Augustine, Gregory and Bernard on Contemplation and the Contemplative Life* (London: Constable, 2: 1951), p. 97.

17. Teresa wants to explain that the soul has no clearer consciousness of the union with the Lord which was granted to her, but that she does not have the unshakable conviction that such a union took place; and she now is longing for a continuous union. See Emmanuel Aegerter, *Le Mysticisme* (Paris: Flammarion, 1952), p. 91.

18. Arturo Serrano Plaja, *Los místicos* (Buenos Aires: Atlántida, 1943), p. 141.

19. Santa Teresa is here reminiscent (without any conscious historical connection) of the "mysticism of silence" attributed to the German fourteenth-century Dominican Tauler. See Giovanni Maria Bertini, *I mistici medievali* (Milano: Garzanti, 1944), pp. 110–11.

20. Fray Efren de la Madre de Dios, ODC, and Fray Otilio del Niño Jesús, ODC, Introduction to *Obras completas de Santa Teresa de Jesús* (Madrid: Autores cristianos, 1961), I, 7.

## Chapter Four

1. The commentators insist that Teresa did not think of physical evils, thus invalidating her teaching of suffering. See Father Gabriel of St. Mary Magdalen, *The Way of Prayer. A Commentary on St. Teresa's "Way of Perfection"* (Milwaukee: Spiritual Life Press, 1965), p. 138.

## Chapter Five

1. Marcel Lépée, *Sainte Thérése Mystique. Une Divine Amitié* (Paris: Desclée, 1951), p. 178. See Chapter IX, "Les Visions," pp. 178–207.

2. Helmut Hatzfeld, "Textos teresianos aplicados a la interpretación de El Greco," in *Estudios literarios sobre mística española* (Madrid: Gredos, 1955), pp. 291–330, 1968, pp. 243–76.

3. Walter Nigg, *Maler des Ewigen* (Zürich: Artemus, 1951).

4. Sister Miriam Thérèse Olabarrieta, SCN, *The Influence of Ramon Lull on the Style of the Early Spanish Mystics and Santa Teresa* (Washington, D.C.: Catholic University Press, 1963).

5. Henri Béchard, SJ, *The Visions of Bernard de Hoyos* (New York: Vantage Press, 1959), p. 49.

6. Carl E. Schmöger (ed.), *The Life of Our Lord . . . From the Revelations of the Venerable Anna Catharina Emmerick as Recorded in the Journals of Clemens Brentano* (Fresno: Academy Library Guild, 1954), I, 194.

7. Father Gabriel of St. Mary Magdalen, ODC, *Visions and Revelations in the Spiritual Life* (Westminster: Newman, 1950), p. 122.

8. Anita Teilhard, *Spiritual Dimensions* (London: Rutledge, 1961). Illustrations between pp. 112–13 and 120–21.

9. Karl Rahner, *Visions and Prophecies* (New York: Herder, 1963), pp. 49 ff.

10. P. Victoriano Larrañaga, *La Espiritualidad de San Ignacio de Loyola. Estudio comparativo con la de Santa Teresa de Jesús* (Madrid: 1944).

11. D. P. Walker, *The Decline of Hell. Seventeenth Century Discussions of Eternal Torment* (London: Rutledge, 1946).

## Chapter Seven

1. J. D. Berruete et J. Chevalier, *Sainte Thérèse et la vie mystique* (Paris: Denoël, 1934). See p. 97 in the chapter on "Physionomie morale."
2. *Loc. cit.*

## Chapter Eight

1. Hilda Graef, *The Story of Mysticism* (Garden City, N.Y.: Doubleday, 1965).
2. Elmer O'Brien, *Varieties of Mystic Experience* (New York: Holt, 1964).
3. Grete Lüers, *Die Sprache der deutschen Mystik des Mittelalters im Werke der Mechtild von Magdeburg* (Munich, 1926).
4. E. H. Palmer, *Oriental Mysticism* (London: Luzac, 1938).
5. Henry Corbin, *L'Imagination créatrice dans le soufisme d'Ibn Arabi* (Paris: Flammarion, 1958).
6. Sister Miriam Thérèse Olabarrieta, SCN, *The Influence of Ramon Lull on the Style of the Early Mystics and Santa Teresa* (Diss., Washington, D.C.: Catholic University of America, 1963).
7. Mother M. Majella Rivet, OSU, *The Influence of the Spanish Mystics on the Works of Saint Francis de Sales.* (Diss., Washington, D.C.: Catholic University of America, 1941), pp. 65–102.
8. For the exact references to the quotations or allusion to quotations see Chapter III of Helmut Hatzfeld, *Estudios literarios sobre mística española* (Madrid: Gredos, 1955), pp. 145–201, 1968, pp. 120–166.

## Chapter Nine

1. Robert Ricard, *Estudios de literatura religiosa española* (Madrid: Gredos, 1964), p. 10.
2. Ramón Menéndez Pidal, "El lenguaje del siglo XVI", in *España y su historia,* II (Madrid, 1957), 153–54.
3. Juan Luis Alborg, *Historia de la literatura española. Edad media y Renacimiento* (Madrid: Gredos, 1966), pp. 12–22.
4. Julián Marías, "La originalidad española," in Germán Bleiberg (ed.), *Spanish Thoughts and Letters in the Twentieth Century* (Nashville: Vanderbilt University Press, 1966), pp. 317–30.
5. Jorge Manrique, *Cancionero.* See Clásicos Castellanos, Ed. (Cortina, 1929), p. 170.
6. Miguel Artigas, "Santa Teresa cantada por los grandes poetas españoles," in *La Basílica Teresiana:* 9 (1922), 75–90.
7. *Loc. cit.*

## Chapter Ten

1. Helmut Hatzfeld, *Estudios literarios sobre mística española* (Madrid: Gredos, 1955), Capítulo V, pp. 253–90, 1968, pp. 210–242.

2. The quotations from Marie de l'Incarnation are based on Dom Albert Jamet (ed.), *Marie de l'Incarnation, Écrits spirituels et historiques* (Paris-Québec: Desclée de Brouwer, 1929 ff.).

## Chapter Eleven

1. Works dealing with this classical parallel are, among many others:

Juan Domínguez Berrueta, *Santa Teresa de Jesús y San Juan de la Cruz* (Madrid, 1915);

Irene Behn, *Spanische Mystik* (Düsseldorf: Patmos, 1957);

Rev. Fr. Brice, CP, *Teresa, John and Thérèse* (New York: Pustet, 1946).

2. E. Allison Peers, *St. John of the Cross* (Cambridge University Press, 1932), p. 74. I draw parallels not found elsewhere with the aid of concordances. I quote the writings of both Saints according to works, chapters and paragraphs, the latter if numbered in the editions of San Juan de la Cruz. I use Padre Crisógono de Jesús, OCD (ed.), *Vida y Obras de San Juan de la Cruz. Biblioteca de autores Cristianos* (Madrid, 1950).

# Selected Bibliography

### BIBLIOGRAPHIES

JIMÉNEZ SALAS MARÍA. *Santa Teresa de Jesús: Bibliografía fundamental.* Madrid: Conşejo Superior, 1962.

SIMON DÍAZ, JOSÉ. *Manual de bibliografía de la literatura española.* Barcelona: Gili, 1963, pp. 275–79.

### MANUSCRIPTS

Most of the works of Santa Teresa exist in autograph manuscripts. See: *Antolín, Guillermo. Los autógrafos de Santa Teresa.* Madrid: Helénica, 1914.

### FIRST EDITIONS OF SINGLE WORKS (Spanish)

*Libro primero de la Madre Teresa de Jesús con un tratado de su vida.* Zaragoza: Tabano, 1591.

*Libro llamado castillo interior.* Salamanca: Foquel, 1588.

*Tratado que escribió la Madre Teresa de Jesús a las hermanas religiosas (Camino de perfección).* Evora: de Burgos, 1583.

*Conceptos del amor de Dios. Con anotaciones de Fray Gerónimo Gracián.* Bruselas: Velpio, 1611.

*Libro de Fundaciones . . . ,* ed. Fray Gerónimo Gracián. Bruselas: Velpio, 1610.

*Avisos espirituales. . . .* Córdoba: Cea, 1598.

### FIRST EDITIONS OF SINGLE WORKS (English)

*The Life of the Mother Teresa of Jesus,* translated by William Malone, SJ. Antwerp, 1611. Modern editions by David Lewis. London: Baker, 1911 and paperback by Allison Peers. New York: Sheed and Ward, 1960.

*The Interior Castle,* translated by J. Dalton. London, 1852. Modern editions by the Benedictines of Stanbrook. London: Baker, 1921 and paperback by Allison Peers. New York: Sheed and Ward, 1961.

*The Way of Perfection and Conceptions of Divine Love,* translated by J. Dalton. London, 1852. Modern edition by the Benedictines of Stanbrook. London: Baker, 1911.

*The Second Part of the Life of the Holy Mother Saint Teresa* or *The History of the Foundations.* Sine loco, 1669. Modern edition: *The Book of Foundations,* translated by David Lewis. London: Baker, 1913.

## COMPLETE EDITIONS OF THE WORKS

First edition (Spanish), *Los Libros de la Madre Teresa de Jesús.* Salamanca: Foquel, 1588.

First Edition (English), *The Works of Saint Teresa,* translated by Abraham Woodhead, 1669.

Modern Critical Standard Edition: *Obras de Santa Teresa de Jesús* editadas y anotadas por el R. P. Silverio de Santa Teresa, CD Burgos: El Monte Carmelo, 1915–1924, 9 vols.

The same without commentary in one volume: *Obras completas de Santa Teresa de Jesús.* Con un estudio preliminar de Luis Santullano. Madrid: Aguilar, 1930. 2d. ed. 1940, 10th ed. 1966.

The same with critical revision of the text: *Obras completas. Nueva revisión del texto original* por los P.P. Efrén de la Madre de Dios, OCD y Otilio del Niño Jesús, OCD, Madrid: Biblioteca de Autores Cristianos, 3 vols., 1951–1959. 2d. ed. 1961.

English translation of *Obras,* ed. P. Silverio: Edgar Allison Peers (ed.) *The Complete Works of Saint Teresa of Jesus.* London: Sheed and Ward, 3 vols., 1944–1946.

*The Letters of Saint Teresa of Jesús,* translated and edited by E. Allison Peers. London: Burns and Oates, 2 vols., 1951.

## STUDIES OF SANTA TERESA (English)

BEEVERS, JOHN. *Santa Teresa of Avila.* Garden City, N.Y., 1961. A short introduction to her personality, written with an existential commitment and decisive quotes from Peer's translation, but without any notes or references.

P. BRUNO DE JESÚS MARIE. *Three Mystics. El Greco, St. John of the Cross, St. Teresa of Avila.* London: Sheed and Ward, 1952. The illustrations and numerous quotations are very helpful. The treatment of El Greco as a mystic is very debatable.

DICKEN, E. W. TRUEMAN. *The Crucible of Love. A Study in the Mysticism of Santa Teresa and St. John of the Cross.* New York: Sheed and Ward, 1963. A parallel between the two greatest Spanish mystics and their "Systems," centered around their Love of God.

HAMILTON, ELIZABETH. *The Great Teresa. A Journey to Spain.* London: Chatto and Windus, 1960. Informative and critical. With illustrations and bibliography. Many personal Spanish travel reminiscences linked to the topic.

HOORNAERT, R. *Saint Teresa in her Writings*. London: Trend & Co., 1931. The best study as far as the literary achievements are concerned.

PEERS, EDGAR ALLISON. *A Handbook of the Life and Times of St. Teresa*. Westminster: Newman, 1954. Excellent reference work for all background questions.

——. *Mother of Carmel*. New York: Morehouse, 1946.

——. *Spanish Mysticism*. London: Methuen, 1924. Knowledgeable introduction. Excellent anthology with translations.

RAMAGE, SEBASTIAN V. *An Introduction to the Writings of Santa Teresa*. Chicago: Regnery, 1963. A condensed recapitulation of the essentials.

SACKVILLE-WEST, V. *The Eagle and the Dove. A Study in Contrasts. St. Teresa of Avila and Ste Thérèse de Lisieux*. Garden City, N.Y., 1944. Rationalistic. Rejects mysticism as not revealing new divine secrets.

WALSH, W. T. *Saint Teresa of Avila*. Milwaukee: Bruce, 1946. Extensive Life and Work presentation from Catholic viewpoint. Somewhat unctuous and sensational.

STUDIES OF SANTA TERESA (Other Languages)

CASTRO, AMÉRICO. *Santa Teresa y otros ensayos*. Madrid: Central de Ediciones y Publicaciones, 1929. Renaissance and Platonism in Santa Teresa.

CRISÓGONO DE JESÚS, SACRAMENTADO. "Doctorado místico de Santa Teresa de Jesús. Trabajo que mereció accésit en el Certamen celebrado en Avila en 1923," *A B C*, Madrid (17 de Marzo, 1923).

——. *Doctrina de Santa Teresa*. Avila: Imp. Sigirano Díaz, 1940.

ETCHEGOYEN, GASTON. *L'Amour divin; essai sur les sources de Sainte Thérèse*. Burdeos-Paris: Féret et fils, 1923. Important for the readings of Santa Teresa.

MANCINI, GIANCARLO GUIDO. *Espressione letteraria dell' insegnamento di Santa Teresa de Avila*. Modena, 1955. Stresses the pedagogical character of Teresa's style.

MENÉNDEZ PIDAL, RAMÓN. *La lengua de Cristóbal Colón, el estilo de Santa Teresa y otros estudios sobre el siglo XVI*. Madrid: Espasa Calpe, 1942. A linguistic rather than a stylistic study.

OECHSLIN, LOUIS. *L'intuition mystique de Sainte Thérèse*. Paris: Presses Universitaires de France, 1946. The best book on Teresa's mystical psychology.

RICARD, ROBERT. "Notes et materiaux pour l'étude du 'Socratisme chrétien' chez Sainte Thérèse et les spirituels espagnols," *Bulletin Hispanique:* v. 49 (1947) 5–37; 170–204; v. 50 (1948) 2–26.

——. *Estudios de literatura religiosa española.* Madrid: Gredos, 1964. Important for the concept of Christian Socratism (self-knowledge) in Santa Teresa.

URBANO, FRAY LUIS. *Las analogías predilectas de Santa Teresa de Jesús.* Madrid, 1924. A fair assessment of the similes.

VERMEYLEN, ALPHONSE. "Blaise Pascal et Santa Teresa," *Sainte Thérèse en France* . . . Louvain, 1959. Traces Teresa in French mystics. Influence smaller than believed.

# Index

*195*